MW00652705

Library Resource Center
Renton Technical College
3000 N.E. 4th St.
Renton, WA 98056

OPTICAL NETWORKS
Third Generation
Transport Systems

UYLESS BLACK

PRENTICE HALL SERIES IN ADVANCED
COMMUNICATIONS TECHNOLOGIES

To join a Prentice Hall PTR internet mailing list, point to:
http://www.phptr.com/register

Prentice Hall PTR
Upper Saddle River, New Jersey 07458
http://www.phptr.com

621
.3821
BLACK
2002

Library of Congress Cataloging-in-Publication Data

A CIP catalog record for this book can be obtained from the Library of Congress.

Editorial/Production supervision: Laura Burgess
Acquisitions editor: Mary Franz
Cover designer: Nina Scuderi
Cover design director: Jerry Votta
Manufacturing manager: Maura Zaldivar
Marketing manager: Dan DePasquale
Compositor/Production services: Pine Tree Composition, Inc.

© 2002 by Uyless Black
Published by Prentice Hall PTR
A division of Pearson Education, Inc.
Upper Saddle River, New Jersey 07458

Prentice Hall books are widely used by corporations and
government agencies for training, marketing and resale.

The publisher offers discounts on this book when ordered in
bulk quantities. For more information contact:
> Corporate Sales Department
> Prentice Hall PTR
> One Lake Street
> Upper Saddle River, New Jersey 07458

> Phone: 800-382-3419
> Fax: 201-236-7141
> email: corpsales@prenhall.com

All product names mentioned herein are the trademarks or
registered trademarks of their respective owners.

All rights reserved. No part of this book may be reproduced, in any form
or by any means, without permission in writing from the publisher.

Printed in the United States of America
10 9 8 7 6 5 4 3 2 1

ISBN: 0-13-060726-6

Pearson Education LTD.
Pearson Education Australia PTY, Limited
Pearson Education Singapore, Pte. Ltd.
Pearson Education North Asia Ltd.
Pearson Education Canada Ltd.
Pearson Educatión de Mexico, S.A. de C.V.
Pearson Education—Japan
Pearson Education Malaysia, Pte. Ltd.
Pearson Education, Upper Saddle River, New Jersey

For my nephews and friends,
James Ross Black and Rick Black
Two very impressive teachers, coaches, and individuals

The ultimate challenge for the world's transport networks does not deal with the subject matter of this book. While many issues remain regarding third generation transport networks, it is believed that most of the technical problems associated with them have been identified and will be solved.

The biggest challenge of transport networks in general, and the public Internet (and private intranets specifically), is not the sending of user data across communications links to machines such as Web servers. The challenge is (a) knowing where the needed data are located in thousands of locations across the planet, (b) assembling and presenting these data as useful information to a user, and (c) doing so all in a few seconds, or even fractions of a second.

Considering how much data are stored in an automated fashion in thousands of servers across public and private networks, the challenge is not insignificant.

Regarding this challenge, I have told my readers in earlier books, "Knowledge is power, if we know where to find the data." For an internet, the Internet, and other modern communications networks, it should be added, ". . . and the data can be assimilated into meaningful information."

This adage fits the situation today with modern communications networks: "Knowledge is power, if we know where the data are located that make up that information, and if the information can be presented to the user in a rapid and intelligible manner."

Rapid and intelligible means the Internet's future servers and other nodes must become much faster *and* much smarter.

It does little good if a third generation transport network presents data to us at several trillion bits per second, when the Web servers (and other nodes) are laden with slow processors *and* the inability to filter and assimilate these trillions of bits of "potential" information into "meaningful" information.

My point is that the WWW should not mean "World Wide Wait." Nor should it stand for the "Whole World is Wallowing in Data" and we can't find it!

It will take a while before the Web's clients and servers, the supporting Web content providers, and the Internet Service Providers will be able to give a retrieval (say, something less than a few hundred hits) back to the user in any semblance of a truly intelligent search.

But, make no mistake, this is where we are headed. Eventually (assuming sufficient bandwidth is made available to the mass population), many more people will be using the Internet in their daily activities. The Internet's Web will prove to be too cost-effective, convenient, and enticing for many competing alternatives.

One such alternative is hard copy mail. The tragic events of September 11 and thereafter will spur the use of electronic communications and email even more than they are used today.

Electronic viruses in an email attachment are nasty things, but they pale in comparison to the damage that can be done by chemical or biological viruses in a mail package.

It is not my intent to start this book on a down note, but it should be recognized that the subject matter of this book, transport networks, have played an indispensable part in our personal and professional lives for many years.

With the recent recognition of the vulnerability of many aspects of an open society to terrorists, the role of the transport networks and their protection becomes even more important in our lives. Indeed, they are now absolutely vital to our existence in an automated, industrialized society.

Contents

Preface

This book describes third generation digital carrier transport networks. The primary focus of the book is on the role of optical fiber and optical routers in these networks, with the emphasis on wave division multiplexing (WDM). Third generation transport networks also entail considerable interworking with Multiprotocol Label Switching (MPLS), and this topic is covered in several chapters. As well, the ITU and the IETF are defining new multiplexing hierarchies for the third generation transport network, and these efforts are described in this book.

You might be wondering what are first and second generation transport networks? I classify first generation systems, introduced in the 1960s, as those that were/are built with predominately T1 and E1 architectures. I classify second generation systems, introduced in the 1980s, as those that were/are built with SONET and SDH architectures. Although these topics are covered in this book, the emphasis is on networks that go beyond these older technologies.

The emphasis of this book is on newer technologies, being introduced as you read this preface, with the focus on optical internets: those dealing with IP over optical; label switching with WDM; optical cross-connects; optical routers; optical bandwidth on demand; and the emerging Optical Transport Network (OTN), published by ITU-T and amplified by the IETF. For the newcomer, Chapter 3 provides tutorials on the basics of optical technology, including the operations of optical fiber and lasers.

I want to emphasize that this book has only one chapter on the technology of optical fiber itself. Scores of books are available on this subject, and my intent is to move beyond the descriptions of a light signal on a fiber. I think Chapter 3 will be sufficient for the newcomer on the subject of optical fiber, and I provide you with some excellent references if you wish to delve into more details about the subject.

INTERNET DRAFTS: WORK IN PROGESS

A considerable portion of this book is devoted to explaining many Internet-based specifications pertaining to IP-based optical networks.

Keep in mind that the Internet drafts are works in progress, and should be viewed as such. You should not use the drafts with the expectation that they will not change. Notwithstanding, if used as general tutorials, the drafts discussed in this book are "final enough" to warrant their explanations. Indeed, many of my clients use these drafts in their product planning and design.

For all the Internet standards and drafts the following applies:

Copyright © The Internet Society (1998). All Rights Reserved.

This document and translations of it may be copied and furnished to others, and derivative works that comment on or otherwise explain it or assist in its implementation may be prepared, copied, published and distributed, in whole or in part, without restriction of any kind, provided that the above copyright notice and this paragraph are included on all such copies and derivative works. However, this document itself may not be modified in any way, such as by removing the copyright notice or references to the Internet Society or other Internet organizations, except as needed for the purpose of developing Internet standards in which case the procedures for copyrights defined in the Internet Standards process must be followed, or as required to translate it into languages other than English.

The limited permissions granted above are perpetual and will not be revoked by the Internet Society or its successors or assigns.

1

Introduction

This chapter introduces the optical network. We begin with a survey of three generations of digital transport networks, followed by a discussion of the extraordinary capacity of optical fiber. The optical network marketplace is examined with a look at current and projected installations. Next, we examine the key nodes (machines) that make up the optical network, then we look inside a node to learn about its components. The chapter concludes with a general explanation of the attributes of optical fiber.

THREE GENERATIONS OF DIGITAL TRANSPORT NETWORKS

The focus of this book is on third generation digital transport networks, usually shorted to 3G, or 3rd generation, transport networks. The main characteristics of three generations of digital transport networks are provided in Table 1–1. The information in this table will be helpful as you read the remaining chapters in this book. Most of the terms in the table are self-explanatory, or, if not, are explained in this chapter.

The first column in the table is the name (or names) usually associated with the technology. The first generation systems are known as T1 or E1. The second generation systems are called SONET (for the Synchronous Optical Network) or SDH (for the Synchronous Digital Hierarchy). These terms are explained in more detail in later parts of this book. However, the

Table 1-1 Three Generations of Digital Transport (Carrier) Networks

Name	Family	Designed for	MUX/SW Schemes at Inception	Principal Media at Inception	Capacity	Typical Payload	Protocol Inter-Working?
T1/E1	First	Voice, Non-BOD, Static	TDM/E/E/E	Copper: (Early 1960s)	Mbit/s	Fixed Length	No
SONET/SDH	Second	Voice, Non-BOD, Static	TDM/O/E/O	Copper, Fiber: (Mid–1980s)	Gbit/s	Fixed Length	Somewhat: PPP, IP, ATM
OTN	Third	Voice, Video, Data, Tailored QOS, BOD, Dynamic	WDM/O/O/O	Fiber (Late 1990s to Early 2000s)	Tbit/s	Fixed or Variable Lengths	Yes: PPP, IP, ATM, MPLS

industry has not yet settled on a handle for the third generation digital carrier network, but the term Optical Transport Network (OTN) is widely used. The second column identifies the generation family.

The third column shows what kinds of user payloads the networks are designed to support. Although the first and second generation networks are designed to support voice traffic, they can and do transport data and video images. But they are not "optimized" for data and video traffic. In contrast, the 3G transport network is designed to support voice, video, or data payloads. When used with multiprotocol label switching (MPLS), the resource reservation protocol (RSVP), and DiffServ, as well as some of the new specifications dealing with optical bandwidth on demand, they are also designed to provide tailored quality-of-service (QOS) features for individual customers. The point will be made repeatedly in this book that the 3G transport network no longer consists of fixed, static "pipes" of capacity; it can dynamically change to meet the changing requirements of its users.

The third column also contains the notations of Non-BOD or BOD. The first and second generation systems are not designed to provide bandwidth of demand (BOD). The bandwidth is configured with crafting operations at each node. 3G systems are more dynamic and allow bandwidth to be requested on demand.

The fourth column lists the predominant multiplexing schemes: TDM or WDM. The fourth column also lists the manner in which the networks switch traffic when they were first deployed (at their inception). First generation systems were solely E/E/E operations: (a) they accepted electrical signals (the first E), (b) processed them (the second E), and (c) sent them to another node (the third E). Second generation systems are O/E/O operations: (a) they accept optical signals (the first O), (b) convert them to electrical signals for processing (the E), and (c) convert the electrical signals back to optical signals for transmission (the second O). Third generation systems are intended to be all optical (O/O/O), in that they process optical payloads, and do not need to convert the bits to electrical images for processing. Today, all three generations are mainly O/E/O oriented.

The fifth column lists the principal media used by the technologies at their inception, as well as the time that these networks were first introduced into the industry. All three generations now use a combination of copper, fiber, and wireless media.

The sixth column lists the typical capacity of the generation. It is evident that each succeeding family has increased its transport capacity by orders of magnitude.

The seventh column goes hand-in-hand with the third column ("Designed For"). The first and second generation networks were designed for fixed-length voice traffic, based on the 64 kbit/s payload, with a 125-μsec clocking increment. The third generation network supports this signal, but also supports variable-length payloads, an important capability for carrying data traffic. As well, the first and second generation networks can carry variable-length traffic, but they are not very efficient in how they go about transporting variable-length data traffic.

The eighth column explains whether any of the generations were designed to interwork with and directly support other protocols. T1/E1 was not so designed; again, 1st generation transport systems were set up to support voice traffic. Any efforts to devise methods of carrying other payloads were an afterthought and in vendor-specific procedures. With the advent of 2nd generation systems with SONET/SDH, efforts were made by the standards groups to define procedures for carrying certain kinds of data traffic, and many manufacturers adapted these standards into their products.

3rd generation transport networks are geared toward supporting many kinds of payloads, and specifically the Internet, ATM, and MPLS protocol suites. As we shall see as we proceed though this book, extensive research has resulted in many specifications defining how MPLS contributes to the operations of the third generation digital (optical) transport network.

All Features Are Not Yet Available

Not all the features and attributes cited in Table 1–1 are available in 3G transport networks. In fact, third generation transport networks are just now appearing in the marketplace, and some capabilities that are touted for them are still in the lab. Nonetheless, many people think full-featured 3rd generation transport networks will be in the marketplace by around 2004. Certainly, pieces are emerging, such as bandwidth on demand, and of course, WDM and terabit networks. Other parts of 3G transport networks have yet to be implemented. For example, O/O/O operations are far from reaching commercial deployment on a mass scale.

Optical Fiber Capacity

To gain an appreciation of the transmission capacity of optical systems operating today, consider the facts in Table 1–2. Prior to the advent of optical fiber systems, a high-capacity network was capable

Table 1–2   Magnitudes and Meanings

Magnitude	Term	Initial	Meaning
$1\,000\,000\,000\,000\,000\,000 = 10^{18}$	exa	E	Quintillion
$1\,000\,000\,000\,000\,000 = 10^{15}$	peta	P	Quadrillion
$1\,000\,000\,000\,000 = 10^{12}$	tera	T	Trillion
$1\,000\,000\,000 = 10^{9}$	giga	G	Billion
$1\,000\,000 = 10^{6}$	mega	M	Million
$1\,000 = 10^{3}$	kilo	k	Thousand
$100 = 10^{2}$	hecto	h	Hundred
$10 = 10^{1}$	deka	da	Ten

of operating (sending and receiving traffic) at several million bits per second (Mbit/s). These electrical/electromagnetic transmissions take place over some form of metallic medium such as copper wire or coaxial cable, or over wireless systems such as microwave. In contrast, optical fiber systems transmit light signals through a glass or plastic medium. These systems are many orders of magnitude "faster" than their predecessors, with the capability of operating in the terabits-per-second (Tbit/s) range.

As depicted in Figure 1–1, a terabit fiber carries 10^{12} bits per second. At this rate, the fiber can transport just over 35 million data connections at 28.8 kbit/s, or about 17 million digital voice channels, or just under 500,000 compressed TV channels (or combinations of these channels).

**1 terabit/s
(a million Mbit/s)**

Approximately:
- **35 million data connections at 28 kbit/s or**
- **17 million digital voice telephony channels or**
- **1/2 million compressed TV channels**

Figure 1–1   Capacity of one fiber with a 1 Tbit/s rate.

Even the seasoned telecommunications professional pauses when think-
ing about the extraordinary capacity of optical fiber.

A logical question for a newcomer to optical networks is, why are
they of much greater capacity than, say, a network built on copper wire,
or coaxial cable? The answer is that optical signals used in optical networks operate in a very high position and range of the frequency spectrum, many orders of magnitude higher than electromagnetic signals.
Thus, the use of the higher frequencies permits the sending of many
more user payloads (voice, video, and data) onto the fiber medium.

Figure 1–2 shows the progress made in the transmission capacity of
optical fiber technology since 1982 [CHRA99]. The top line represents experimental systems, and the bottom line represents commercial systems.
The commercial results have lagged behind the experimental results by
about six years. The dramatic growth in the experimental capacity was
due to improved laboratory techniques and the progress made in dispersion management, a subject discussed later in this book. As the figure

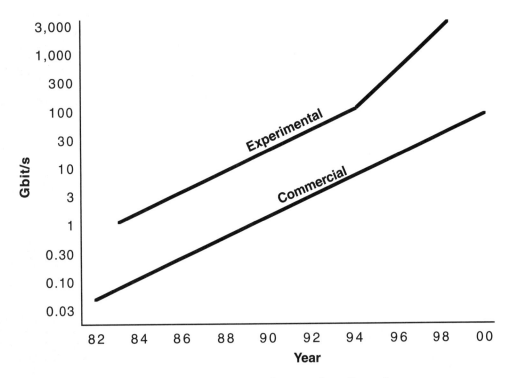

**Figure 1–2   Transmission capacity as a function of year
[CHRA99].**

shows, the transmission capacity of optical fiber has been growing at an extraordinary rate since the inception of the technology.

A BRIEF INTRODUCTION TO WDM AND TDM

We would like to keep this introductory chapter free from technical detail as much as possible. However, it is necessary to introduce two terms before proceeding further: (a) wave division multiplexing (WDM), and (b) time division multiplexing (TDM). Later chapters will embellish on this introduction. Refer to Figure 1–3 during this discussion.

WDM:

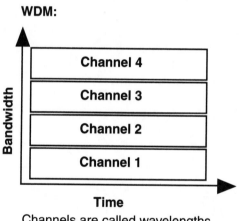

Channels are called wavelengths

TDM:

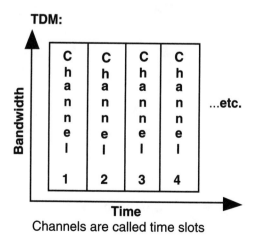

Channels are called time slots   **Figure 1–3   WDM and TDM.**

WDM is based on a well-known concept called frequency division multiplexing or FDM. With this technology, the bandwidth of a channel (its frequency domain) is divided into multiple channels, and each channel occupies a part of the larger frequency spectrum. In WDM networks, each channel is called a *wavelength*. This name is used because each channel operates at a different frequency and at a different optical wavelength (and the higher the frequency, the shorter the signal's wavelength). A common shorthand notation for wavelength is the Greek symbol lambda, shown as λ.

The wavelengths on the fiber are separated by unused spectrum. This practice keeps the wavelengths separated from each other and helps prevent their interfering with each other. This idea is called channel spacing, or simply spacing. It is similar to the idea of guardbands used in electrical systems. In Figure 1–3, the small gaps between each channel represent the spacing.

Time division multiplexing (TDM) provides a user the full channel capacity but divides the channel usage into time slots. Each user is given a slot and the slots are rotated among the users. A pure TDM system cyclically scans the input signals (incoming traffic) from the multiple incoming data sources (communications links, for example). Bits, bytes, or blocks of data are separated and interleaved together into slots on a single high-speed communications line.

Combining WDM and TDM

Most optical networks (or, for that matter, most networks in general) use a combination of WDM and TDM by time-division multiplexing fixed slots onto a specific wavelength, as shown in Figure 1–4. This concept is quite valuable because it allows multiple users to share one

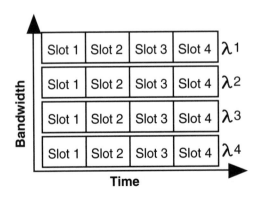

Figure 1–4   Combining WDM and TDM.

WDM wavelength's capacity. With some exceptions, the capacity of one wavelength exceeds an individual user's traffic capacity needs.

These introductory definitions should be sufficient for us to use them in this chapter. In later chapters, TDM and WDM are examined in considerable detail.

THE OPTICAL MARKETPLACE

The optical technology is a high-growth market. As Figure 1–5 shows, it is expected to more than double between 2000 and 2003. Most of the growth will be for terrestrial WDM and optical networks, and submarine cable systems. The growth of conventional TDM systems will continue (shown in Figure 1–5 as SONET/SDH, and explained in

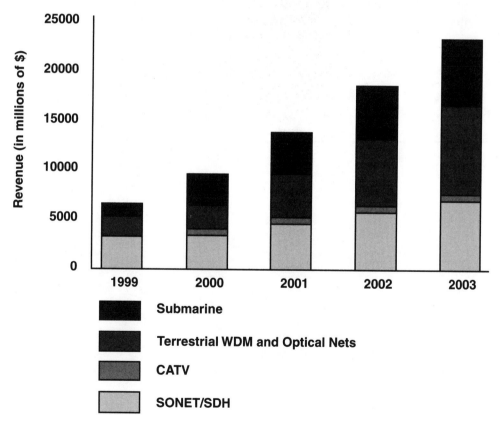

Figure 1–5   Worldwide market for optical components.

Chapter 5), but at a lesser rate than the other areas. Optical systems are being incorporated into CATV networks, but this growth will be modest because the coaxial cable plant to the homes cannot be re-wired in a cost-effective manner. A residence does not need the bandwidth of fiber (at least not for the foreseeable future).

Figure 1–6 shows another study comparing the projected transmission capacity and the demand through 2004 [STRI01]. The figures pertain to the national backbone in the United States and not to the access loops. This study holds that the building-out of optical networks discussed earlier will provide excess capacity for the early part of this decade, and if one examines the gap between demand and capacity, it is reasonable to expect that capacity will exceed demand well beyond 2004.

There are those in the industry who disagree. They state that the upcoming applications will require huge amounts of bandwidth, and that this supposed excess capacity will be consumed by these applications. There is no question that some applications do indeed require a lot of bandwidth. A prime example is interactive high-quality Web traffic, exhibiting the integration of high-resolution, real-time voice, video, and data.

The Local Loop Bottleneck Must Be Solved

It is my view that the upcoming applications, and their demand for large chunks of bandwidth, are not going to be realized to any large

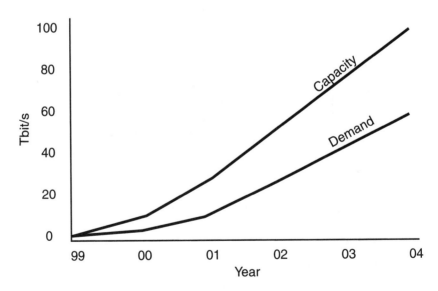

Figure 1–6   Demand vs. capacity [STRI01].

degree until bandwidth is available on the access line (the local loop) to the end user. It does little good to download a Web response to a user at a terabit rate within the network when the vast majority of access lines are restricted to V.90 speeds (56 kbit/s). Certainly, some businesses can afford to purchase large bandwidths from the business to the terabit backbones. But many businesses cannot afford to purchase this bandwidth, nor can the majority of residential users. In addition, broadband access loops are not available to most residences anyway.

The situation in the United States is interesting, and quite frustrating to many customers, because many of them are limited to very low capacity links to the Internet. What is the incentive for the local access providers (the telephone local exchange carriers (LECs), CATV operators, and wireless providers) to expand their local access plant to the megabit or terabit rate? After all, with some minor exceptions (and in spite of the 1984 and 1996 legislative efforts), these companies have a lock on their market. Some people believe that these companies do not have a lot of incentive to invest in the upgrading of their plants.

Maybe so, but the local access providers will expand their plant if they think there is sufficient demand to enable them to make money on their investment. So, beyond the issues of government-sponsored monopolies, is there really that much demand for the deployment of high-capacity systems into the mass marketplace?[1] Most Internet users use the Internet for email or simple text-oriented Web retrievals, and many have been conditioned to the slow response time in their interactions with their networks.

The present situation can be illustrated with a diagram shown in Figure 1–7.[2] The circle in this figure illustrates the relationships of: (a) user applications' requirements for bandwidth (labeled "Applications" in the figure), (b) the capacity of the user or network computers (labeled "CPU" in the figure), and (c) the capacity of the communications media to support traffic (labeled "Bandwidth" in the figure).

Historically, the bottleneck in this circle has varied. At times, it has been the lack of CPU (and memory) capacity in the user's computer. At

---

[1]By mass marketplace, I mean deployment into residences on a large scale, well beyond the 15–20% penetration rate for the current efforts of telephone company and the cable company.

[2]I call this illustration the "eternal circle," because it shows a seemingly never-ending dependency-relationship between the three components.

Library Resource Center
Renton Technical College
3000 N.E. 4th St.
Renton, WA 98056

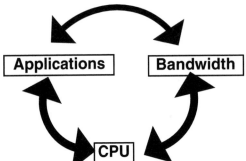

Figure 1-7   The eternal circle.

other times, it has been the lack of capacity in the network to support the capacity requirements of the users' applications.

Figure 1–7 shows the relationships with two-way arrows, which suggests that these three operations are interrelated and dependent upon each other. But which comes first? Does the application's requirement for more capacity lead to faster CPUs and/or the expansion of network bandwidth? Or does the introduction of more bandwidth encourage the development of faster computers and more powerful applications? There are no clear answers to these questions. Sometimes one pushes the other, and at other times the opposite occurs.

However, at this time in the telecommunications industry, we can state the following:

- Within the optical network (the backbone or core network) the bottleneck is the "CPU," because its electrical-based architecture (in switches, routers, and bridges) cannot handle a large number of connected optical fiber WDM links that operate in the terabit range. Thus, the creation of all-optical photonic switches (PXCs) is a high priority in the industry.
- At the edge of the network, and to the end user, the bottleneck is the "bandwidth," but not because of the optical fiber. The bottleneck is due to the continued use of the telephone-based copper plant, and the mobile phone links (and the very slow process of getting it upgraded).
- The "applications" part of the Eternal Circle is a question mark to some people. If the network operators finally provide the bandwidth all the way to the mass market (the residence), will sophisticated three-dimensional, voice/video/data applications be developed to

take advantage of the increased capacity? I believe the answer is a resounding yes, assuming the network operators can keep the price affordable to most households.

Expansion of Network Capacity

One of the more interesting changes occurring in the long-distance carrier industry in the United States is the extraordinary growth of bandwidth capacity. This growth is occurring due to the maturation of the WDM technology, and its wide-scale deployment. It is also occurring due to the aggressive deployment of fiber networks by the "non-traditional" carriers; that is, those carriers who have come into the industry in the last few years.

Figure 1–8 shows the growth of long-distance capacity since 1996, and projections through 2001. The shaded bars show total mileage, and the white bars show total capacity, in terabits per second.

Some people question if this bandwidth will be used. Others see it as an opportunity to discount excess capacity, at the expense of the traditional carriers, who are enjoying healthy profits from their long-distance

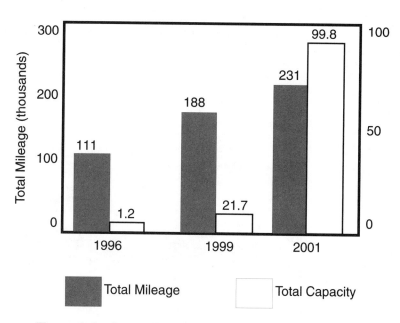

Figure 1–8   Long-distance growth in the United States.

revenues. It will be interesting to see how the scenarios develop over the next few years. Some marketing forecasts state that this situation will lead to a "fire sale" of DS1 and DS3 lines.

WIRELESS OPTICAL SYSTEMS

Another entry into the optical technology is a multichannel optical wireless system from [BELL99]. Figure 1–9 shows a system that operates at 10 Gbit/s using four wavelengths. It can transmit over 2.7 miles of free space. Each wavelength operates at 2.5 Gbit/s. It requires a line-of-sight topology. Other vendors are offering this system, including Nortel Networks.

The systems uses WDM with custom-built telescopes, and standard optical transmitters and receivers. Light signals are sent from a transmitting telescope to a receiving telescope and are focused onto the core of an optical fiber using coupling optics within the second telescope.

The system is attractive in situations where the deployment of fiber cable is not feasible, for example, across restricted-access terrain, or bodies of water. It can be deployed much more quickly than fiber cable systems. It can also offer a cost-effective solution to line-of-sight channels in conference and convention centers.

In most countries, optical wireless requires no governmental licensing or frequency allocation schemes.

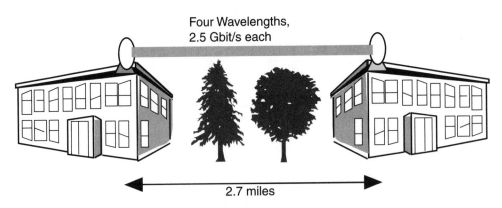

Figure 1–9   Wireless optical systems.

KEY OPTICAL NODES

We now leave the subject of the optical network marketplace, and focus our attention on the nodes (machines) that comprise the network. Figure 1–10 shows the key nodes in an optical network. The topology is a ring, but the topology can be set up either as a ring, a point-to-point, multipoint, or meshed system. In most large networks, the ring is a dual ring, operating with two or more optical fibers. The structure of the dual ring topology permits the network to recover automatically from failures on the optical links and in the link/node interfaces. This is known as a *self-healing ring* and is explained in later chapters.

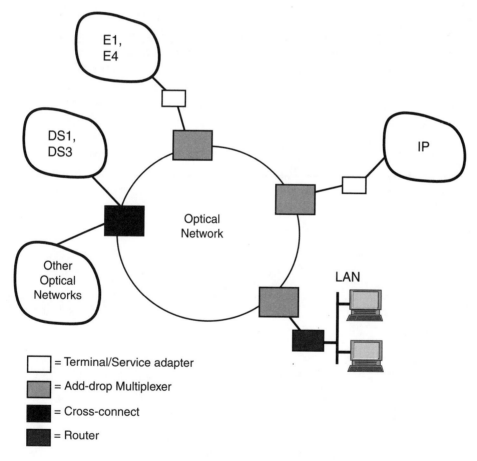

Figure 1–10   Key nodes in the optical network.

End-user devices operating on LANs and digital transport systems (such as DS1, E1, etc.) are attached to the network through a service adapter. This service adapter is also called an access node, a terminal, or a terminal multiplexer. This node is responsible for supporting the end-user interface by sending and receiving traffic from LANs, DS1, DS3, E1, ATM nodes, etc. It is really a concentrator at the sending site because it consolidates multiple user traffic into a *payload envelope* for transport onto the optical network. It performs a complementary, yet opposite, service at the receiving site.

The user signals, such as T1, E1, ATM cells, etc., are called *tributaries*. The tributaries are converted (mapped) into a standard format called the *synchronous transport signal (STS)*, which is the basic building block of the optical multiplexing hierarchy. The STS signal is an electrical signal. The notation STS-n means that the service adapter can multiplex the STS signal into higher integer multiples of the base rate, The STS signals are converted into optical signals by the terminal adapter and are then called OC (optical carrier) signals.

The terminal/service adapter can be implemented as the end-user interface machine, or as an add-drop multiplexer (ADM). The ADM implementation multiplexes various STS input streams onto optical fiber channels. OC-n streams are demultiplexed as well as multiplexed with the ADM.

The term *add-drop* means that the machine can add or drop payload onto one of the fiber links. Remaining traffic that is not dropped passes straight through the multiplexer without additional processing.

The *cross-connect (CS)* machine usually acts as a hub in the optical network. It can not only add and drop payload, but it can also operate with different carrier rates, such as DS1, OC-n, E1, etc. The cross-connect can make two-way cross-connections between the payload and can consolidate and separate different types of payloads. For example, the cross-connect can consolidate multiple low bit-rate tributaries into higher bit-rate tributaries, and vice versa. This operation is known as *grooming*.

Key Terms for the Cross-connect

The convention in this book is to use three terms to describe the optical cross-connect. There is a spate of terms to describe a cross-connect. I counted six terms in one paper alone. To make sure there is no ambiguity about the optical cross-connect in this book, the following terms are used:

- *Optical/Electrical cross-connect (OXC):* Receives optical signals, converts them to electrical signals, makes routing/switching and/or ADM decisions, then converts the electrical signals back to optical signals for transmission. These operations are also noted as O/E/O. This technique is also called an opaque operation.
- *Photonic cross-connect (PXC):* Performs the functions of the OXC, but performs all operations on optical signals. These operations are also noted as O/O/O, and are also called transparent operations.
- *Cross-connect (XC):* A more generic term, used when it is not necessary to distinguish between the OXC or the PXC.
- *Switch:* Some recent literature distinguishes between a cross-connect and a switch. This literature states that cross-connect is an outdated term! Well, the term switch has also been around for quite a while. Anyway, the book uses the terms cross-connect and switch synonymously.

Other terms and different definitions of optical nodes are used by various vendors, network operators, and standards groups. In some cases, they are the same as those just cited; in other cases, they are different. Where appropriate, I will distinguish and explain these other terms.

OTHER KEY TERMS

Other terms need to be defined and clarified in order for readers to understand the other chapters in this book. For the first few times I use these terms, I will refer you back to these definitions, or repeat them. Unfortunately, the industry is not consistent in the use of some of these terms; some varying interpretations are explained below.

- *Fiber link set:* This term refers to all the fibers (if there are more than one) connecting two adjacent XCs or other fiber nodes. The link set may consist of scores of individual optical fibers and hundreds of wavelengths.
- *Edge, ingress, egress nodes:* These terms refer to the placement of the XCs at the boundaries of the network. The term edge encompasses both ingress and egress. Ingress obviously means the XC sending traffic into the network, and egress is the node sending traffic out of the network.

- *Interior, transit, or core nodes:* These three terms refer to an XC that is located inside the optical network and communicates with other XCs for internal network operations or with the edge nodes for communications (perhaps) outside the network.
- *Optical switched path (OSP):* The optical path between two adjacent optical nodes. The OSP is one logical channel of a fiber link set.
- *Lightpath and trail:* The term lightpath defines an end-to-end optical path through one or more optical nodes or networks to the end users. This term is also used in some literature to identify the optical path between two adjacent nodes, so it must be interpreted in the context of its use. Also, some literature uses the terms lightpath and trail synonymously.
- *Label switched path (LSP):* The end-to-end MPLS path across one or more MPLS nodes (and perhaps optical as well) networks to the end users.

Another Look at the Optical Node

Figure 1–11 shows a more detailed view of the optical network node and its components [NORT99b]. This example shows the light

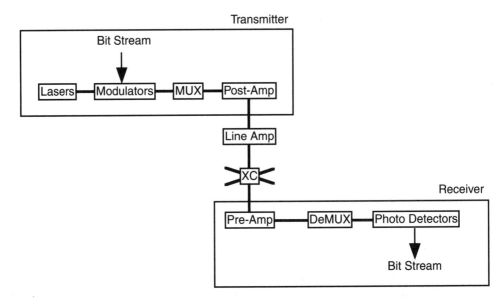

Figure 1–11   Optical components in more detail [NORT99b].

signal transmitted from the left side to the right side of the figure. The events for the operation are explained below, with references to the chapters in this book that provide more detailed explanations.

- First, laser devices generate light pulses tuned to specific and precise wavelengths, such as 1533 or 1557 nanometers (nm). Lasers are explained in Chapter 3.

- Next, the optical modulators accept the electrical signal (an incoming bit stream), and convert it to an optical signal. In addition to the conversion, the modulator uses the incoming bit stream to make decisions about turning the light stream on and off to represent the digital 1s and 0s of the incoming stream. Chapters 3 and 4 provide more information on this process.

- The multiplexer (MUX) combines different TDM slots or WDM wavelengths together. Chapters 5, 6, and 7 explain multiplexing in considerable detail.

- The signal is passed to an optical post-amplifier (Post-Amp). This amplifier boosts the strength of the power of the signal before it is sent onto the fiber. See Chapters 3 and 7 for more information on amplifiers.

- On the fiber, a dispersion compensation unit (not shown in Figure 1–11) corrects the dispersion of the signal as it travels through the fiber. As explained in more detail in Chapters 3 and 7, dispersion is the spreading of the light pulses as they travel down the fiber, which can cause interaction (and distortion) between adjacent pulses.

- As the signal travels down the fiber, it loses its strength. Therefore, the signal power is periodically boosted with an amplifier (Line Amp) to compensate for these losses, again as explained in Chapters 3 and 7.

- There may be an XC on the link to switch the signals to the correct destination. The manner in which the signals are relayed through a cross-connect is one of keen interest in the industry and is examined in Chapters 8, 9, 10, 12, and 14.

- At the final receiver, optical pre-amplifiers (Pre-Amp) boost the strength of the signal once again (Chapters 3 and 7).

- A demultiplexer separates the multiple wavelengths (Chapters 5, 6, and 7).

- Optical photodetectors convert the optical wavelengths into an electronic bit stream (Chapter 3).

EVOLUTION OF OPTICAL SYSTEMS

To set the stage for subsequent chapters, Figure 1–12 shows the evolution of optical systems since the late 1980s/early 1990s to the present time [GILE99].

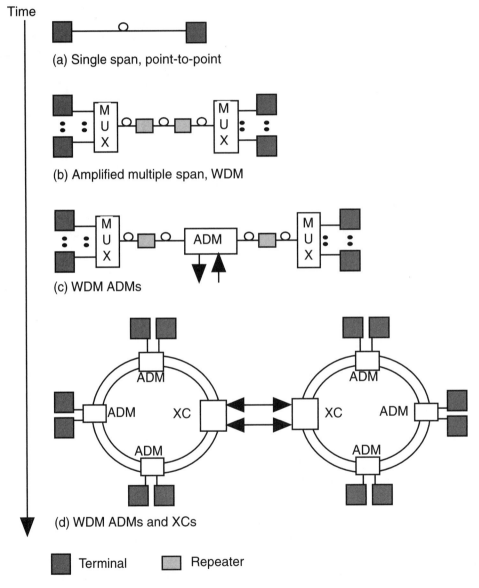

Figure 1–12   Evolution of optical systems [GILE99].

The early systems had a single channel point-to-point topology, as shown in Figure 1–12 (a). The short fiber spans did not use optical amplifier repeaters, so the span lengths rarely exceeded 40 km. The restriction of length was due partially to the limit of laser transmitter power of 1 mW. Optical systems at this time used a single fiber to increase the overall transmission capacity of the point-to-point link.

The discovery of erbium-doped fiber amplifiers (repeaters) was a major milestone in the ability to extend the fiber link. The optical amplifier allowed the optical transmission to extend to wide areas (see Figure 1–12 (b)).

Now that a link could span thousand of kilometers, it became feasible to deploy add-drop multiplexers (ADMs) to allow the connection of points along the link, shown in Figure 1–12 (c). (Of course, ADMs in optical networks have been around for over ten years, but wavelength ADMs (WADMs) are more recent.) As of this writing, the fixed-wavelength ADM (of selected channels) is the state-of-the-art implementation for WADMs. But WADMs that are dynamically reconfigurable are the next phase for WADMs.

As shown in Figure 1–12 (d), cross-connects (XCs) permit a more powerful grooming of traffic between optical networks (in this example, optical rings). This configuration has been deployed for over a decade in TDM optical systems; wavelength XCs, noted as PXCs in this book, are the next stage of the evolution.

KEY ATTRIBUTES OF OPTICAL FIBER

Finally, as a prelude to the remainder of the book, we conclude this chapter by reviewing the major attributes of optical fiber.

The advantages of fiber optics (compared to copper cable) include superior transmission quality and efficiency. Since the optical signal has none of the characteristics association with electrical signals, optical fiber does not suffer from common electromagnetic effects such as experiencing interference from other electrical components, such as power lines, electrical machines, and other optical links.

Because it does not emanate energy outside the fiber, the optical signal is more secure than copper and wireless media, which are easy to monitor and glean information from the residual energy emanating from these media.

Glass fiber is very small and of light weight, a significant attribute for network operators who must install communications links in buildings, ducts, and other areas that have very limited space for the communications links.

We learned earlier that fiber has a very wide bandwidth which allows for the transport of very large payloads, some in the terabits-per-second range.

Since the fiber is comprised of glass with a very small diameter, it is fragile and is somewhat difficult to connect and splice. Also, because glass is not a conductor of electrical current, it cannot carry power to the regenerators (which are used to strengthen signals on long spans). This situation is changing, as passive optical networks are deployed (a subject for Chapter 8).

SUMMARY

Optical fiber and optical-based networks have revolutionized the world of telecommunications, principally because of their extraordinary transmission capacity. They have replaced almost all the older media, such as copper, in the large backbone networks in the world, such as the telephone networks, and the Internet. Unfortunately, due to the dominance of copper wire in the telephone local loop plant, they have not been installed (to any significant) extent in residences. Nonetheless, optical fiber technology will continue to grow, and with the advent of WDM and powerless amplifiers, their presence will become commonplace in all high-speed networks.

2

The Telecommunications
Infrastructure

This chapter introduces the basic components that make up a telecommunications network. The focus is on the components that are germane
to the subject of optical networks. We begin with the part of the network which connects businesses and residences in a local/metropolitan
area. This discussion is followed by an examination of the long-haul
backbone network architecture. Next, the role of layered protocols in
transport networks is explained. The chapter concludes with a discussion
of the digital carrier systems, with examples of the digital multiplexing
hierarchy.

The first part of this chapter is meant as a basic tutorial, so the
more advanced reader can skip to the section titled "Considerations
for Interworking Layer 1, Layer 2, and Layer 3 Networks." This section should be read by all.

THE LOCAL CONNECTIONS

Most businesses and residences are able to communicate with each other
via the telephone and, increasingly, the CATV networks, as well as with
mobile phones. See Figure 2–1. These communications connections are
typically called local interfaces, local loops, subscriber loops, metropolitan networks, or simply the user-network interface (UNI).

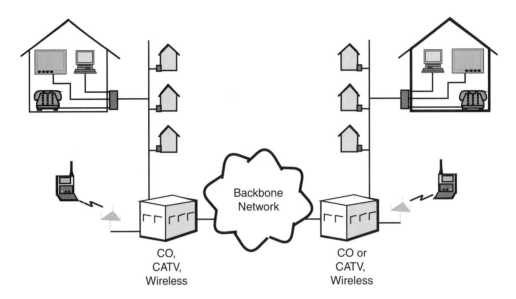

Figure 2–1   The local exchanges.

For the telephone company (telco) connection, the user gains access to the telephone system through the ubiquitous copper wires that run from the telco central office (CO) to the user's telephone. For the cable TV connection, the TV coaxial cable is the channel installed between the user and the cable provider. Of course, for the mobile phone user, access is accomplished through the air.

Increasingly, optical fibers are replacing some of the copper wire and coaxial cable installations, primarily to office buildings. Thus far, there is limited interest in extending fiber to residences, although a few new residential developments have deployed fiber to the home (FTTH). The main thrust is the deployment of fiber to the curb (FTTC), where the optical signals are converted to electrical signals for transmission back and forth on the copper wire or coaxial cables at the user's premises.

THE BACKBONE CONNECTIONS

For transport of the customer's traffic across a wide geographical area, the long-haul backbone network is employed, as shown in Figure 2–2. The common term in the industry for this network is a digital transport network or transport network, and it is the subject of this book.

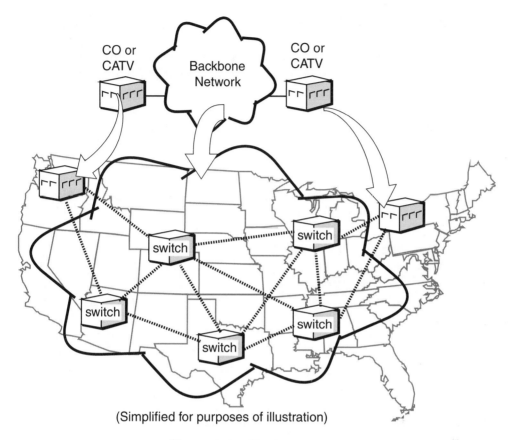

(Simplified for purposes of illustration)

Figure 2–2   The backbone.

The term network in Figure 2–2 is a misnomer because the world's "transport network" consists of thousands of networks that are owned by network service providers such as the telephone companies, and the postal, telephone, and telegraph ministries (PTTs) in many parts of the world. Some Internet service providers (ISPs) have deployed their own networks as part of this backbone structure. Other companies build networks and rent them to other service providers; these companies are often called a carrier's carrier.

The blank network "cloud" at the top of Figure 2–2 has been filled in at the bottom of the figure, showing the positions of communications nodes and links. The communication among the nodes in the network is accomplished with procedures defined by a network-to-network interface (NNI).

Whatever the form taken, the important aspects of the backbone are the requirements for (a) supporting massive amounts of traffic (in the terabit-per-second rate), (b) assuring that the customers' traffic arrives safely at its destination, and (c) making sure the received traffic is of high quality (the voice image is pristine, the data message has no errors, the TV picture is clear). As explained in Chapter 1, the optical fiber technology is an indispensable tool to support these three critical requirements.

The dashed lines inside the backbone in Figure 2–2 are usually optical fiber, or some form of high-capacity radio medium, such as satellite or microwave. For the past ten years, the backbone links have been migrating to optical fiber.

The switches residing in the network are responsible for relaying the customer's traffic through the network to the final destination. With few exceptions, the switches are configured to examine a called party telephone number or a destination IP address to make their forwarding decision.

At this stage of the development of optical networks, these switches are O/E/O devices; as noted in Chapter 1, they convert the optical signal to electrical images so they can examine the information in the traffic to glean the telephone number or the IP address to make their routing decision. Then they convert the electrical signal back to optical for transmission to the outgoing optical link. As explained in more detail in subsequent chapters, the movement is toward photonic (PXC) switches (O/O/O devices) due to their capacity and speed.

THE DIGITAL MULTIPLEXING HIERARCHY

It was noted that the backbone network must support millions of customers and transmission rates in scores of terabits per second. In addition, this huge customer payload must be organized in a structured manner if it is to be managed properly. One key aspect of supporting, organizing, and managing this traffic is through digital multiplexing technologies.

The idea of digital multiplexing is to use multiplexing levels. As seen in Figure 2–3, at the lowest level, the user's traffic is not multiplexed. The most common example is a customer's voice traffic operating at 64 kbit/s (it is called a DS0 signal). In many networks (at a PBX in a building, or at the telephone central office), 24 DS0 signals are multiplexed together to make better use of, say, the copper wires going to the telephone office. These combined signals are called DS1 (and, in many circles, T1). To exploit the transmission capacity of other media, such as microwave, coaxial cable, and certainly optical fiber, 28 DS1s are multiplexed into what is called DS3 (or T3, in many circles).

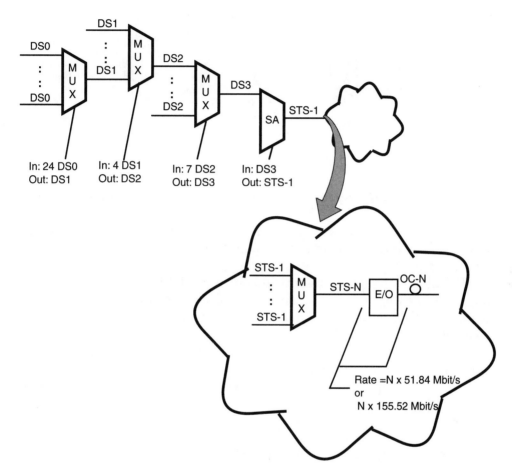

Figure 2–3   The North American multiplexing hierarchy.

Figure 2–3 shows another stage of the multiplexing called the DS2 signal. This operation is usually invisible to a customer; that is, a customer can purchase DS0, DS1, and DS3 payloads, but DS2 is usually not part of a commercial offering. It is placed in this figure because it plays a role in some of the SONET operations discussed in later chapters.

On the right side of Figure 2–3 is yet another stage of the operations. The DS3 signal is mapped into an STS-1 signal (synchronous transport signal number 1) by a service adapter (SA). The purpose of this operation is to add some overhead bytes to the DS3 and to align the DS3 properly with the network's other payloads.

The network cloud is expanded at the bottom part of Figure 2–3. Another multiplexer combines multiple STS-1s into another higher capacity

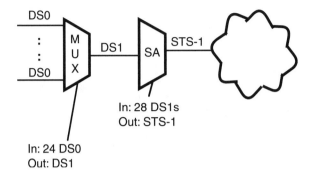

Figure 2–4   Another way to multiplex the users' signals.

payload, STS-N. The N can take different values (two values of N are shown in the figure), depending on specific configurations in the network, a topic explained in greater detail in Chapter 5.

Finally, an electrical-to-optical converter (E/O) converts the electrical signal to an optical signal, now called the OC-N signal. The small circle on the OC-N link is a common notation to identify optical (in contrast to electrical) links.

There are other ways to groom the traffic for transport across the optical network. As suggested in Figure 2–4, it is possible (and a common practice) to multiplex 28 DS1s into separate tributaries and carry them in the STS-1 signal.

THE DIGITAL SIGNALING HIERARCHIES

During the past 30 years, three different digital signaling hierarchies have evolved in various parts of the world. These hierarchies were developed in Europe, Japan, and North America, and are first generation digital transport systems. See Figure 2–5. Fortunately, all are based on the basic clocking rate of 125 μsec, and the basic 64 bit/s signal. Therefore, the basic architectures interwork reasonably well. However, their multiplexing hierarchies differ considerably, and the analog/digital conversion schemes are not the same.

Japan and North America base their multiplexing hierarchies on the DS1 rate of 1.544 Mbit/s. Europe uses an E1 2.048 Mbit/s multiplexing scheme. Thereafter, the three approaches multiplex these schemes in multiples of these rates (plus some overhead bits).

The Synchronous Digital Hierarchy (SDH) is the official international standard for second generation digital carrier networks. It is based

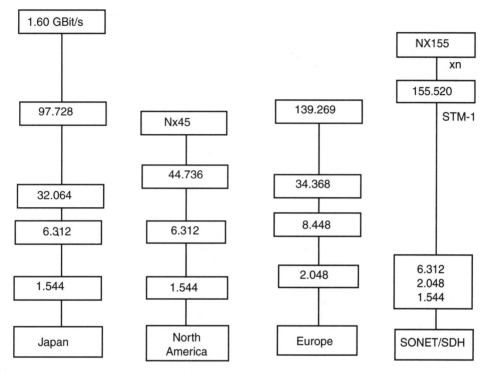

Note: Unless noted otherwise, speeds in Mbit/s

Figure 2–5   The digital multiplexing hierarchy.

on SONET, and specifies a different multiplexing hierarchy. The basic SDH rate is 155.52 Mbit/s. It then uses a N x 155.52 multiplexing scheme. A smaller rate than 155.52 Mbit/s is available for SONET. The smaller rate is 51.840 Mbit/s.

Shortly after the inception of T1 in North America in the early 1960s, the ITU-T published the E1 standards, which were implemented in Europe and most other parts of the world. Japan followed with a hierarchy similar to the North American specifications at the lower hierarchical levels, but not at the higher levels.

T1 is based on multiplexing 24 users onto one physical TDM circuit. T1 operates at 1,544,000 bit/s, which was (in the 1960s) about the highest rate that could be supported across twisted wire-pair for a distance of approximately one mile. Interestingly, the distance of one mile (actually, about 6000 feet) represented the spacing between manholes in large cities. They were so spaced to permit maintenance work such as splicing cables and the placing of amplifiers. This physical layout provided a convenient means to replace the analog amplifiers with digital repeaters.

T1 OR DS1; T3 OR DS3?

The term T1 was devised by AT&T (before divestiture in 1984) to describe a specific type of carrier technology. Strictly speaking, the term DS1 is the correct post-divestiture term. To keep matters simple, this

North American Multiplexing Hierarchy				
Type	*Digital Bit Rate*	*Voice Circuits*	*T1*	*DS3*
DS1	1.544 Mbit/s	24	1	-
DS1C	3.152 Mbit/s	48	2	-
DS2	6.312 Mbit/s	96	4	-
DS3	44.736 Mbit/s	672	28	1
DS4	274.176 Mbit/s	4032	168	6

European Multiplexing Hierarchy			
Type	*Digital Bit Rate*	*Voice Circuits*	*System Name*
E1	2.048 Mbit/s	30	M1
E2	8.448 Mbit/s	120	M2
E3	34.368 Mbit/s	480	M3
E4	139.264 Mbit/s	1920	M4
E5	565.148 Mbit/s	7680	M5

Japanese Multiplexing Hierarchy			
Type	*Digital Bit Rate*	*Voice Circuits*	*System Name*
1	1.544 Mbit/s	24	F1
2	6.312 Mbit/s	96	F6M
3	34.064 Mbit/s	480	F32M
4	97.728 Mbit/s	1440	F100M
5	397.20 Mbit/s	5760	F400M
6	1588.80 Mbit/s	23040	F4.6G

Figure 2–6   The digital multiplexing schemes.

book uses the term T1 synonymously with the term DS1, and the term T3 synonymously with DS3. Figure 2–6 shows the more common digital multiplexing schemes used in Europe, North America, and Japan, and the terms associated with these schemes.

THE LAYERED PROTOCOL MODEL
IN THE TRANSPORT NETWORK

Throughout this book, it is convenient to use the OSI layered protocol model to explain aspects of transport networks. If you are new to layered protocols and the OSI model, see [BLAC91]. Figure 2–7 depicts a view of this model and the relationships of the layers of transport networks, MPLS, and the principal Internet protocols for the model.

The first observation is that transport networks operate at the physical layer (layer 1) of the model. Originally, the OSI model defined the physical layer as one that had restricted, physical functions such as signal generation/reception, clocking, the definition of the media (fiber, copper), and so on. While this statement still holds, the 2G and 3G physical layers are quite powerful, and define many other operations, such as extensive diagnostics, backup/recovery, and bandwidth provisioning.

OSI	1G, 2G, 3G Transport Networks	MPLS	Internet
Application			Web, Email, etc.
Presentation			Not Used
Session			Not Used
Transport			TCP/UDP
Network			IP
Data Link		MPLS	MPLS
Physical	T1, E1, SDH, OTN, etc.	T1, E1, SDH, OTN, etc.	T1, E1, SDH, OTN, etc.

Figure 2–7   The layered model and other layered protocols.

For this book, the layer 1 remains the same for MPLS and IP operations. In addition, it is assumed the IP (and the upper layers above IP) will operate over MPLS, unless otherwise stated.

CONSIDERATIONS FOR INTERWORKING LAYER 1, LAYER 2, AND LAYER 3 NETWORKS

One of the fundamental concepts in the 3rd generation transport network is the interworking of the layer 1, layer 2, and layer 3 entities; in effect, the graceful interactions among what are called circuit-switched operations at layer 1 and packet/frame/datagram operations at layers 2 and 3.[1] This book covers this topic in many sections in subsequent chapters. For this discussion, it is noteworthy that 3G optical networks are essentially layer 1 networks, and they display some of the characteristics of 1G and 2G circuit-switched networks. The salient aspects of these systems for this book include the following points:

1. Circuit-switched nodes (such as an SS7 switch) may have thousands of physical links (ports).
2. These ports (unlike IP networks) do not have IP addresses. They are usually identified by (a) a switch-specific port number (interface) and (b) a channel ID on the port; for TDM, a slot number (say, DS0 # 6, or STS-1 # 2), and for WDM, a wavelength ID (say, wavelength # 4 on the fiber).
3. Neighbor nodes do not need to know about their neighbor's internal port number ID; they need to know the channel ID on the port in order to recognize each piece of traffic. The exception to this statement is when many links are bundled together as a fiber link set; in this situation, the neighbor nodes need to know the specific link in the set.
4. Many of the circuit-switches' features are configured manually, and many of the operations in the switch remain static throughout the sending and receiving of user traffic.

---

[1]The terms packet and frame are often used interchangeably. If they are distinguished from each other, frame refers to a unit of traffic associated with layer 2 (and in some transport networks, even layer 1), and packet refers to any unit of traffic associated with layers 3 and above. The term datagram is always associated with an IP packet at layer 3.

5. The switching technology on circuit-switches is based on a very fast hardware-oriented cross-connect fabric, wherein the input and output ports are very tightly synchronized to the receiving and sending of discrete, fixed-length TDM slots of traffic.

These important points are revisited in Chapter 10; see "Considerations for Interworking Layer 1 Lambdas and Layer 2 Labels."

SUMMARY

Most businesses and residences communicate with each other via the telephone, the CATV cable, and mobile phones. If the connections are made over a wide area, the long haul networks (the 1st, 2nd, or 3rd transport networks) come into play. Most of the long haul media is optical fiber, but the local connections from the long haul network to a customer are a mix of copper wire, coaxial cable, optical fiber, and wireless technologies.

Multiplexing is an indispensable tool for aggregating (and managing) customers' traffic into high bit rates for transport across the specific medium. Different multiplexing hierarchies have evolved over time, but the trend is to migrate to one multiplexing scheme—a subject for later chapters.

3

Characteristics of Optical Fiber

This chapter is a tutorial on optical fiber. Hundreds of books and papers are devoted to this subject. The approach is to provide the newcomer with the requisite information needed to understand the role they play in 3G optical transport networks and in the emerging optical Internet. For those readers who want to delve into the engineering aspects of this technology, I provide several references as we proceed through the chapter.

THE BASICS

Before one can grasp the underlying concepts of fiber optics, several aspects of light should be considered. It is instructive to note that light is part of the electromagnetic spectrum. The light that is visible to the human eye is only a fraction of the entire spectrum range, and light frequencies are several orders of magnitude higher than the highest radio frequencies. Different colors or wavelengths that constitute light are nothing more than different frequencies that propagate at various speeds over a medium. The prism can be used to demonstrate this phenomenon. When white light (which is the composite of all visible colors) enters the prism, it refracts and bends differently because of the individual speeds of the various frequencies or colors. Because of this refraction process, the colors exit separately. So, in a sense, the prism is an optical demultiplexer.

Fiber optics is the technology of transmitting information over optical fiber in the form of light. The light energy consists of *photons*, which is the quantum of radiant energy. The electrical signal to be transmitted is converted at the source into a light signal, which is then modulated and sent to a light-emitting diode or a laser for transmission through the fiber. At the receiving end, the detector converts the modulated light signal back to its electrical equivalent.

The fiber used in communications is usually a fine strand of glass weighing on the order of one ounce per kilometer, and it is as thin as human hair (50–150 microns in diameter for multimode and 8 microns for single-mode fiber, discussed shortly). Plastic fiber also exists, and it is applied to short distance needs.

Some of the advantages of fiber optics noted in Chapter 1 (compared to copper cable) include superior transmission quality and efficiency, as well as the elimination of crosstalk, static, echo, and delay problems. Fiber also minimizes environmental effects such as weather, water, and freezing. Once again, optical fiber is very small and of light weight. It has a wide bandwidth which allows for the transport of very large payloads.

THE WAVELENGTH

Light is a form of energy radiation at very high frequencies. For example, the frequency of the color blue operates at 600 THz. In optical networks, the practice is not to use frequencies in defining an optical channel, but to use the term *wavelength*. The wavelength is defined by the length in nanometers (nm) of the optical signal. Figure 3–1 shows how a wavelength is measured. It is the distance (measured in meters) between successive iterations of the oscillating light signal. The frequency of the signal is the number of waves that are sent on the fiber (and measured at a fixed point) in one second. Frequency is designated by the term hertz (Hz).

Wavelength

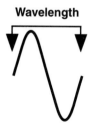

Figure 3–1   The wavelength.

Table 3–1   Common Terms

Multiplication Factor		Prefix	Symbol	Meaning
0.1 =	10^{-1}	deci	d	Tenth
0.01 =	10^{-2}	centi	c	Hundredth
0.001 =	10^{-3}	milli	m	Thousandth
0.000 001 =	10^{-6}	micro	μ	Millionth
0.000 000 001 =	10^{-9}	nano	n	Billionth
0.000 000 000 001 =	10^{-12}	pico	p	Trillionth
0.000 000 000 000 001 =	10^{-15}	femto	f	Quadrillionth
0.000 000 000 000 000 001 =	10^{-18}	atto	a	Quintillionth

The higher the frequency of the signal, the shorter the wavelength. This fact is demonstrated by:

Frequency (in Hz) = Speed of light in a vacuum (in meters) / Wavelength (in meters)

Thus, a frequency of 192.1 THz operates with a wavelength of 1560.606 nm (191.1 THz = 299,792,458 / .000001560606). As another example, a frequency of 194.7 THz operates with a wavelength of 1539.766 nm (194.7 THz = 299,792,458 / .000001539.766).

Table 3–1 should prove helpful as you read this book about wavelengths. As you can see, a nanometer wavelength is one billionth of a meter. A typical optical wavelength is 1552.52 nm.

THE BASIC COMPONENTS

Like other media technologies, a fiber optic system has three basic components (see Figure 3–2): the optic fiber or light guide, the transmitter or light source, and the receiver or light detector.

The Source of the Signal

For producing the light signal, the emission can be a spontaneous emission or a stimulated emission [DUTT98].[1] The spontaneous emission takes place when a electron (well, many electrons) is brought to a very

---

[1]For the reader who needs basic information on optical fiber beyond this chapter, Dutton's book is top-notch. It is, overall, the best-written book that I know of on the subject. It has very little overlap with the subject matter in this book, so it would serve as a good companion to the book you are now reading.

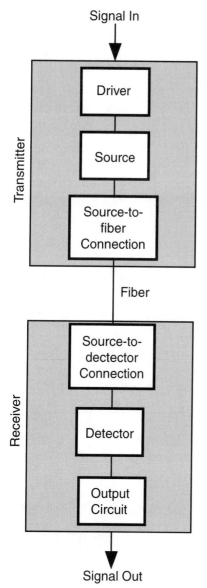

Figure 3–2   The basic fiber setup.

high energy level, and an unstable state. The electron will return spontaneously (in a few pico seconds) to a stable state, and will emit a photon in doing so. The optical wavelength is determined by the amount of energy the electron releases.

A laser operates with stimulated emission. For this process, the electron enters and stays in a high-energy state for a few microseconds. Then it changes its state spontaneously. During this state, it can be stimulated by a photon to emit its energy in the form of another photon. Thus, the laser produces the light signal which is sent into the fiber.

The Detector

Several kinds of optical detectors are used in optical systems. The photoconductor is a good example. It is a piece of undoped semiconductor material that has electrical contacts attached to it, with voltage applied across the contacts. When a photon arrives from the fiber, it is absorbed by the material, resulting in the creation of an electron/hole pair. The electron and the hole migrate toward one of the electrical contacts, with the electron attracted to the positive contact, and the hole migrating to the negative contact, thus creating the electrical energy.

STRUCTURE OF THE FIBER

Figure 3–3 (a) shows the parts that make up an optical fiber cable. The optical fiber works on the principle of total internal reflection. Once light begins to reflect down the fiber, it will continue to do so. The fiber is constructed of two layers of glass or plastic, one layer surrounding the other, as shown in Figure 3–3 (a). These layers are then enclosed in a protective jacket. The jacket surrounding the core and cladding is some type of polymer protective coating. The inner layer, the *core*, has a higher refractive index (n_1) than the outer layer (n_2), the *cladding,* as depicted in Figure 3–3 (b). Light injected into the core and striking the core-to-cladding interface at greater than the critical angle will be reflected back into the core.

The overall size of the optical fiber is quite small. As one example, in a single mode fiber (explained shortly), the core is about 10 micrometers in diameter (0.000010m). The cladding is around 125 mmeters (0.000125 mm).

Angles

Figure 3–4 shows several aspects of the fiber and the optical signal. Two aspects of the signal's propagation are of interest here: the angles of incidence (identified as θ_1) and reflection (identified as θ_{1r}). The light signal propagates down the fiber going through a series of reflections off the cladding, back into the core, then to the cladding, then back into the core, and so on.

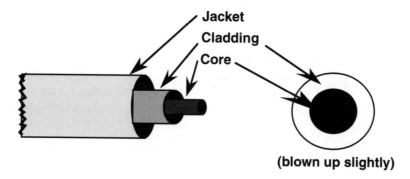

(a) Structure of Optical Fiber

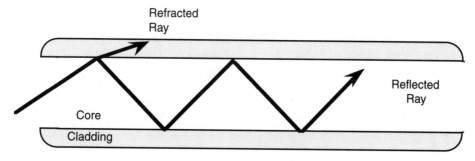

(b) Signal Propagation

Figure 3–3   Structure of the fiber.

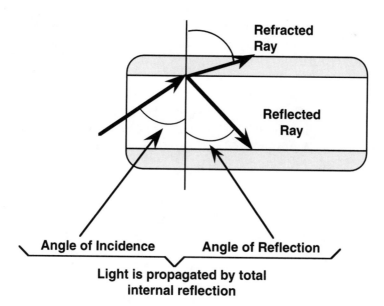

Light is propagated by total
internal reflection

Figure 3–4   Total internal reflection.

Since the angles of incidence (θ_1) and reflection (θ_{1r}) are equal (a law of geometrical optics), the light will continue to be reflected down the core. This concept is not unlike a very long and very narrow billiards table. A ball shot at an angle into the cushion will bounce off at the same angle and continue bouncing from cushion to cushion down the length of the table, always at the same angle. Light striking the interface at less than the critical angle will pass into the cladding and will be absorbed and then dissipated by the jacket. (However, a significant amount of the energy of the light can propagate down the cladding.)

As the angle of incidence increases, so too does the angle of reflection. For larger values of θ_1, there is no refracted ray; thus, all the energy from the incident ray is reflected, and is called total internal reflection. The angle of refraction is the angle of the refracted signal (θ_2). To summarize this verbal description [RAMA98]:

$$\theta_{1r} = \theta_1$$
$$n_1 \sin\theta_1 = n_2 \sin\theta_2$$

FIBER TYPES

This part of the chapter examines the optical fiber technology in more detail, and I highly recommend [REFI99], if you want more details on this subject. Several of the examples in this section are sourced from this reference. I have already given my recommendation for [DUTT98] (see Footnote 1). Two other fine technical references on this subject are [ARGA92] and [RAMA98]. Any examples that are sourced from these references will be cited as appropriate.

Let's examine the concept of *mode*. See Figure 3–5. In its simplest form, a mode is a path that a light signal takes though a fiber. A multimode fiber is one in which the guided light ray takes different paths through the cable. A single-mode fiber is one in which the guided light ray takes one path through the cable.

The simplest fiber type is the multimode fiber. This fiber has a core diameter ranging from 125–400+ μm (.005 to over .016 of an inch), which allows many modes, or rays of light propagation. The most common multimode fiber deployed in the late 1970s and early 1980s had a core diameter of 50 μm. This fiber was used on interoffice and long-distance trunks. Today, multimode fiber is used almost exclusively for private premises systems in which distances are usually less than 1 km.

The larger core diameter in multimode fiber permits more modes. Since light reflects at a different angle for each mode, some rays will

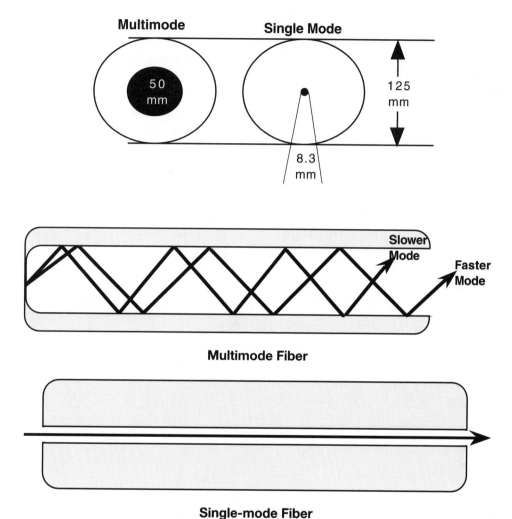

Figure 3–5   Basic fiber types.

follow longer paths than others; that is, each mode travels down the path at slightly different velocities.

The ray that goes straight down the core without any reflecting will arrive at the other end sooner than other rays. Other rays arrive later, and the more times a ray is reflected, the later it arrives. Thus, light entering the fiber at the same time may arrive at the other end at slightly different times. When this phenomenon occurs, we say that the light has "spread out." This spreading of light is called *modal dispersion*. The effect of modal dispersion is that the signal (the digital pulse) becomes smeared as it travels down the fiber.

A way to eliminate modal dispersion is to reduce the core's diameter until the fiber will propagate only one mode efficiently. In effect, the energy of the light signal travels in the form of one mode. This approach is used in the single-mode fiber, which has a core diameter of only 2–8 µm, with the most common diameter of about 8.3 µm. These fibers are by far the most efficient. Their advantages are minimum dispersion, high efficiency, and high operating speeds.

Single-mode fiber eliminates modal dispersion, but another potential problem may occur. It is called *chromatic dispersion*. The idea of chromatic dispersion is the same as modal dispersion. Even in single-mode fiber, different frequency components (wavelengths) travel at different speeds in the fiber. We will have more to say about chromatic dispersion shortly.

KEY PERFORMANCE PROPERTIES OF FIBER

Optical fiber's key performance properties discussed in this section are (a) attenuation, (b) chromatic dispersion, and (c) polarization mode dispersion. We start with a look at the decay of the signal's strength, called attenuation.

ATTENUATION

Figure 3–6 shows the spectral attenuation performance of a typical silica-based optical fiber. The attenuation decreases with increasing wavelength, except at wavelengths above 1.6 µm, due to bending-induced loss and silica absorption. Also, notice the three peaks in the figure. They are attenuation absorption peaks associated with the hydroxyl ion (OH-). The figure also shows five wavelength windows (labeled 1st through 5th), which represent implementations of several optical fiber wavelengths.

If low power levels are introduced into an optical fiber, the signal propagation behaves as if the medium were linear. This means that the power of the signal determines attenuation and the refractive index. However, high power levels have the effect of creating nonlinear effects; they are dependent upon the power level itself. Thus, at higher power levels, optical fiber exhibits nonlinearities. These nonlinearities, known

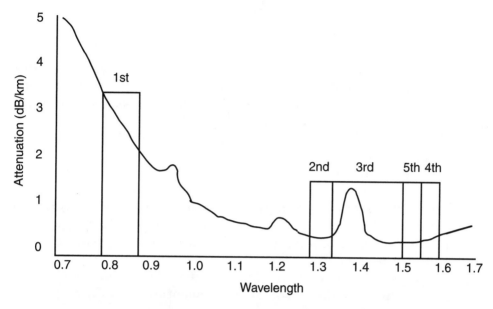

Figure 3–6   Attenuation performance of silica-based optical fiber [REFI99].

as *thresholds* when they reach the point of manifesting themselves, place limitations on the transmission capacity of optical fiber systems.

Early systems operated in the first window using multimode fiber at about 0.85 µm, and later in the second window at about 1.3 µm. Initially, single-mode fiber also operated in the second window with attenuation at about 0.35 dB/km or less. In the late 1990s, lasers supporting longer wavelengths (1.55 µm) became available operating in the third window with attenuation at around 0.2 dB/km.

The third window is where DWDM operates today, and commercial systems will soon support transmissions in the fourth window. The fifth window may come into use in the future.

AMPLIFIER SPONTANEOUS EMISSION (ASE)

Due to the attenuation of the optical signal, optical amplifiers must be placed on the link to boost the strength of the signal. This situation results in the following effects [CHIU01]. First, amplifiers do not perform perfectly, and during their amplification operation, they emit power not associated with the signal. This effect is called amplifier spontaneous emission (ASE).

ASE degrades the optical signal-to-noise ratio (OSNR). An acceptable optical SNR level (SNRmin) that depends on the bit rate, transmitter-receiver technology, and margins allocated for the impairments, needs to be maintained at the receiver. Vendors often provide some general engineering rule in terms of maximum length of the segment and number of spans. For example, current transmission systems are often limited to up to 6 spans each 80km long.

Assume that the average optical power launched at the transmitter is P. The lightpath from the transmitter to the receiver goes through M optical amplifiers, with each introducing some noise power. Unity gain can be used at all amplifier sites to maintain constant signal power at the input of each span to minimize noise power and nonlinearity. A constraint on the maximum number of spans can be obtained with well-known and published equations. If you want to delve into these details, refer to [KAMI97]. Some examples of implementations of fiber spans are discussed in Chapter 7.

CHROMATIC DISPERSION

Chromatic dispersion was introduced earlier. Recall that it is the effect of the different wavelengths traveling at different speeds in the fiber. In effect, the spectral components of the pulse travel at different speeds.

The first component of chromatic dispersion is called *material dispersion*. It arises because the refractive index of silica is frequency-dependent; that is, the dispersive characteristics of the dopants and the silica mean that the frequency components of the signal travel at different velocities.

The second component is called *waveguide dispersion*. It deals with the fact that the refractive index (the refractive indices of the cladding and the core) changes with wavelength. Waveguide dispersion is explained as follows [RAMA98]:

- The energy of the light propagates in the core and in the cladding.
- The effective index of a mode lies between the refractive indices of the core and the cladding.
- The value of the index between the two depends on the proportion of power that is in the core and the cladding. If most of the power

is in the core, the effective index is closer to the core refractive index; otherwise, it is closer to the cladding reflective index.

• The power distribution of a mode between the core and the cladding is a function of the wavelength.

• If the wavelength changes, the power distribution changes, resulting in the effective index or propagation constant of the mode to change.

Figure 3–7 shows the dispersion material component and two types of waveguide components: dispersion-unshifted fiber (USF) and dispersion-shifted fiber (DSF). The DSF component includes a variation of DSF, called non-zero-dispersion fiber (NZDF). These fibers are explained next, with references back to this figure.

Chromatic dispersion is measured in units of ps/nm-km. The term ps refers to the time spread of the pulse; nm is the spectral width of the pulse, and km is the length of the fiber cable.

A method to combat chromatic dispersion is called *dispersion-shifted* fiber (appropriate for single-mode fiber). It is designed to exhibit zero dispersion in the 1.55 μm wavelength.

Figure 3–8 compares the chromatic dispersion characteristics of three different single-mode fibers:

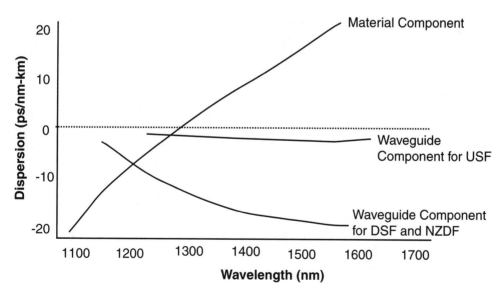

Figure 3–7   Material and waveguide dispersion components [REFI99].

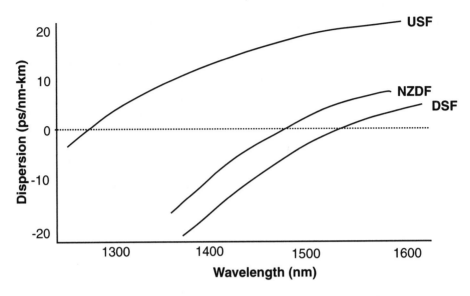

Figure 3–8   **Chromatic dispersion versus wavelength [REFI99].**

- *Dispersion-unshifted fiber (USF):* Zero-dispersion wavelength resides near 1.31 µm.
- *Nonzero-dispersion fiber (NZDF):* Zero-dispersion wavelength resides near 1.53 µm (may range to 1.565 µm). The initials for nonzero-dispersion fiber are also noted as NDF.
- *Dispersion-shifted fiber (DSF):* Zero-dispersion wavelength resides near 1.55 µm.

This discussion leads us to a more detailed explanation of the types of optical fibers in use. The International Telecommunication Union (ITU) has published recommended standards for four types of single-mode fibers.

Dispersion-unshifted fiber (USF) is an older technology that was introduced in 1983 (ITU G.652). It exhibits zero chromatic dispersion at 1310 nm. USF is very widely-used in the industry, and is also referred to as standard or conventional fiber. It is found as CATV operating in the second- and third-wavelength windows. It exhibits high chromatic dispersion at 1550 nm, and does not operate well at rates beyond 2.5 Gbit/s.

Dispersion-shifted fiber (DSF) was introduced in 1985 (ITU G.653). It exhibits zero chromatic dispersion at 1550 nm. Its attenuation performance (third window) is attractive. Due to its attractive attenuation and chromatic dispersion characteristics, it was considered a good candidate for 1550 nm systems. This initial view has been changed in view of the nonlinear effects of optical signals (discussed later). Notwithstanding, the technology is found in submarine systems and long-distance telephone networks. However, DSF does not perform well with multiple wavelengths in the third wavelength window, and it is being replaced by nonzero-dispersion fiber (NZDF), which will be discussed shortly.

1550 nm loss-minimized fiber is a special form of DSF and is published as ITU Recommendation G.654. It has very low loss in the 1550 nm signal. However, USF is expensive and difficult to manufacture. Its principal use has been in nonrepeated submarine systems.

Nonzero-dispersion fiber (NZDF or NDF) was introduced in the early 1990s. It is designed for DWDM systems, and it has been standardized by the ITU, as well as the Telecommunications Industry Association (TIA). It operates over a portion of the third wavelength window, with the chromatic dispersion small enough to support individual channel rates of 10 Gbit/s over distances of over 250 km. The chromatic dispersion ranges between 1 and 6 ps/nm-km in the 1550 nm wavelength window. Today, NZDF is deployed extensively in submarine as well as long-haul terrestrial networks.

Polarization-mode Dispersion (PMD)

The third property (actually, impairment characteristic) of optical fiber is called *polarization-mode dispersion* (PMD; see Figure 3–9). This problem occurs because the fiber is not consistent along its length. Due to bending and twisting, as well as temperature changes, the fiber core is not exactly circular. The result is that the modes in the fiber exchange power with each other in a random fashion down the fiber length, which results in different group velocities; the signal breaks up. In effect, the light travels faster on one polarization plane than another.

The distribution of the energy of the signal over the state of polarizations (SOPs)[1] changes slowly with time [RAMA98]; that is, the instantaneous values conform to a Maxwellian function whose mean value increases with the square root of the fiber's length:

---

[1]The SOP refers to the distribution of light energy in two polarization modes. This idea is found in any electromagnetic signal. Light energy (the pulse), traveling down the fiber that is uniform along its length, is divided into two polarization modes, one on the x-axis and one on the y-axis. In ideal conditions, the two modes have the same propagation constant.

$$(\Delta\tau) = D_{PMD}\sqrt{L}$$

where $\Delta\tau$ is the time-averaged differential time delay, L is the length of the length, and D_{PMD} is the fiber PMD parameter, measured in ps/$\sqrt{km}$.

For a uniform fiber, the time spread is constant. In reality, the light energy of the pulse, propagating at different velocities, leads to pulse spreading, or PMD. The two modes are on the x-axis (slow mode) and y-axis (fast mode), as shown in this figure. The right side of the figure shows the PMD experienced with non-consistent fiber.

The various standards groups are now publishing parameters on PMD. The International Electrotechnical Commission (IEC) is working on a standard under IEC SC86A Working Group 1.

It should be noted that PMD might (depending on who is talking) be a problem in systems that use older optical fiber. For example, problems can occur using older fiber with transmissions rates in the 10 Gbit/s range, and some in the industry think that running high rates (such as 40 Gbit/s) is not operationally feasible. As illustrationed, [CHIU01] defines the following PMD performance parameters. For older fibers with a typical PMD parameter of 0.5 picoseconds per square root of km, based on the constraint, the maximum length of the fiber segment should not exceed 400 km and 25 km for bit rates of 10 Gbit/s and 40 Gbit/s, respectively. For newer fibers with a PMD parameter of 0.1 picosecond per square root of km, the maximum length of the transparent segment (without PMD compensation) is limited to 10000 km and 625 km for bit rates of 10 Gbit/s and 40 Gbit/s, respectively. In general, the PMD re-

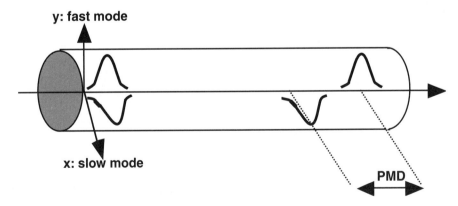

Figure 3–9   PMD [REFI99].

quirement is not an issue for most types of fibers at 10 Gbit/s or lower bit rate.

Components are available to reduce the effect of PMD. They are called PMD compensators, and are now available for rates as high as 40 Gbit/s. But they cost money, and some companies think the problem is overblown. As of this writing, the issue of PMD and how serious a problem it is has not been resolved. Many of the solutions are still in the vendors' labs. So, stay tuned, and stay alert to the issue.

LASERS

Lasers were introduced briefly at the beginning of this chapter. The term laser is a shortened form for "light amplification by stimulated emission of radiation." Lasers are used in high-capacity optical networks to send the optical signals to the fiber. They are very small semiconductor devices designed to transmit very specific and precise wavelengths. These transmitters operate on the principal of an "excited state," which means that the electrons in certain parts of the semiconductor material have more energy than other electrons. When the electron loses some of its energy and falls to a ground state, the energy released is in the form of photon, light energy. Appling electrical current to the laser produces many electrons in an excited state. Of course, as these many electrons decay to a ground state, they give off light energy in the form of many photons.

SUMMARY

While the optical fiber medium is clearly superior to copper and wireless media in regards to bandwidth and signal quality, optical signals still suffer from transmission impairments. They are broadly classified as attenuation, chromatic dispersion, and polarization-mode dispersion. The effects of these problems depend on the type of fiber used, as well as other factors such as the wavelength(s) transmitted on the fiber, the spacing (and nature) of the amplifiers, and the condition of the fiber cable.

4

Timing and Synchronization

This chapter explains the synchronization and clocking functions used in optical networks. Asynchronous and synchronous networks are examined. Clock variations and controlled and uncontrolled clocking slips are analyzed, and compared to each other. After these subjects are covered, clock distribution systems are examined. The chapter concludes with a discussion of synchronization messages.

TIMING AND SYNCHRONIZATION IN DIGITAL NETWORKS

With the advent of digital networks and the transmission and reception of binary pulses (1s and 0s), it became important to devise some method for detecting these signals accurately at the receiver. Figure 4–1 illustrates the problem.

The ideal system is one in which the binary pulses arrive at the receiver in a very precise and concise manner. This means that the receiver knows the exact time that the signal (a binary 1 or 0) manifests itself at the receiver interface. This synchronization between the transmitter and the receiver is achieved because each machine knows about the other's "clock," that is, at which frequency the sending machine sends its traffic to the receiving machine. Fortunately, it is a relatively easy task to determine this timing, because the receiver can derive (extract) the clock from the incoming bit stream by examining when the pulses arrive at the receiver. For example, in Figure 4–1(a), the signal and the clock are perfectly aligned when the signal reference mark occurs with the zero crossing in the physical clock wave form. However, errors can occur if the clock is not aligned with the signal, as seen in Figure 4–1(b). This problem is usually called phase variation, and it may translate into an incorrect interpretation of the binary 1s and 0s in the transmission stream.

Therefore, it is not enough that signals be aligned in the same frequency domain (the same rate of ticking of the clocks). The signals must also be aligned in the phase domain (the same instant that the clocks emanate the tick).

In older systems that operated at a relatively low bit rate, the clocking did not have to be very accurate because the signal on the line did not change very often. As the digital networks became faster and more bits were transmitted per second, the time the bits were on the channel decreased significantly. This meant that if there was a slight inaccuracy in the timing of the receiver's sampling clock, it might not detect a bit or, more often, it might not detect several bits in succession. This situation leads to a problem called slips. Slipping is the loss of timing and the resultant loss of the detection of bits.

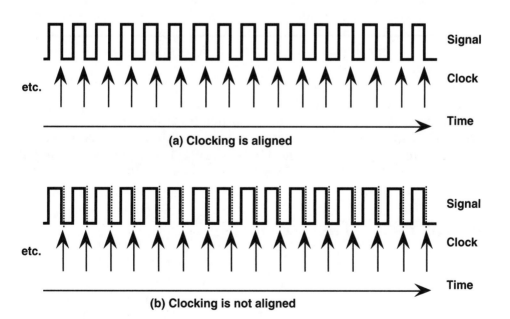

(a) Clocking is aligned

(b) Clocking is not aligned

Figure 4–1   Clocking and phase variation.

EFFECT OF A TIMING ERROR

Without the use of clocking mechanisms, an error will be passed to customers, perhaps through multiple nodes in the network. This creates a ripple effect throughout the network, but its effect depends on the type of traffic being transmitted. The typical impact of clocking errors on different types of user traffic is:

Type of Traffic	Result of Error
Digital data	Reduced throughput
Encrypted data	Resend key
Fax	Missing lines/distorted page
Video	Picture freeze, or dropouts
Voice	Audible click
Voice band data	Carrier drop

THE CLOCKING SIGNAL

In its simplest terms, a clocking signal carries information about time. This information is represented by the signal crossing a reference mark. In Figure 4–1, for example, when the signal crosses a certain voltage level, this crossing allows the receiver to determine when the clocking signals occur.

Different terms are used to describe the clocking signal. The one used in most of the literature is the unit interval (UI), which corresponds to one cycle of the clocking signal. Another term is the phase, which is measured in radians (1 UI = 2 radians). UI is equal to the reciprocal of the data rate. As examples, one UI for a DS1 1.544 Mbit/s rate is 648 nsec and one UI for a DS3 44.736 Mbit/s rate is about 22 nsec.

TYPES OF TIMING IN NETWORKS

The systems that existed in the 1950s and early 1960s were not synchronized to any common clocking source because they consisted of analog circuits and did not need a precise timing setup. However, as digital networks were deployed, and especially with the advent of the T1 technology, timing became a greater concern.

These early digital networks were not synchronized to a common frequency, and thus they were called asynchronous networks. Each machine in the network ran its own "free-running clock," and the clocks between two machines could vary by many unit intervals.

Today, optical networks are called synchronous networks because the timing is tightly controlled. In reality, they are actually plesiochronous networks. The prefix plesio means "nearly." Each portion of the network, as shown in Figure 4–2, is synchronized to a highly accurate primary reference source (PRS) clock. Because of the superior level of performance and the fact that this technique is fairly inexpensive, PRS clocks are a cost-effective way to improve network performance. In Figure 4–2, a portion of this network is referenced with primary reference source x (PRS x) and another portion is synchronized with PRS y. Thus, the term plesiochronous distinguishes this type of network from a truly synchronous network, which has only one PRS. The distinction between synchronous and plesiochronous is not used much today, so we will use the term synchronous throughout the book.

Ideally, a single synchronous network uses one PRS, which is also known as the master clock. As shown in Figure 4–3, the components derive their clocking from this master clock. Timing is derived first from the master clock, and then from a slave (in this example, a toll office).

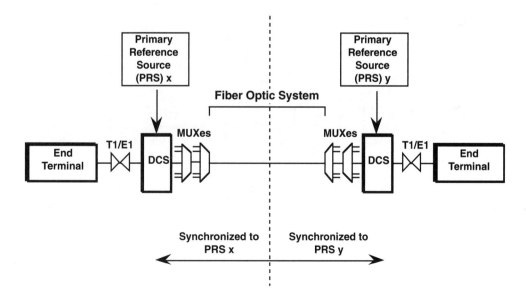

Figure 4–2   Synchronous networks.

Then, the timing is passed to digital switches, digital cross-connects, end offices, etc. Therefore, timing is "cascaded down" to other equipment, such as channel banks and multiplexers.

Figure 4–3 also shows the employment of different types of clocks called stratum n clocks. Each stratum n clock is required to perform within a certain degree of accuracy. The stratum 1 clock must meet the most stringent timing requirements, whereas the stratum 4 clock needs to meet only the least stringent requirements.

The Synchronous Clock Hierarchy

Table 4–1 summarizes the synchronous network clock hierarchy and shows long-term accuracy for each stratum level, as well as typical locations of the clocking operations. Long-term accuracy for the stratum 1

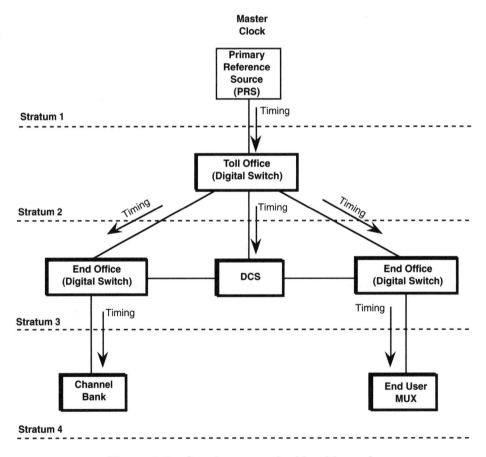

Figure 4–3   Synchronous clocking hierarchy.

Table 4–1   Clock Hierarchy for Synchronous Networks

Clock Stratum	Typical Location(s)	Free-Run Accuracy (Minimum)
1	Primary Reference Source (PRS)	± 1.0 X 10^{-11*}
2	Class 4 office	± 1.6 X 10^{-8}
3 and 3E[1]	Class 5 office, DCS	± 4.6 X 10^{-6}
4 and 4E[1]	Channel bank, end-user Mux	± 32 X 10^{-6}

* = Also annotated as .00001 ppm (parts per million)

[1]Stratum 3E and 4E clocks are not part of ANSI standards (ANSI T1.101). They are used by (the former) Bellcore (GR-1244-CORE) and stipulate more stringent requirements with regard to wander and holdover (a loss of a previously connected external reference). These enhanced clocks are compatible with the ANSI T1.101 clocks.

clocks is $\pm 1.0 * 10^{-11}$. The next level of accuracy is the stratum 2 clock, which is usually located in class 4 toll offices. The long-term accuracy for these clocks is $\pm 1.6 * 10^{-8}$. Next in the order of accuracy are the stratum 3 clocks, typically located in the class 5 end office or a digital cross-connect (DCS). The long-term accuracy of these clocks is $\pm 4.6 * 10^{-6}$. The last level of the synchronous network clock hierarchy is the stratum 4 clock. These clocks are usually located in channel banks or multiplexers at the end-user site. Their accuracy is $\pm 32 * 10^{-6}$.

TIMING VARIATIONS

While synchronous networks exhibit very accurate timing, some variation will exist between the network elements within a network as well as network elements between networks. This variation is generally known as phase variation.

Phase variation is usually divided into *jitter* and *wander*. Jitter is defined as a short-term variation in the phase of a digital signal, which includes all variations above 10 Hz. In effect, jitter is the short term for variation of the digital signal's optimal position in time. Causes of jitter include common noise, the bit stuffing processes in multiplexers, or faulty repeaters.

In contrast, wander is the long-term variation in the phase of a signal and includes all phase variations below 10 Hz. Wander may also include the effects of frequency departure, which is a constant frequency difference between network elements. Wander is almost inevitable in any network due to the slight variations in clock frequency differences, transmission delay on the path, or bit stuffing operations.

Jitter and wander are dealt with in many digital networks through the use of buffers. These buffers exist at each interface in any machine where the signal is processed (multiplexed, switched, etc.). Buffers act as windows to receive and transmit traffic. Additionally, for digital systems, they can be used to accommodate to frequency departure or phase variations. Buffers are carefully designed to handle the most common variations.

Frequency Accuracy

Most systems in North America describe clocking accuracy as the degree that a clock's frequency deviates from its ideal value. It is defined as:

$$FF_{os} = (f - f_d)/f_d$$

where FF_{os} = fractional frequency offset, f = actual frequency output of a clock, and f_d = ideal or desired frequency.

In addition to the requirements cited above, Bellcore establishes the following requirements for holdover stability and the pull-in/hold-in range. The legend in Box 3–1 explains the column entries in Table 4–2.

Table 4–2   Other Timing Requirements

Stratum	Holdover Stability	Pull-in/Hold-in Range
1	N/A	N/A
2	$\pm 1 * 10^{-10}$/day	$\pm 1.6 * 10^{-8}$
3E	$\pm 1 \times 10^{-10}$/day*	$\pm 4.6 * 10^{-6}$
3	<255 slips ($\pm 3.7 \times 10^{-7}$)*	$\pm 4.6 * 10^{-6}$
4E	NA	$\pm 32 * 10^{-6}$
4	NA	$\pm 32 * 10^{-6}$

* For initial 24 hours

Box 4–1   Legend for Table 4–2

Holdover: Operating condition of a clock once it has lost a previously
                   connected clocking reference. During this time, the ma-
                   chine must exhibit the stability cited in this column.
Pull-in range: The largest band of input signal frequency for which the
                   clock will acquire lock. Assures that synchronization can be
                   achieved with a clock of equal stratum level that may be op-
                   erating at the limits of its permissible frequency offset, while
                   the clock-under-test is operating at the opposite frequency
                   offset limit.
Hold-in range: The largest band of input signal frequency for which the
                   clock will maintain lock. Specified so that a clock of a given
                   stratum level will be able to maintain lock with a reference
                   from a clock of the same stratum level as the upstream
                   clock varies in frequency.

METHODS OF CLOCK EXCHANGE

Clearly, it is in the best interest of all concerned to use a common clocking source for all machines in the network. Some systems use this approach and some systems do not. This part of the chapter expands on our
earlier discussions about clocking and describes several methods of
achieving synchronization between machines.

Five methods of clock exchange can be employed in a network. They
are as follows: (a) free-running, (b) line-timed, (c) loop-timed, (d) external, and (e) through-timed. Some systems use a combination of these
methods. The reader should check vendors offerings carefully, because
each vendor probably uses these operations in slightly different ways. In
addition, the design of each network element may place limitations on
how some of the clocking distributions operations are implemented.

Free-Running

The free-running method has each machine generate its own timing
from a (highly stable) crystal oscillator. In most systems, this oscillator
has a long-term accuracy better than ±4.6 ppm. Figure 4–4 shows a free-
running/free-running configuration. We use the term free-running twice
to denote that both machines on the line are running with an oscillator.

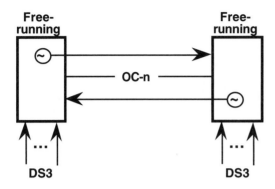

Figure 4–4   Free-running/free-running configuration.

⊙ **Free-running Oscillator**

With this approach, no external clocking source is used, which has its advantages and disadvantages. The advantage is obviating the expense of connecting to an external timing source. The disadvantage is the requirement for buffers to compensate for the delta between clock differences (i.e., an incoming DS3 signal and the outgoing signal to the other machine). Nonetheless, this approach is quite effective for point-to-point linear configurations with asynchronous (in this example, DS3) interfaces.

Line-Timed

The line-timed mode derives clocking from the signal on the incoming line. The clock extraction from this signal is fed into the local timing generator module, which, in turn provides the timing to the outgoing signals. This configuration is shown in Figure 4–5. The line-timed mode is simple, but it does not perform very well in configurations where several machines are connected linearly to each other in a path. Clocking inaccuracies tend to accumulate at each node and can lead to distorted signals.

Loop-Timed

Loop-timed mode is also called gateway or master/slave mode. It is used in systems where different timing generator modules are employed or where machines tied to different stratum levels must interact with each other.[2] The frequency sent from the master unit (in Figure 4–6 (a),

---

[2]Bellcore defines loop-timing as a timing mode for nodes that have only one synchronous interface. Therefore, it is a special case of line-timing. We consider this definition helpful but too restrictive.

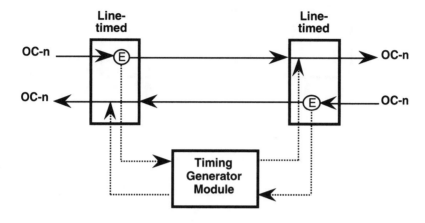

Line-timed   Line-timed

OC-n   OC-n

OC-n   OC-n

Timing
Generator
Module

Ⓔ = Clock extraction from line signal,
      dashed lines indicate clocking signals

Figure 4–5   Line-timed configuration.

the free-running unit) is used to derive the clock at the slave unit (in Figure 4–6(a), the loop-timed unit). The slave unit loops the receive clock back across the line as the transmit clock. The loop-timed mode may also employ an external clock, as shown in Figure 4–6(b). The external clock is typically a stratum 3 level clock or better. This configuration in this figure is also called the phase locked/loop-timed mode. Another configuration is shown in Figure 4–6(c). The slave unit can also furnish clocking utilizing the Building Integrated Timing Supply (BITS, described later in this chapter).

External

We introduced the external clocking mode in the previous section. As the name implies, the machines time their transmitted signals from internal oscillators that are locked to an external clocking source. This configuration requires local office clocks at each end terminal, so it is used in many interoffice applications. The clock sources illustrated in Figure 4–7 must be stratum 3 or better, and they may emanate from more than one primary reference source (that is, they may be plesiochronous systems). Figure 4–7 (b) shows that this configuration can provide synchronization outputs to the office BITS clock (or to other central office equipment).

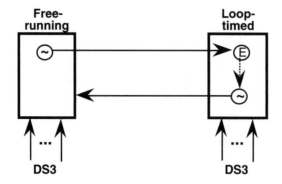

(a) Loop-timed at one end/free-running at the other end

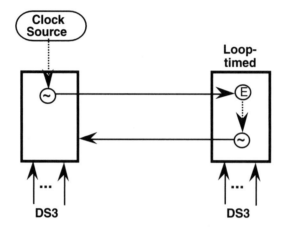

(b) Loop-timed at one end/external at the other end

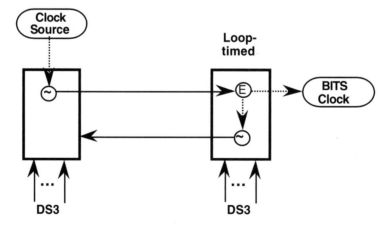

(c) Loop-timed at one end/external at the other end, and timing to BITS.

Figure 4–6   Loop-timing.

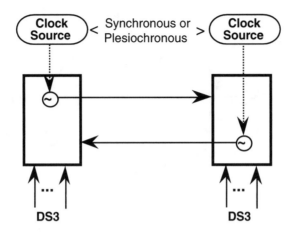

(a) External at both ends

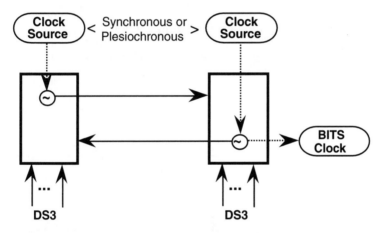

(b) External at both ends, and timing to BITS

Figure 4–7   External timing.

Through-Timed

The last example of timing distribution is called through or through-timed mode. We use a ring topology for this example. Two configurations are shown in Figure 4–8. In Figure 4–8(a), a free-running clock distributes timing signals to the other nodes on the ring. These nodes on the ring are through-timed. This term means that the network element derives its transmitted timing in the "east" direction from a received line signal in the "west" direction, and the transmit timing in the west

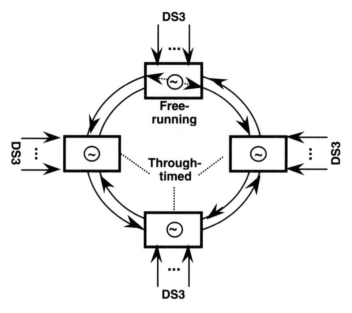

(a) Free-running clock and through-timed

Figure 4–8 (a)   Through-timed.

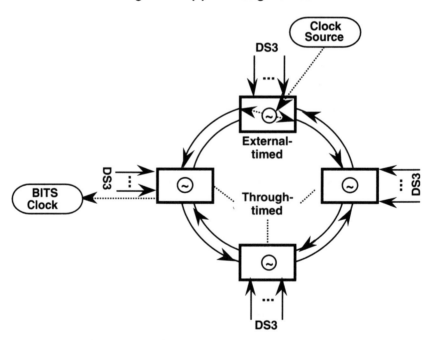

(b) External clock and through-timed

Figure 4–8 (b)   Through-timed, continued.

direction from the received line signal in the east direction. Through-timing is typically employed when the network node is passing the signal transparently through the node and does not want to change the timing. Through-timing is used in signal regeneration and echo cancellers.

Timing can be provided with an external clock as well, as depicted in Figure 4–8(b). This figure shows also that timing on the ring can be distributed to BITS.

DISTRIBUTION OF TIMING USING SONET AND DS1

Figure 4–9 shows a configuration for using both DS1 and SONET to distribute timing information. DS1 has been used over the years to distribute timing information throughout the network. As seen in this figure, the information is sent between the master (source) and slave clocks. These DS1 signals may also carry traffic. As networks have been upgraded to lightwave systems, SONET has become the preferred facility to transmit these signals among COs, interoffice networks, and access networks. The incoming OCn signal provides timing information, which is traceable back to a highly accurate reference clock, exhibiting low jitter and wander. The DS1 timing signal can also be used to feed the local BITS clock, or, if BITS is not available, the DS1 signal can be provided directly to other equipment.

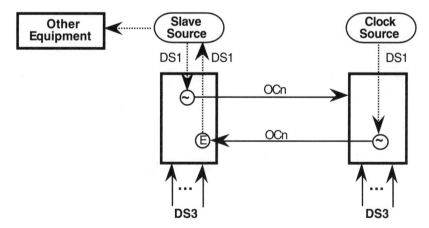

Figure 4–9   Using DS1 and SONET to distribute timing information.

TIMING DOWNSTREAM DEVICES

We have learned that synchronization can be provided with an external synchronization interface (ESI) and "cascaded" downstream to other nodes. An earlier discussion showed how this occurs in a ring configuration. Figure 4–10 shows several linear configuration options for downstream timing. These options are not all-inclusive.

Figure 4–10 depicts where timing is inserted in the line and the number of interfaces (as (n)) that are clocked by building integrated supply timing (BITS). In Figure 4–10(a), a terminal provides primary and backup BITS to 10 external interfaces, with the timing cascading down through add-drop multiplexers (ADMs) to an end terminal. Figure 4–10(b) is provided to emphasize that timing signals can be branched

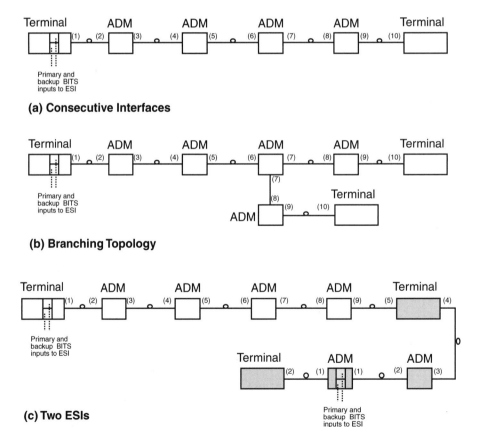

Figure 4–10   External synchronization interfaces (ESI).

across more than one link and to more than one end terminal. Figure 4–10(c) shows how two ESIs are terminated in one terminal. This configuration might occur if a terminal is connected to two different network providers. BITS does not define which ESI is the authoritative clock source—that issue must be resolved by the network providers. Some providers are reluctant to have their machines clocked by other providers. Others will not allow the customer to provide the clock.

THE BUILDING INTEGRATED TIMING SUPPLY (BITS)

The building integrated timing supply (BITS) is now being employed throughout the United States to provide synchronization for digital networks. BITS has two timing references: a primary source called reference A and a secondary source called reference B. Regardless of the source reference, timing must be traceable to a stratum 3 clock or better.

BITS can provide timing for a wide range of equipment, such as channel banks, cross-connects, SONET terminals, digital loop carriers (DLCs), signaling system #7 (SS7) components, asynchronous transfer mode (ATM) machines, frame relay nodes, and switched multimegabit data service (SMDS) devices.

BITS provides a composite clock for equipment with extractable timing of 64/8 kHz. It also provides DS1 timing as well as other timing, if needed. Figure 4–11 shows the 64/8 kHz composite clock. The term 64/8

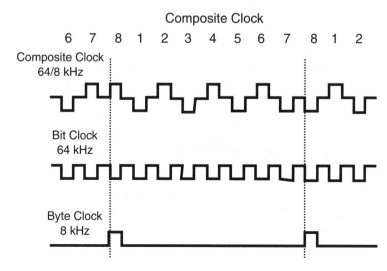

Figure 4–11   BITS clocks.

refers to a 64 kHz bit clock and a 8 kHz byte clock which can be derived from the composite clock stream. The 64 kHz bipolar clock is derived with every 8th bit bipolar violation (BPV). Additionally, the 8 kHz byte clock is derived by counting the BPVs in the byte clock.

Therefore, two types of phase criteria must be satisfied: (a) bit phase and (b) byte phase. We learned earlier that phase is any stage in a series of changes, and two signals are said to be "in phase" when the two signals are in the exact same stage; that is, at the same percent of amplitude (rising or falling) at the same time.

Figure 4–12 shows how a composite clock actually clocks data across a channel unit in an office. The system clocks data in at one end and out at the other end. Therefore, if a 1 data bit is clocked out as a 0, then the results are, of course in error. This error occurs when a transmitter's clock is out-of-phase with the receiver's clock. This situation can occur when two channel banks are referenced to two different composite clocks. While they both may be operating with the same frequency of 64 kHz, their signals are lacking phase sync.

While achieving correct bit phase synchronization is quite important, when used alone, bit phase synchronization does not guarantee accurate sync operations at the machine. Figure 4–13 shows that byte clock phase synchronization must also be provided by the network. The top part of the figure shows that the byte sent from the sender is in exact phase with the receiver's clock. Therefore, the sender and the receiver have both the same frequency and the same phase relationships. The lower part of the figure shows that the sender's and receiver's frequen-

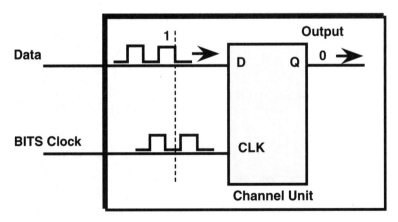

Out-of-phase Condition

Figure 4–12   Bit sync.

Both frequencies are the same and in phase:

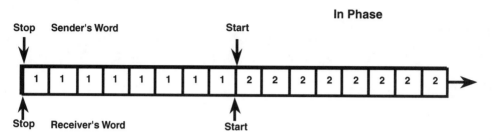

Both frequencies are the same but out-of-phase:

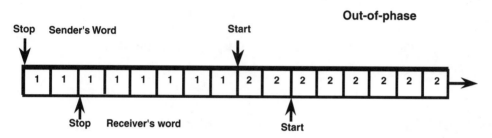

Figure 4–13   Byte sync.

cies are the same but their signals are out of alignment. Simply stated, the receiver is using a different set of 8 bits as a byte from the sender.

As we learned earlier, the byte BPV of the composite clock must be exactly the same with regard to amplitude polarity and the time it is measured. Figure 4–14 shows an out-of-phase signal from the perspective of transmitter and receiver.

Be aware that phase sync failure will not cause office alarms; therefore, no protection switching operation is invoked nor is an alternate data path chosen. Additionally, carriers normally do not monitor loss of a composite clock, but they will receive information via customer complaints.

In contrast to a system that does not employ BITS, timing problems are filtered out at a tandem office and Bellcore standards allow no more than four slips per day per circuit.

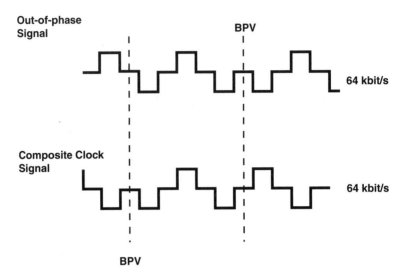

Figure 4–14   Composite clock and out-of-phase signal.

SYNCHRONIZATION STATUS MESSAGES (SSMS)
AND TIMING LOOPS

One of the overhead bytes of the SONET header (overhead bytes are discussed in Chapter 5) contains the synchronization status message (SSM). SSM indicates the status and quality level of the SONET signal. It allows the network provider to define which clocking source (and its accuracy) is being used in the network. The SSM operation is often referred to as S1-byte synchronization messaging.

The SSM operation is quite helpful in a situation where a node (say, node A) loses its synchronization clock from a primary source [NORTa99]. In Figure 4–15(a), node A is providing clocking information to node B from BITS 1. Further, node B is also receiving clocking from yet another node, say, node C. However, the message sent from B to A is coded as "Don't use." This prevents A and B from going into a timing loop.

In Figure 4–15(b), node A loses its BITS 1 timing, or the timing is degraded (say to stratum 3). Node A informs node B of this situation with a message stating that is running a statum 3 (holdover mode). Node B realizes that its clocking from node C is better than that from node A. Therefore, it sends a message to node A informing A that C has

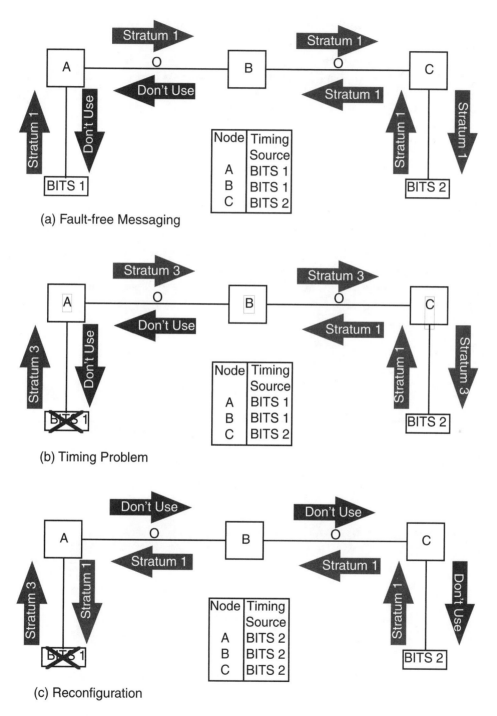

(a) Fault-free Messaging

Node	Timing Source
A	BITS 1
B	BITS 1
C	BITS 2

(b) Timing Problem

Node	Timing Source
A	BITS 1
B	BITS 1
C	BITS 2

(c) Reconfiguration

Node	Timing Source
A	BITS 2
B	BITS 2
C	BITS 2

Figure 4–15   Synchronization messaging examples.

access to statum 1 clocking. This message is relayed from node A to the BITS source.

Now, all components are clocked from BITS 2, as depicted in Figure 4–15 (c). All nodes are receiving their timing from BITS 2, through node C.

SUMMARY

Synchronization and clocking functions are vital operations in digital networks. Older carrier systems were asynchronous in nature, but today, all implementations in backbone networks use highly accurate and precise synchronous clocks. With these newer systems, clock variations and slips are tightly controlled (and are rare in occurrence relative to—especially—1G systems). Third-generation optical transport networks operating in the terabit range require very precise and accurate synchronization services.

5

SONET and SDH

This chapter surveys the second generation digital transport network technology, as implemented in SONET and SDH. The topic is introduced by explaining the origins of SONET and SDH, and how the two standards came about. The chapter then concentrates on the principle features of SONET and SDH, citing their main functions and how they perform these functions.

Following are some points to keep in mind during the reading of this chapter. SONET and SDH use the terms frame and envelope to describe a discrete unit of traffic on a communications link. The terms are used interchangeably. The term synchronous payload envelope (SPE) denotes that part of the envelope that contains the user traffic; the remainder of the envelope contains overhead bytes used to help manage the SPE.

HOW SONET AND SDH CAME INTO BEING

SONET and SDH were developed to replace the aging T1 and E1 technologies that were first deployed in the early 1960s to provide a high-speed (1.544 Mbit/s and 2.048 Mbit/s, respectively) digital carrier system for voice traffic.

Extensive research had been underway for more than a decade on many of the features that are found in SONET/SDH. One notable achievement began in 1984. It focused on the efforts of several standards

71

groups and vendors to develop optical transmission standards for what is known as the *mid-span meet* (also known as *transverse compatibility*). The goal was to publish a specification that would allow different vendors' equipment to operate with each other at the fiber level.

In addition, due to the breakup of the Bell System in 1984, there were no standards developed beyond the T3 technology. Prior to the divestiture, all equipment was built by AT&T's manufacturing arm, Western Electric (WECO), which ensured that there would be no compatibility problems of any components in the telephone network.

After the breakup, there was little incentive for the other carriers (such as MCI and Sprint) to purchase AT&T-based equipment. Indeed, there was an incentive *not* to purchase AT&T equipment, since AT&T, MCI, and Sprint had become competitors with each other for long-distance services. This situation led to the rapid growth of alternate equipment vendors (such as Nortel Networks), who were developing advanced digital switching technologies.

The 1984 divestiture paved the way for alternate long-distance carriers through the equal access ruling. The alternate carriers were given equal access to the local exchange carrier (LEC) infrastructure and connections to AT&T for end-to-end long-distance service. The LEC could connect to MCI, Sprint, and others through their switching facilities, at an interface in the LEC or long-distance carrier offices called the point of presence (POP).

During this time, higher capacity schemes beyond T3 became proprietary, creating serious compatibility problems for network operators who purchased equipment from different manufacturers. In addition, the early 1980s witnessed the proliferation of incompatible and competing optical fiber specifications.

The various standards groups began the work on SONET after MCI sent a request to them to establish standards for the mid-span meet. The SONET specifications were developed in the early 1980s and Bellcore submitted its proposals to the American National Standards Institute (ANSI) T1X1 Committee in early 1985, based on a 50.688 Mbit/s transfer rate. The initial SONET work did not arouse much interest until the Metrobus activity became recognized.

Later, using the innovative features of Metrobus, the SONET designers made modifications to the original SONET proposal, principally in the size of the frame and the manner in which T1 signals were mapped into the SONET frame.

From 1984 to 1986, various alternatives were considered by the ANSI T1 Committee, who settled on what became known as the synchronous transport signal number one (STS-1) rate as a base standard. Finally, in 1987, the ANSI T1X1 committee published a draft document on SONET.

PARTICIPATION BY ITU-T

During this time, the international standards body now known as the International Telecommunication Union-Telecommunication Standardization Sector (ITU-T) had rejected the STS-1 rate as a base rate in favor of a base rate of 155.520 Mbit/s. For a while, it appeared that the North American and European approaches might not converge, but the SONET frame syntax and structure were altered one more time to a rate of 51.84 Mbit/s, which permitted this rate to be multiplexed (concatenated) by an integer of three to the European preference of 155.52 Mbit/s. This work has resulted in almost complete compatibility between the North American and European approaches. The ITU-T Recommendations are now considered the "official" standards and are collectively called the Synchronous Digital Hierarchy (SDH).

Once the major aspects of the standards were in place, vendors and manufacturers began to develop SONET and SDH equipment and software. These efforts came to fruition in the early 1990s and, as of this writing, SONET and SDH have been deployed throughout the world.

REASONS FOR SUCCESS OF SONET/SDH

The SONET and SDH provide a number of attractive features when compared with the first generation transport networks. SONET/SDH is an optical-based carrier (transport) network utilizing synchronous operations between the network components/nodes, such as multiplexers, terminals, and switches. SONET/SDH's high speeds (some systems operate at the gigabit rate) rely on high-capacity fiber. Much of the T1 and E1 technology was geared toward the use of copper (twisted pairs) media, which operate at more modest transmission rates.

As just stated, the SONET/SDH network nodes are synchronized with each other through very accurate clocking operations, which insures that traffic is not "damaged," or lost due to clocking inaccuracies. T1/E1 clocking systems are very accurate, and they now use the same clocking mechanisms as SONET/SDH, but they were not originally so designed.

SONET/SDH is quite robust and provides high availability with self-healing topologies. In the event that a link is lost due to node or fiber failure, SONET/SDH can recover by diverting the traffic to back up facilities. Most T1/E1 systems can be configured for backup, but "robustness" is not an inherent part of a T1/E1 architecture.

SONET and its ITU-T counterpart SDH are international standards. As such, they pave the way for heterogeneous, multivendor systems to operate without conversions between them (with some exceptions).[1]

Unlike T1/E1, SONET/SDH give the network node a direct access to low-rate multiplexed signals, without the need to demultiplex the signals back to the original form. In other words, the payloads residing inside a SONET/SDH signal are directly available to a SONET/SDH node.

SONET/SDH provide extensive Operations, Administration, and Maintenance (OAM) services to the network user and administrator. Indeed, about 4% of the bandwidth in a SONET/SDH network is reserved for OAM. A T1 system allows only one bit per 193 bits for OAM&P, and E1 provides only one byte per frame. With this comparison in mind, it is easy to conclude that SONET and SDH have the capability for more extensive and powerful network management operations than T1 or E1.

THE SONET MULTIPLEXING HIERARCHY

We have emphasized several times that one of the most important functions of a transport network is the multiplexing of user traffic on low-capacity links into much larger payloads on higher capacity links. We also explained that a multiplexing hierarchy is essential to keep the many payloads (a) organized and (b) identified on the media. This section explains how SONET accomplishes this critical operation.

The synchronous transport signal-level 1 (STS-1) forms the basis for the optical carrier-level 1 signal. OC-1 is the foundation for the complete synchronous optical signal multiplexing hierarchy. The higher level signals are derived by the multiplexing of the lower level signals. The high-level signals are designated as STS-N (or electrical signals) and OC-N (for optical signals), where N is an integer number.

As illustrated in Table 5–1, OC transmission systems are multiplexed by the N values of 1, 3, 9, 12, 18, 24, 36, 48, to 192. Presently, signal levels OC-3, OC-12, OC-48, and OC-192 are most widely supported multiples of OC-1. Table 5–1 also shows the number of DS1 and DS3 signals that are carried in the OC envelopes.

---

[1]First generation digital carrier systems (such as T1 and E1 in Europe) are not standardized on a worldwide basis, and different systems exist in various parts of the world.

Table 5–1   SONET Transmission and Relationship to Asynchronous Payloads

Electrical	Optical Hierarchy	Transmission Line Rate (Mbit/s)	DS-3 Equiv.	DS1 Equiv.	DS0 Equiv.
STS-1	OC-1	51.840	1	28	672
STS-3	OC-3	155.520`	3	84	2,016
	OC-9	466.560	9	252	6,048
	OC-12	622.080	12	336	8,064
	OC-18	933.120	18	504	12,096
	OC-24	1,244.160	24	672	16,128
	OC-36	1,866.240	36	1,008	24,192
	OC-48	2,488.320	48	1,344	32,256
	OC-96	4,976.640	96	2,688	64,512
	OC-192	9,953.280	192	5,376	129,024

SONET AND SDH MULTIPLEXING STRUCTURE

Table 5–2 illustrates the similarities and differences of the SONET and SDH multiplexing structure. We use this table to compare the basic terminology used in the SONET and SDH multiplexing operations. The multiplexing operations of SONET and SDH are quite similar. Part of the challenge to understanding their relationships is to understand that the two hierarchies use different terms to describe very similar functions.

Table 5–2   Comparison of SONET/SDH Rates and Services

SONET	SDH	Bit Rate-Mbit/s	Mux. Rate
VT1.5		1.728	4 x 1.728 = 6.912
	VT2	2.304	3 x 2.304 = 6.912
VT3		3.456	2 x 3.456 = 6.912
VT6		6.912	1 x 6.912 = 6.912
STS-1	STM-0	51.84	7 x 6.912 or 1 x 51.84 = 51.84
STS-3	STM-1	155.52	3 x 51.84 = 155.52
STS-12	STM-4	622.08	4 x 155.52 = 622.08
STS-48	STM-16	2488.32	4 x 622.08 = 2488.32
STS-192	STM-64	9953.28	4 x 2488.32 = 9953.28

SONET uses the term virtual tributary (VT) to describe a specific user payload that it transports across a communications link. SDH uses the term virtual container (VC) to describe the user payload. For example, a VT might consist of a DS1 payload, and a VC might consist of an E1 payload. In some SDH documents, the term VT is also used.

Other key terms for the SDH signals are as follows: container (C-n), virtual-container (VC-n), tributary unit (TU-n), TU group (TUG-n), administrative unit (AU-n), and AU Group (AUG). The "n" following the various designations represents an integer number. The designations can have different numeric values following them. So "n" is substituted with a numerical value depending on what part of the SDH mapping hierarchy is being discussed.

SDH payloads are called synchronous transport modules (STMs), and are: STM-1, STM-4, STM-16, and STM-64. This notion also applies to both the container (C) designations and virtual container (VC) designations, as they can be represented with double digits. However, with the STM signals, the decimal number following the letters STM represents its multiplexing level.

In SONET, STS-3 is comprised of 3 DS-3s plus the SONET overheads, STS-12 has the bandwidth capabilities of 12 DS-3s, STS-48 has 48 DS-3s worth of bandwidth, and finally, there are 192 DS-3s equivalency of bandwidth in an STS-192 signal. Note that each jump in level is equal to four times, just as it is in the SDH STM hierarchy.

THE SONET/SDH FRAME STRUCTURE

An effective way to keep the many payloads organized on the fiber is to make certain that each bit and each byte is concisely and precisely structured and identified. This task is accomplished by defining how the user payloads and supporting overhead bytes are placed onto the fiber at the sending node and how they are removed at a receiving node. In this section, we learn how the organization is accomplished.

The basic transmission unit for SONET and SDH is the envelope (frame), as illustrated in Figure 5–1. It is comprised of 8 bit bytes (octets) that are transmitted serially on the optical fiber. For ease of documentation, the payload is depicted as a two-dimensional map. The map is comprised of n rows and m columns. Each entry in this map represents the individual octets of a synchronous payload *envelope*. (The "F" stands for flag, and is explained later.)

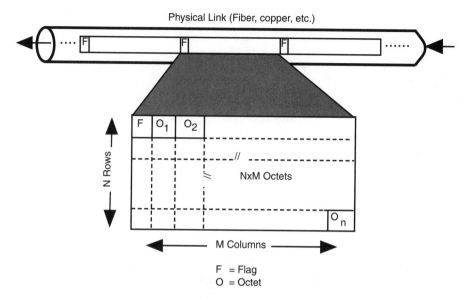

Figure 5–1　The SONET/SDH envelope (frame).

The octets are transmitted in sequential order, beginning in the top left-hand corner through the first row, and then through the second row, until the last octet is transmitted, which is the last row and last column.

The envelopes are sent contiguously and without interruption, and the payload is inserted into the envelope under stringent timing rules. In addition, a user payload may be inserted into more than one envelope, which means that the payload does not need to be inserted at the exact beginning of the part of the envelope that is reserved for this traffic. It can be placed in any part of this area, and a pointer is created to indicate where it begins.

This approach allows the network to operate synchronously while accepting asynchronous traffic. That is, traffic arriving at a node (say, a cross-connect) does not need to be synchronized with the clock at this node. By simply placing the user payload into the payload envelope as the user traffic arrives, the pointer can be set to indicate where the payload is. Thereafter, the payload is encapsulated into the SONET/SDH and sent on its way, using the ongoing network clocks to keep things synchronized.

Rationale for the 51.840 Mbit/s Envelope

In the second generation transport technology, all multiplexing rates start at the SONET rate of 51.840 Mbit/s or the SDH rate of 155.520 Mbit/s. As noted, the SONET basic rate was the foundation for all higher level rates in SONET and SDH. Therefore, it will be helpful to understand how this rate is created and the reasons for using the rate in the first place.

A key consideration in the design of SONET and SDH was to be able to support the T1 and E1 125 μsecond clocking increment. This timing unit is fundamental to the North American, Japanese, and European digital voice transport system because the universal 64 kbit/s voice channel is derived as:

- A voice signal is sampled at 8,000 times per second.
- Therefore, each sample duration is 125 μsec (1 sec / 8000 = .000125).
- 8 bits per samples × 8,000 samples per second = 64,000 bit/s.

The basic transmission unit for SONET is the STS-1 frame. See Figure 5–2. The frame consists of 90 columns and 9 rows of 8-bit bytes

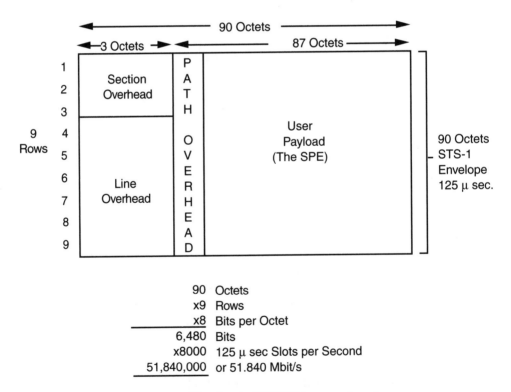

Figure 5–2 The basic SONET frame structure.

(octets). Therefore, the frame carries 810 bytes or 6480 bits. SONET transmits at 8000 frames/second. Therefore, the frame length is 125 μsec. This approach translates into a transfer rate of 51.840 Mbit/s (6,480 x 8000 = 51,840,000). Obviously, this approach interworks well with the 64 kbit/s digital voice signal. And don't forget, SONET and SDH were designed to support digital voice traffic.

Overhead and User Areas in the Envelope

Notice that the first three columns of the frame contain transport overhead, which is divided into 27 bytes with 9 bytes allocated for section overhead and 18 bytes allocated for line overhead. The other 87 columns comprise the STS-1 envelope capacity (although the first column of the envelope capacity is reserved for STS path overhead). Several fields are used for signaling control, administrative alarms, etc. Several other fields are used to identify the type of equipment being used as well as the types of payloads that reside in the envelope. Other bytes are used for pointers to locate the position of the user payload in the frame. This overhead is explained shortly.

The 87 columns are also called the synchronous payload envelope (SPE). The actual user payload consists of 86 columns or 774 bytes. Therefore, the user payload operates at 49.536 Mbit/s (774 x 8000 = 49,536,000). Obviously, the user payload can support VTs up to the DS3 rate (44.736 Mbit/s).

The STS-1 frame is transmitted row by row from left to right. Each byte is transmitted with the most significant bit first.

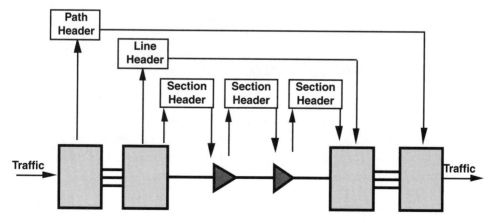

Figure 5–3   SONET functional components.

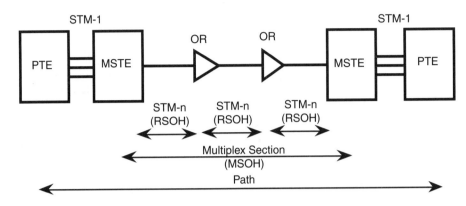

Figure 5–4   SONET functional components.

SONET AND SDH FUNCTIONAL COMPONENTS

Figure 5–3 shows the major functional components on a SONET link: the section, line, and path operations. The concept is to partition activities and responsibilities among the three major components. This modular approach facilitates the ability to add and remove components, because from a protocol standpoint (logical operations), the three components are somewhat independent of each other, and their operations are described shortly.

Figure 5–4 shows the major SDH components. Once again, the similarities between SONET and SDH are evident, but SDH further distinguishes differences in the path overheads. The first one is the higher order path overhead (HO-POH) and the second is the lower order path overhead (LO-POH). There is some difference in how these overhead octets are used. In the SONET arena, the overheads are referred to as section, line, and path overheads. There is no distinction among types of Path overheads.

SONET AND SDH PROBLEM DETECTION

SONET and SDH define many rules and actions for the detection of problems and failures on a link or in a node. Additionally, they provide information on how the detection of these problems is signaled to various parts of the span. Figure 5–5 shows how the detection of certain events can trigger alarm signals. There are six failure conditions:

- Loss of signal (LOS)
- Loss of frame (LOF)

- Loss of pointer (LOP)
- Alarm indication signal (AIS)
- Far end receive failure (FERF)
- Remote alarm indication (RAI)

The detection of LOS, LOF, or LOP at the section terminating equipment (STE) or line terminating equipment (LTE) causes the generation of alarms on that device's output port to the downstream network element. For example, if an STE detects a LOS or LOF, its output port generates an AIS of all 1s to the downstream LTE, which in turn generates an AIS with H1, H2 to the path terminating equipment (PTE); this in turn generates an AIS with V1, V2 to the VT PTE. The VT PTE might then generate a DSn AIS on the tributary. These events also invoke upstream signals. The LTE sends a foreign receive failure using a K2 to its

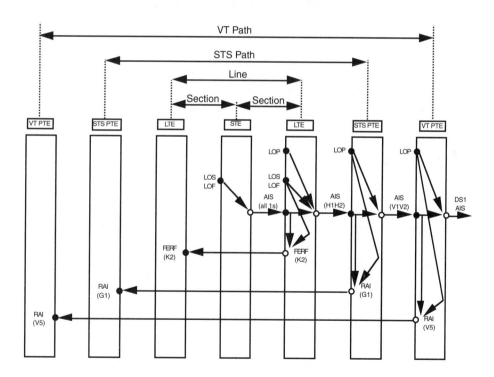

● Detection

○ Transmission

Figure 5–5   Examples of alarm signals.

associated LTE upstream. Likewise, the VT PTE sends an RAI from V5 to its peer VT PTE.

LOCATING AND ADJUSTING PAYLOAD WITH POINTERS

SONET and SDH use a pointer concept to deal timing (frequency and phase) variations in a network. The purpose of pointers is to allow the payload to "float" within the payload area of the envelope. Figure 5–6 shows this idea. The pointer is an offset value that shows the relative position of the first byte of the payload.

During the transmission across the network, if any variations occur in the timing, the pointer needs only to be increased or decreased to compensate for the situation.

Several options are available for how the payload is mapped into the frame. The option just discussed is called the floating mode, for obvious reasons.

Another option is called the locked mode. With this approach, the pointers are not used and the payload is fixed within the frame. It cannot float. This approach is much simpler, but it requires that timing be maintained throughout the network. Since all signals have a common orientation, the processing of the traffic is efficiently performed.

VIRTUAL TRIBUTARIES IN MORE DETAIL

Virtual tributaries (VTs) are used to support sub-STS-1 levels, which are simply synchronous signals used to support low-speed signals. To support different mixes of VTs, the STS-1 SPE can be divided into seven

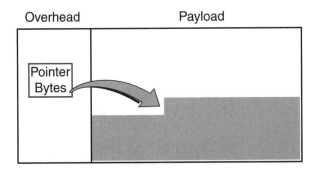

Figure 5–6   Payload pointers.

groups. Each group occupies 12 columns and 9 rows of the SPE and may actually contain 4, 3, 2, or 1 VTs. For example, a VT group may contain one VT 6, two VT 3s, three VT 2s, or four VT 1.5s. Each VT group must contain one size of VTs, but different VT groups can be mixed in one STS-1 SPE.

The four sizes of the VT are as follows: VT 1.5 = 1.728 Mbit/s, VT 2 = 2.304 Mbit/s, VT 3 = 3.456 Mbit/s, VT 6 = 6.912 Mbit/s.

Figure 5–7 shows a VT 1.5 group. The 1.5 bytes occupy three columns and nine rows. The actual user traffic consists of 24 bytes in

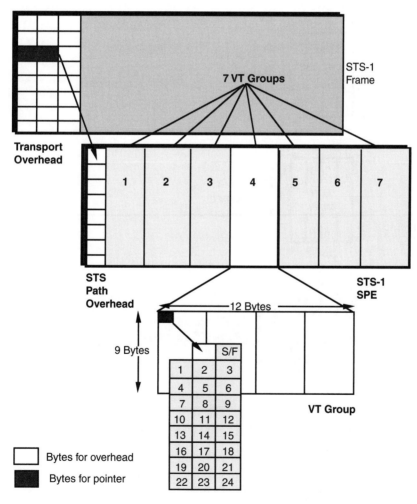

Figure 5–7   Payload management with VTs.

accordance with a T1 24 slot frame. The remaining three bytes are used for SONET control. A VT 1.5 group supports four VT 1.5 transmissions to occupy the full 12 columns of the VT structure.

At the bottom of Figure 5–7 reside the 24 user samples of a, say, voice signal. Each sample is 8 bits, and, since the SPE is sent 8,000 frames a second, one sample of the voice image is carried in each SPE. Once again, supporting the 64,000 bit/s voice signal is fundamental to the operation of a digital transport network.

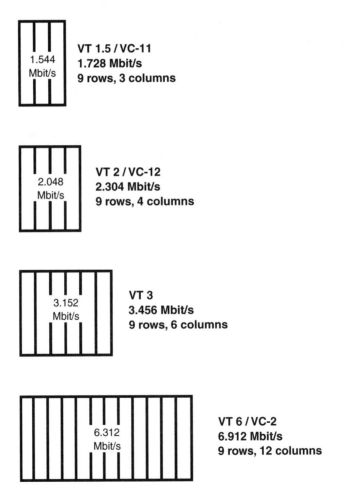

Figure 5–8   VTs and VCs.

VIRTUAL TRIBUTARIES AND VIRTUAL CONTAINERS

The various administrations and standards groups from Japan, North America, and Europe worked closely together to accommodate the three different regional signaling standards. The initial SONET standards published in the United States in 1984 were reviewed by Japan and the European PTTs to see if these requirements would meet their needs. During this time, the ANSI T1 committee had become involved with Bellcore in the development of SONET.

The original SONET standard made no provision for the European rate of 140 Mbit/s and, for a time, the various administrations and standards groups tried to accommodate all multiplexing rates of all three regions. Discussions continued through the European Telecommunications Standard Institute (ETSI) and agreement was reached on a subset of the multiplexing schemes of the three regions. ETSI stressed the importance of the intermediate rates of 8 and 34 Mbit/s, in contrast to the ease of doing international networking. Reason prevailed and compromises were reached. The importance of international internetworking came to the fore and multiplexing schemes based on 1.5, 2.48, 6.312 were accommodated. Figure 5–8 shows the structure of the virtual tributaries (VT) and virtual containers (VC). VT1.5 is called VC1–11 in Europe and it accommodates the T1 rate. VT2 is called VC-12 in Europe and it accommodates the Europe CEPT 1 rate of 2.048 Mbit/s. VT3 is not employed in Europe. It is used in North America to optimize multiplexing DS1c transport signals. VT6 is called VC-2 in Europe and it accommodates the 6.312 Mbit/s rate from all three regions.

THE OVERHEAD BYTES

Figure 5–9 shows the structure and names of the SONET OAM headers and the bytes within the headers. The reader may recall that each major component is responsible for creating a header at the transmitting network element and processing the header at the receiving network element. Let's start with a general look at the section overhead bytes:

- *A1 and A2 (framing):* Flags used by a receiving machine to synchronize onto the SONET signal.
- *J0 (trace):* Used for STS-1 identification; a unique number that is assigned to each STS-1 of an STS-n signal.

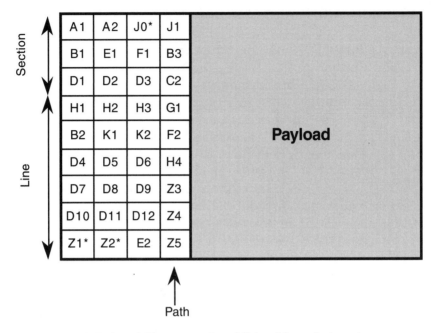

Notes: for J0*, Z1*, and Z*, see text for additional byte designations

Figure 5–9   Abbreviated names for the OAM bytes.

- *B1 (bit interleaved parity):* A parity check on the previously sent STS-1 frame with the answer (the parity) in the current frame. The BIP-8 byte checks for transmission errors over a section. If excessive errors are occurring, alarms and diagnostics (as shown in Figure 5–5) may be generated.
- *E1 byte (orderwire):* A 64 kbit/s voice channel which can be used for maintenance communications among terminals, hubs, and regenerators.
- *F1 (user):* Set aside for the network provider to use in any manner deemed appropriate.
- *D1, D2, and D3 (data communications channel (DCC)):* Used for data communications channels and are part of 192 kbit/s operations that are used for signaling control, administrative alarms, and other OAM&P. In later chapters, discussions will explain how the DCC can be used for MPLS, and other more advanced operations.

The line overhead bytes occupy the bottom 6 octets of the first three columns in the SONET frame. Line overhead is processed by all equipment except for the regenerators. Here is a general view of their functions:

- *H1 and H2 (pointers):* Indicate the offset in bytes between the pointer and the first byte of the SPE. This pointer allows the SPE to be located anywhere within the envelope, as long as capacity is available.

- *H3 (pointer action):* Used to frequency justify the SPE; that is, to allow for possible slight timing differences that may exist between nodes.

- *B2:* Use is identical to the BIP byte found in the section header, except that this byte pertains only to the line header.

- *K1 and K2 automatic protection switching (APS):* Used for detecting problems with the line terminating equipment, and for alarms and signaling failures, as well as network recovery.

- *D4-D12:* (data communications channel): Used for line communication and are part of a 576 kbit/s message which is used for maintenance control, monitoring, alarms, etc. Originally, the Common Management Information Protocol (CMIP) was defined for use in the bytes, and some vendors still use CMIP. Others use the Transaction Language 1 (TL 1) in these bytes, or in the F1 byte. Still others use the Simple Network Management Protocol (SNMP).

- *Z1 and Z2 bytes:* Originally these bytes were reserved for future growth, and are now partially defined. The Z1 byte is also designated as the S1 byte. It is used to convey synchronization information about the SPE, and it allows the node to make decisions about potential clocking sources. The Z2 byte is also designated as byte M0 or byte M1. Its use is to convey information about error conditions back to the source of the SPE.

- *E2 (orderwire):* Explained earlier.

The path overhead remains with the payload until the payload is demultiplexed at the far-end node (the STS-1 terminating equipment). This processing is usually at the customer premises equipment (CPE). The functions of the path overhead bytes are as follows:

- *J1(path trace):* Used to repetitively transmit a 64 byte fixed length string in order for the recipient path terminating equipment to verify a connection to the sending device.

- *B3:* Function is the same as that of the line and section BIP fields, except that it performs a parity check calculated on all bits in the path overhead.

- *C2 (path signal label):* Used to indicate the construction of the STS payload envelope. The path signal label can be used to inform the network that different types of systems are being used, such as ATM, FDDI, etc.

- *G1 (path status):* Carries maintenance and diagnostic signals such as an indication for block errors, and several identification functions.
- *F2:* Used by the network provider.
- For certain support functions, the growth bytes of SONET Z3 are to be used for DQDB mapping. Z4 for SONET and SDH is still a growth byte. Z5 for both SONET and SDH is for error monitoring.

SONET AND SDH CONCATENATION

It is possible to concatenate (for example) three STS-1s into one STS-3c frame. This operation is common when payload such as ATM or IP is transported, and a channelized structure is not needed. Beyond STS-3c, SONET and SDH support a variety of concatenation operations, and all are identified with the letter "c" appended to the back of the multiplexing designation. Chapter 6 shows provides more information on concatenation and [BLAC01] has the details if you need them.

SUMMARY

SONET and SDH represent the second generation transport network, and in many networks, especially long-haul networks, the T1/E1 first generation systems no longer exist. However, in order to provide a graceful evolution to SONET and SDH, the 2G networks are backward compatible and able to support 1G operations. Thus, the well-known 125 µsec timing increment is carried over to SONET and SDH. Likewise, the TDM concepts that are fundamental to T1 and E1 are retained in SONET and SDH as well.

The 2nd generation systems are quite different from their predecessors in that they provide (a) much more capacity to users, (b) have powerful OAM capabilities with the three headers, and (c) operate with extensive backup and protection arrangements. We explained points (a) and (b) in this chapter. Point (c) is covered in Chapter 8.

6

Architecture of Optical Transport Networks (OTNs)

This chapter examines the optical transport network (OTN), as defined by the ITU-T. The emphasis is on ITU-T Recommendations G.709, G.872, and several IETF efforts dealing with the OTN. We begin with a look at the concept of a digital wrapper, followed by an introduction to control planes and in-band/out-of-band signaling. We then examine the current digital hierarchy, as defined by the ITU-T, and the North American standards groups. Next, an analysis is made of several mapping and multiplexing arrangements; both subjects are discussed in relation to the SONET/SDH counterparts. The chapter concludes with a study of the OTN layered architecture and how the digital wrapper is being defined by the standards bodies.

THE DIGITAL WRAPPER

User traffic, such as voice, video, and data, is transported through networks by encapsulating the traffic units (the user bits) inside other traffic units. This operation is often called encapsulation, in which the user payload is placed inside the other traffic and is not examined by any node (except for possible errors introduced by the network) until the traffic reaches the final destination. This idea is shown in Figure 6–1.

Many people call encapsulation framing. This term is typically used when referring to the operations that occur between the third layer (such

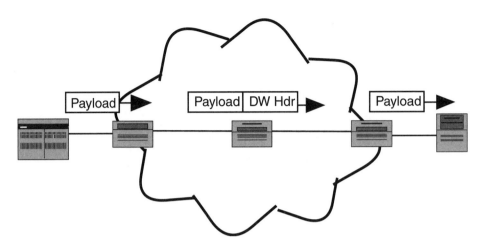

Figure 6–1   Digital wrapper header.

as IP), and second/or first layers of the layered model. As examples, SONET has a framing convention for carrying IP traffic in the layer 1 frames; Ethernet has another convention for encapsulating IP traffic into the layer 2 frames.

The idea of the digital wrapper stems from the concept of encapsulation: wrapping up user traffic, placing headers (maybe trailers) around it, and shipping it through the network. One of the key fields in the digital wrapper is a forward error correction (FEC) value. Its job is to correct bits that have been damaged due to transmission impairments. In a typical OC-192 system, FEC can provide better than 10^{-20} bit error rate (BER) performance with a new fiber system [NORT98]. Using FEC on extended spans can improve the link budget (the accumulated Db values on the end-to-end span) by 2 dB.

Another important field in the digital wrapper header is the protocol ID. It is used to identify the type of traffic that is being transported through the network, such as IP datagrams, OSPF routing packets, and ICMP diagnostic packets.

Many different encapsulation standards exist, and few of them are compatible. As examples, ATM encapsulation is not the same as Frame Relay encapsulation; SONET encapsulation is not the same as Ethernet encapsulation.

So, the idea of the digital wrapper is not new. But the intent is to standardize a digital wrapper for use in the new optical networks.

CONTROL PLANES

A control plane is a set of software and/or hardware in a node that is used to control several vital operations of the network, such as bandwidth allocations, route discovery, and error recovery.

Obviously, the control plane is important. One example of a control plane that has been in existence for some time is the SS7 protocol stack. (In SS7, a control plane is usually called a signaling plane.) Its job is to control the data plane of the telephone network.

The term data plane does not mean the traffic is only data; it might be voice or video traffic. The terms "user plane" and "transport planes" are also used to describe the data plane.

Other examples of control planes are the routing protocols (OSPF, IS-IS, BGP) used in data networks. They enable IP (in the data plane) to forward traffic correctly.

Figure 6–2 shows the relationships of the control plane to the data plane. The control messages are exchanged between nodes to perform a wide variety of operations. For optical networks, some of the more important tasks for the control plane include:

- Exchanging status messages, such as alarms and diagnostics.
- Providing timing messages to keep nodes' clocks in sync with each other.
- Using messages to download information on which wavelengths will be used between two nodes.

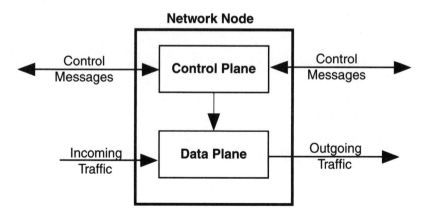

Figure 6–2   The control plane and the data plane.

- Exchanging hello messages to make certain nodes are up and running.
- Setting up and tearing down data plane connections (maybe, depending on the nature of the control plane).
- Building forwarding (cross-connect) tables to allow the data plane to relay traffic from its input link (output port) to its output link (output port).

Second generation digital transport networks such as SONET and SDH have used network management protocols in the data plane (SNMP, CMIP, TL1, or proprietary protocols residing in the DCC bytes) for protection and restoration schemes. This approach has several problems [AWDU01]:

- It leads to relatively slow convergence following a failure. The only way to expedite service recovery in such environments is to pre-provision dedicated protection channels.
- It complicates the task of interworking equipment from different manufacturers, and thus different networks.
- It precludes the use of distributed dynamic routing control capabilities.

The approach for third generation digital transport networks is to define a separate, dedicated control plane that can operate in any of the following fashions:

- The control plane messages can be exchanged on a separate physical fiber link from those of the user traffic.
- Alternatively, the control messages can be sent on the same fiber link as the link used for the user traffic, as well as on the same wavelength (possible, but not encouraged).
- Control messages can also be sent on a separate wavelength on the same fiber that is transporting user traffic on the other wavelengths of that fiber.
- Control messages can be sent and received on separate nodes from those that carry the data traffic (somewhat complex in coordinating nodal activities, but permitted).

We will hold the thoughts about the control plane for later chapters; in the discussions on multiprotocol lambda switching (Chapter 10) and link management protocols (Chapter 11), they will be examined in more detail in relation to these specific protocols. Now, we examine where the messages of the control plane flow between the network nodes.

IN-BAND AND OUT-OF-BAND CONTROL SIGNALING

Many systems carry the control plane messages on the same physical link/circuit as the user traffic. For example, the IP-based protocols use this approach where, say, OSPF control plane traffic and IP user plane traffic use the same link. This approach is an in-band control plane, and it uses in-band signaling.

The 3G transport networks use a separate channel for signaling information. This approach is called out-of-band signaling and it is preferred to in-band signaling because it is more efficient and robust. Later discussions will amplify and reinforce this general statement.

Two types of out-of-band signaling exist. With the first type, known as physical out-of-band signaling, a separate physical channel is used for signaling. The second type is called physical in-band/logical out-of-band signaling. With this approach, signaling and user traffic share the same physical channel, but part of the channel capacity is reserved only for signaling traffic; the remainder of the bandwidth is reserved for user traffic, such as IP payloads.

Figure 6–3 shows the differences between these two methods of out-of-band signaling. In Figure 6–3 (a), two physical links are used between two nodes, which are optical nodes in this example. In Figure 6–3 (b), one physical link is used between two nodes, with the signaling traffic allotted reserved bandwidth on the link. Figure 6–3 (b) is an example of the well-known ISDN, using a TDM control slot on the link called the B channel.

Generally, it is not practical or cost-effective to use two separate links (two separate wire-pairs, two separate fibers, etc.) for each residential customer (or a few customers), which would entail installing more cable in the local distribution plant. Consequently, the ISDN approach represents a compromise; the physical channel is shared, but some bandwidth is dedicated to the logical signaling channel.

In addition, ISDN was designed to support a limited set of users on a local loop. It was later adapted for use in high-capacity backbone networks, and it does not provide for redundant links that are used, say, in

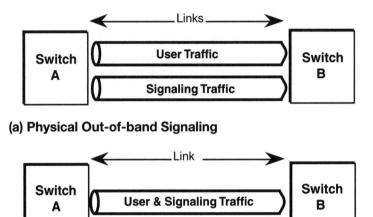

(a) Physical Out-of-band Signaling

(b) Physical In-band/Logical Out-of-band Signaling

Figure 6–3   Comparison of signaling systems.

the core of a 1st, 2nd, or 3rd generation transport network. If the link fails, the user (or a few users) is denied service, but the failure does not affect a large population.

SS7 is an example of an out-of-band control plane. SS7 is usually deployed as a separate network within the overall telephone network architecture for the purpose of establishing and terminating telephone calls. If a user link fails, the signaling link is still operable and can continue to support other user calls.

But what happens if the signaling link fails? As shown in Figure 6–4, SS7 and 3G transport networks can be designed to support more than one signaling link; if one link fails, another link is available to take over without the loss of any signaling traffic. Since the optical backbone

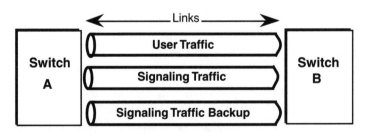

Figure 6–4   Redundant signaling links to provide robustness.

(and, of course, SS7) may support many users (in fact, millions of users), physical signaling with redundant links is quite important.

We can take this discussion one step further and pose another question: "What happens if an optical node fails?" The 3G transport network is sufficiently concerned with downtime (node unavailability), that the network also has redundant nodes, as well as redundant links between the nodes. These topologies are explained in more detail in subsequent chapters.

An In-band Signal on an O/O/O PXC

If an optical node is not capable of O/E/O operations, it can resort to the tried-and-true technique used in telephone systems for many years: the presence or absence (power on/power off) of the physical signal. In fact, many of the restoration mechanisms of optical networks are based on this notion. The presence or absence of a physical optical signal can be used to indicate the absence or presence of problems respectively on the link.

IMPORTANCE OF MULTIPLEXING AND MULTIPLEXING HIERARCHIES

As noted several times in this book, one of the key elements of a digital transport network is multiplexing, the aggregation of lower bandwidth traffic (called tributaries or containers) into higher level tributaries of greater bandwidth. The idea is shown in Figure 6–5, in which lower bandwidth DS0s are multiplexed into higher bandwidth DS1s, which, in turn, are multiplexed into still higher bandwidth DS3s.

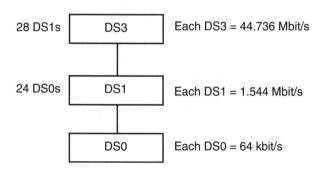

Figure 6–5   Multiplexing levels revisited.

The attractive aspect of this operation is that it allows lower bandwidth payloads to support modest bandwidth needs of certain users, and higher bandwidth payloads to support users that have such needs. At the same time, these tributaries/containers can be combined (multiplexed) for transport across high bandwidth media (optical fiber) at far less expense than transporting individual low bandwidth tributaries. When necessary, the higher level multiplexed tributaries can be demultiplexed (separated) and sent to the appropriate user.

CURRENT DIGITAL TRANSPORT HIERARCHY

SONET and SDH were developed to address several problems that exist with digital transport networks. The one of interest here is the fact that the first generation digital transport multiplexing hierarchy varied (and still varies, but to a lesser extent than before) in the different geographical regions of the world. This disparate approach is complex and makes

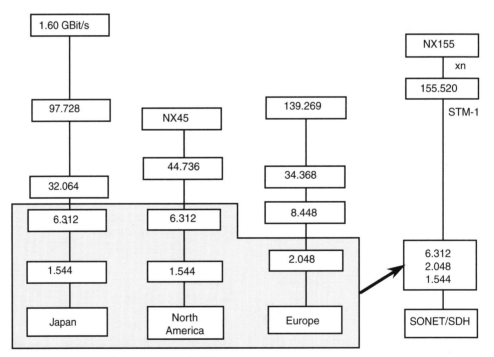

Note: Unless noted otherwise, speeds in Mbit/s.

Figure 6–6   SONET/SDH.

the interworking of the systems difficult and expensive. Moreover, it means that companies that build hardware and software for carrier systems must implement multiple commercial platforms for what could be one technology. SONET and SDH provide a standard from which vendors can build compatible multiplexing transport hierarchies. The SONET/ SDH multiplexing hierarchy is shown in a general way in Figure 6–6, a slight re-rendering of Figure 2–5 in Chapter 2.

While SONET and SDH do not ensure equipment compatibility, they do provide a basis for vendors to build worldwide standards. Moreover, as shown with the shaded area in Figure 6–6, SONET and SDH are backwards compatible, in that they support the transport carriers' first generation transport systems in North America, Europe, and Japan. This feature is important because it allows different digital signals and hierarchies to operate with a common transport system, which is SONET/SDH.

SONET MULTIPLEXING HIERARCHY

Figure 6–7 shows the details of the SONET multiplexing and mapping hierarchy. The convention is to show the flow of operations going from the right side of the page to the left side. The boxes on the right-most side indicate the user payloads that are multiplexed and mapped into the higher levels of virtual tributaries (VTs), VT groups, and synchronous transport signal (STS) signals. The notation xN indicates the level of multiplexing; that is, how many lower level signals are multiplexed into the next higher level signal. The notation of STS-3c indicates that the lower level tributaries have been joined (concatenated) into higher level signals. This concatenation allows the full payload to be treated as one entity and not as individual tributaries. STS-3c is an optional mapping scheme. In SONET, four VT1.5s are multiplexed together to create a VTG (Virtual Tributary Group of 6.912 Mbit/s). Notice that this hierarchy also supports some of the ITU-T signals (e.g., E1 at 34.368 Mbit/s).

SDH MULTIPLEXING HIERARCHY

Figure 6–8 shows the original SDH multiplexing hierarchy as published in the ITU-T G.707 and G.708 recommendations. The basic multiplexing scheme starts on the right side of the figure and progresses to the left side of the figure. This structure is similar to the SONET structure

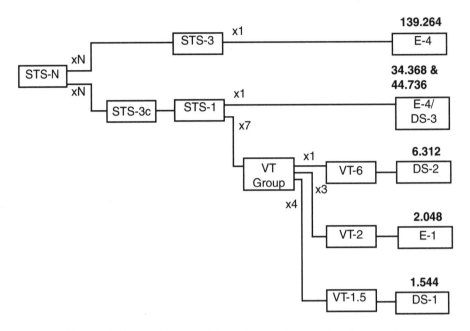

Figure 6–7   SONET multiplexing and mapping hierarchy.

explained earlier. At the lowest level, containers (C) are input to VCs. The purpose of this function is to create a uniform VC payload envelope. Various containers (ranging from 1.544 Mbit/s to 139.264 Mbit/s) are covered by the original SDH standard.

Next, VCs are aligned with TUs. This alignment entails bit stuffing to bring all inputs to a common bit transfer rate. Next, the VCs are aligned to TUs, and pointer processing operations are implemented to denote the position of the tributaries in the payload envelope.

These initial functions allow the payload to be multiplexed into TUGs. As Figure 6–8 illustrates, the Xn indicates the multiplexing integer used to multiplex the TUs to the TUGs. The next step is the multiplexing of the TUGs to higher level VCs, and TUG 2 and 3 are multiplexed into VC-3 and VC-4. These VCs are aligned with bit stuffing for the administrative units (AUs) which are multiplexed into the AU group (AUG). This payload then is multiplexed with an even N integer into the synchronous transport module (STM).

The SONET 1.544 DS1 multiplexing structure, as recommended in ITU-T G.707, is also shown in Figure 6–8. For the purpose of transfer-

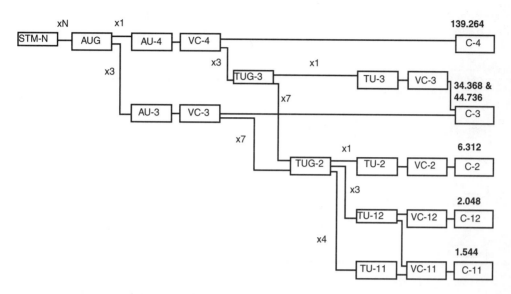

Figure 6–8   The SDH (original) multiplexing hierarchy.

ring information, almost all digital signals of conventional North American multiplexing hierarchy can be employed. Figure 6–8 depicts the SDH terminology as it applies to the North American DS1 (1.544 Mbit/s) signal. This same approach is used to represent the DS1C (3.152 Mbit/s), DS2 (6.312 Mbit/s) and DS3 (44.736 Mbit/s) signals.

Each DS1 consists of 1.544 Mbit/s and is referred to as a container (C). Each container (a C-11) becomes a virtual container (a VC-11) by the addition of path overhead bits (POH) and some stuffed bits in predefined positions. This procedure is called mapping. As noted earlier, the process referred to as aligning relates to the procedure of assembling the virtual container into a tributary unit (a TU-11) in which a pointer is added to indicate the position of the first byte of the virtual container in the tributary unit frame. (Recall that the SONET term for TU-11 is VT1.5.) Thereafter, the process is the same as the other payload mapping and multiplexing operations.

Revised SDH Transport Hierarchy

Figure 6–9 shows the revised SDH digital hierarchy. As the SDH technology matured, and as vendors and network operators gained more

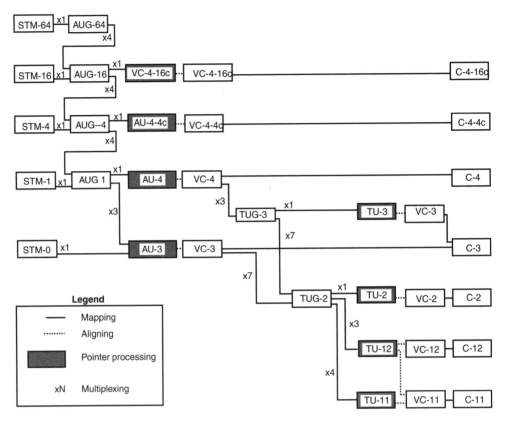

Figure 6–9   The revised SDH digital hierarchy.

experience with SDH, it was recognized that the transport hierarchy
model in Figure 6–9 needed to be expanded to show changes to SDH, no-
tably (a) how concatenation fits into the hierarchy, (b) with the resulting
AUs and AUGs, and (c) how the resulting STMs (on the left side of Figure 6–9) relate to the AUs and AUGs.

Also included in this figure is a legend that explains where the following operations take place: (a) mapping, (b) alignment, (c) pointer processing, and (d) multiplexing. These operations were defined in the
original SDH recommendations, but, to keep matters simple, they were
not included in Figure 6–8. Notice also the STM-N frames on the left side
of the figure.

KEY INDEXES AND OTHER TERMS

Before we proceed into a more detailed discussion of the G.709 and G.872 operations, it is important to introduce and review several terms that are used to explain bit rates, multiplexing levels, wavelengths supported, and information on enhanced functionality. Keep the entries in Box 6–1 in mind as you read the remainder of this chapter. These entries and associated acronyms are explained where appropriate.

Box 6–1   Key Indexes and Terms

Three terms dealing with the physical signal are: (a) 1R: signal is reamplified, (b) 2R: signal is reamplified and reshaped, (c) 3R: signal is reamplified, reshaped, and retimed.

Several index values are used to explain the multiplexing level and the associated bit rate. They are as follows (see Appendix 2 of [BELL01] for more details), and the terms will make more sense as you proceed through the chapter:

The index k is used to represent a supported bit rate, described as OPUk, ODUk, and OTUk. The value of k=1 represents an approximate bit rate of 2.5 Gbit/s, k=2 represents an approximate bit rate of 10 Gbit/s, k=3 an approximate bit rate of 40 Gbit/s and k=4 an approximate bit rate of 160 Gbit/s (under study by the ITU-T).

The exact bit-rate values in kbits/s for the k units are as follows:

- OPU: k=1: 2 488 320.000, k=2: 9 995 276.962, k=3: 40 150 519.322
- ODU: k=1: 2 498 775.126, k=2: 10 037 273.924, k=3: 40 319 218.983
- OTU: k=1: 2 666 057.143, k=2: 10 709 225.316, k=3: 43 018 413.559

The index m is used to represent the bit rate or set of bit rates supported on the interface. The valid values for m are (1, 2, 3, 12, 23, 123).

The index n is used to represent the order of the OTM, OTS, OMS, OPS, OCG, and OMU. This index represents the maximum number of wavelengths that can be supported at the lowest bit rate supported on the wavelength. It is possible that a reduced number of higher bit-rate wavelengths are supported. The case n=0 represents a single channel without a specific wavelength assigned to the channel.

The index r, if present, is used to indicate a reduced functionality of OTM, OCG, OCC, and OCh.

THE NEW OPTICAL TRANSPORT AND DIGITAL TRANSPORT HIERARCHY

Figure 6–10 shows the new digital transport hierarchy, known as the OTN multiplexing hierarchy [G.87200]. It is evident that the multiplexing architecture of OTN is different from the SONET and SDH schemes. All the multiplexing hierarchies still use the right-to-left multiplexing flow, but OTN has a new set of terms and concepts to describe a third generation digital transport network. The remainder of this chapter examines the entities of the OTN, and you will find Figure 6–10 to be a useful reference as your read the remainder of this chapter.

ODUk Mapping and Multiplexing

Since G.709 defines at the optical channel layer three distinct client payload bit rates, an optical channel data unit (ODU) frame has been defined for each of these bit rates. An ODUk refers to a bit rate k framing signal, where k = 1 (for 2.5 Gbit/s), 2 (for 10 Gbit/s) or 3 (for 40 Gbit/s).

As shown in Figure 6–10, in optical channel data unit (ODUk) mapping, the client signal is mapped into the optical channel payload unit (OPUk). The OPUk is mapped into an ODUk and the ODUk is mapped into an optical channel transport unit (OTUk). The OTUk is mapped into an OChr and the OChr is then modulated onto an OCCr.

Therefore, these levels of ODUk multiplexing can be defined:

ODU1 multiplexing:
- Four ODU1 are multiplexed into one OPU2, which is mapped into one ODU2.

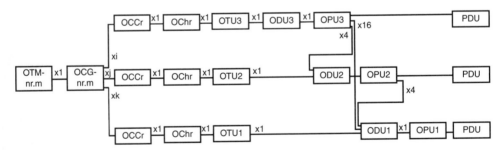

Note: The multiplexing capabilities of OTM, OCC, and OCG can vary, depending on the values of nr, r, and m.

Figure 6–10   The OTN multiplexing hierarchy.

- Sixteen ODU1 are multiplexed into one OPU3, which is mapped into one ODU3.

ODU2 multiplexing:

- Four ODU2 are multiplexed into one OPU3, which is mapped into one ODU3.

THE OTN LAYERED MODEL

Like most communications systems in place today, optical networks are described by a layered model. This approach is also used to describe parts of the SONET/SDH network, as shown in Figure 6–11. Notice that more than one term is associated with two of the layers. SONET uses the term line and SDH uses the term multiplex for one of the layers. For one

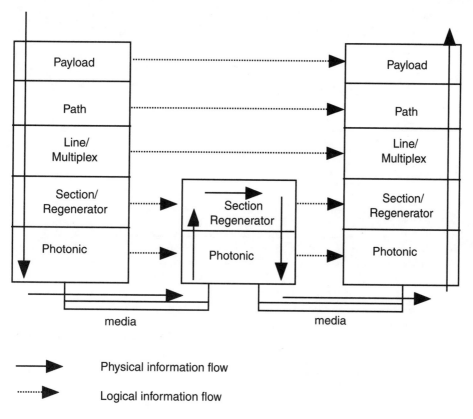

Figure 6–11   The SONET/SDH layered model.

other layer, SONET uses the term section, and SDH uses the term regenerator. The layers have different names, but they are performing the same functions. The functions of the SONET/SDH layers are described in Chapter 5 (with the headers used at these layers).

The ITU-T has published a layered model for next generation optical networks; the general scheme is shown in Figure 6–12 [G.70901] and [G.87200]. The model is designed with several layers. The bottom three layers and a multiplexing operation (shown in the figure as optical channel multiplexing) are collectively called the optical transport hierarchy (OTH). The functions of the layers are:

- *Optical channel (OCh) layer:* Provides end-to-end optical channels between two optical nodes, supporting user (client) payloads of different formats, such as ATM, STM-N, etc. Services include routing, monitoring, provisioning, and backup and recovery features.

- *Optical multiplex section (OMS) layer:* Provides for the support of WDM signals, and manages each signal as an optical channel. Services include wave division multiplexing, and multiplex section backup and recovery.

- *Optical transmission section (OTS) layer:* Provides the transmission of the physical optical signal, based on the specific type of

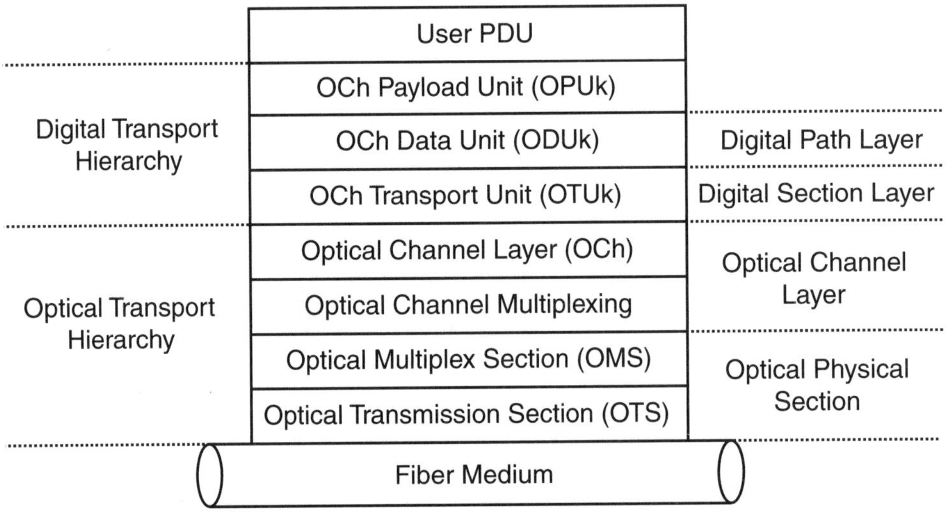

Figure 6–12   The optical network layered architecture.

fiber, such as dispersion-unshifted fiber (USF), dispersion shifted fiber (DSF), etc. Services include the correct signal generation and reception at the section level.

Each optical channel is an optical carrier that supports an optical transport unit (OTU). The bit rates for the OTU are defined by k. An OTUk (where k = 1,2,3) is composed of the entities of OTUk, ODUk, and PDUk. The upper layers are collectively called the digital transport hierarchy, also known as the *digital wrapper* layer. The functions of these layers are:

- *Optical channel payload unit (OPUk):* Provides support to map (digitally wrap) clients' signals (i.e., STM-N signals, IP packets, ATM cells, or Ethernet frames into a structured frame).
- *Optical channel data unit (ODUk) layer:* Provides client-independent connectivity, connection protection and monitoring. The layer is also called the digital path layer.
- *Optical channel transport unit (OTUk):* Provides FEC capabilities and optical section protection and monitoring capabilities. This layer is also called the digital section layer.

The layered model in Figure 6–12 is more elaborate than the SONET/SDH layered model in Figure 6–11 that has been used since the mid-1980s. The reasons for expanding the model is to establish a framework for an optical network to support (a) STDM, data-driven traffic (which is beyond the TDM voice-driven SONET/SDH network), (b) high bandwidth DWDM Tbit/s rates, (c) and enchanted OAM&P without concern for the granularity of the client payload (the user protocol data unit [PDU]) in Figure 6–12.

Another View

Let's look at these entities in a different way. Figure 6–13 shows the user payload (client traffic) encapsulated into an optical payload unit of order k (OPUk). This unit is an octet-based frame consisting of 4 rows and 3810 columns. The first two columns are overhead and the remaining 3808 bytes is for payload. The overhead content varies, depending upon the type of client traffic.

This traffic is encapsulated into an ODUk. This unit is also an octet-based frame, consisting of 4 rows and 3824 columns. Thus, it adds 14 additional columns of ODU overhead, consisting of general communications

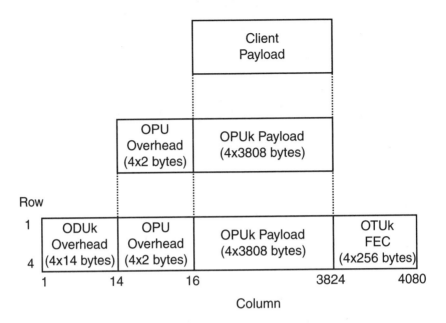

Figure 6–13   OPU, PDU, and OTU.

channels, frame alignment, monitoring and maintenance signals, as well as protection channel bytes.

The OTUk is created from the bytes discussed above, and an additional 256 columns of an FEC field.

Full Functionality Stack: OTM-n.m

Figure 6–14 shows the arrangement for a full functionality stack, designated as OTM-n.m (Optical Transport Module). The OTM-n.m is the information structure used to support OTN interfaces. Up to n OCCs can be multiplexed into an OCG-n.m using wavelength division multiplexing. The OCC tributary slots of the OCG-n.m can be of different sizes, depending on the value of the index m (m = 1, 2, 3, 12, 23, or 123). The OCG-n.m is transported via the OTM-n.m.

Reduced Functionality Stack: OTM-nr.m and OTM-0.r

The OTM also defines stacks that have reduced functionality. This arrangement is used to support optical physical section (OPS) layer connections in the OTN. Two options are permitted, with modifications to the protocol stack. These options are shown in Figure 6–15 and Figure 6–16:

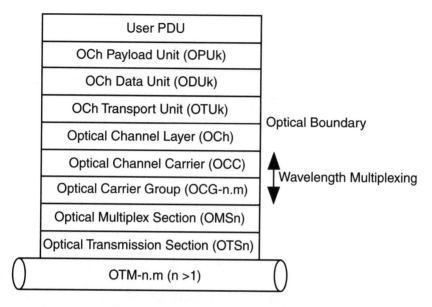

Figure 6–14   Full functional stack.

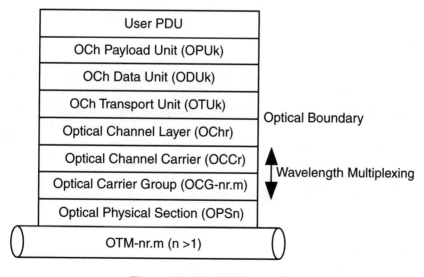

Figure 6–15   OTM-nr.m.

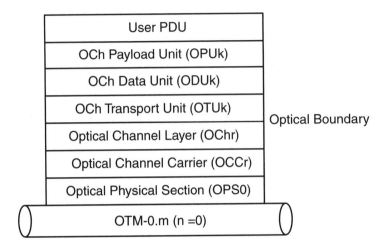

Figure 6–16   OTM-0.

- *OTM-nr.m:* consists of up to n multiplexed optical channels (see Figure 6–15). Up to OCCr are multiplexed into an OCG-nr.m using WDM. The OCCr tributaries of the OCG-r.m can range from m = 1, 2, 3, 12, 23, or 123. The OCG-nr.m is transported via the OTM-nr.m.

- *OTM-0:* consists of a single optical channel without a specific wavelength assigned (see Figure 6–16). This reduced functionality does not support WDM. Only one OCCr tributary slot is provided; thus an OCG-0r.m stack is defined. The OCCr tributary can range from m = 1, 2, 3. The OCCr is transported via the OTM-0.m.

ENCAPSULATION AND DECAPSULATION OPERATIONS

Again, as in other layered protocol models, the OTN defines the relationship of the layers to the traffic units. Figure 6–17 shows this relationship. The arrows on the left side of the figure denote the processing of the traffic going down the layers at the transmit side with the arrow that points down. Conversely, the arrow that points up denotes the processing of the processing of the traffic at the receiving side. For obvious reasons, the operations on the transmit side are called encapsulation, and the operations on the receive side are called decapsulation.

The traffic units on the left side of the figure are called signal types. Here is a description of these signal types. You will also find Figure 6–10 to be helpful during this discussion:

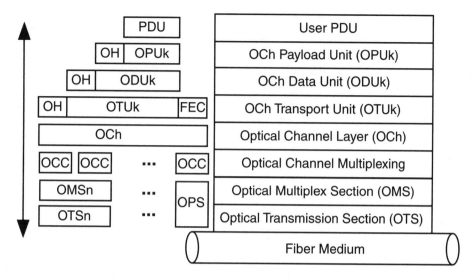

Figure 6–17   Encapsulation and decapsulation.

- *OPUk signal:* Optical channel payload unit (OPU) is defined as a structured signal of order k (k = 1, 2, 3) and is called the OPUk signal. The OPUk frame structure is organized in an octet-based block frame structure with 4 rows and 3810 columns. The two main areas of the OPUk frame (4 x 3810 Bytes) are the OPUk Overhead area (column 15 and 16) and the OPUk payload area (columns 17 to 3824).

- *ODUk signal:* Optical channel data unit (ODU) is defined as a structured signal of order k (k = 1, 2, 3) and is called the ODUk signal. The ODUk frame structure is organized in an octet-based block frame structure with 4 rows and 3824 columns. The two main areas of the ODUk frame are the ODUk Overhead area (columns 1 to 14, with column 1 dedicated to frame alignment and OTUk specific alignment) and the OPUk area (columns 15 to 3824, which are dedicated to the OPUk area).

- *OTUk signal:* Optical channel transport unit (OTU) of order k (k = 1, 2, 3) defines the conditioning for transport over an optical channel network connection. This signal is called the OTUk signal. The OTUk (k = 1,2,3) frame structure is based on the ODUk frame structure and extends it with a forward error correction (FEC). Scrambling is performed after FEC computation and insertion into the OTUk signal. In the OTUk signal, 256 columns are added to the ODUk frame for the FEC and the reserved overhead bytes in row 1, columns 9 to 14 of the ODUk overhead, are used for OTUk specific overhead, resulting in an octet-based block frame structure with 4 rows and 4080 columns (4 x 4080 bytes).

GENERIC FRAMING PROCEDURE (GFP)

The generic framing procedure (GFP) is used to encapsulate any type of traffic over the optical channel. It follows the construction of the digital wrapper. Its implementation is intended to avoid the use of other encapsulation and framing conventions, such as SDH/SONET and Ethernet. GFP is defined to transport any client layer (defined as OTN ODU of unit-k) over fixed rate optical channels.

One of GFP's principal attributes is that it sets forth the rules for conveying idle frames through the optical network, which most other framing procedures do not define. Knowing if the signals in the networks represent traffic (non-idle) or no traffic (idle) is very important. It allows the synchronous optical network to continue its operations even though it may be transporting asynchronous traffic.

The frame format for GFP is shown in Figure 6–18. The four-byte header is a two-byte PDU length indicator (PLI) and a two-byte header error control (HEC) field. The frame check sequence field (FCS) is optional. The idle frame format includes a null PLI and the HEC field.

GFP defines also two frame-oriented mechanisms. The first is frame multiplexing in which frame multiplexing is performed on a frame-by-frame basis. When no frames are waiting, idle frames are inserted. The second is called the GFP frame delineation; framing of the payload is

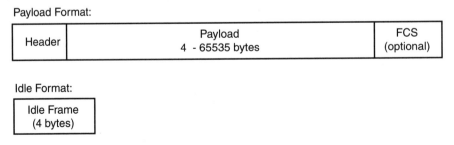

Figure 6–18   The GFP frame format [BELL01].

based on the detection of a correct HEC. After which, PLI is used to find the start of the next frame.

The GFP frames constitute the OPUk payload. The corresponding OPUk overhead is defined by the payload structure identifier (PSI), which includes the following fields: (a) PT: payload type (1-byte) and (b) RES: reserved (254-bytes).

The GFP OPUk (k = 1, 2, 3) capacities are defined so that they can include the following client bit rates: (a) GFP (OPU1): 2,488,320 kbit/s, (b) GFP (OPU2), 9,995,276 kbit/s, and (c): GFP (OPU3): 40,150,519 kbit/s.

The attractive aspect of GFP is by aligning the variable-length byte structure of every GFP frame with the byte structure of the OPUk, there are no restrictions on the maximum frame length. Therefore, a frame may cross the OPUk frame boundary.

SUMMARY

The third generation digital multiplexing scheme is an enhanced revision of the second generation SONET/SDH hierarchy. It has recently been defined, and vendors and network operators are planning the transition to the technology.

We are not finished with the 3G OTN; it is revisited in more detail later, after MPLS and GMPLS have been introduced (if you are in need of this material now, go to Chapter 10, and see "The Next Horizon: GMPLS Extensions for G.709").

Library Resource Center
Renton Technical College
3000 N.E. 4th St.
Renton, WA 98056

7

Wavelength Division Multiplexing (WDM)

Wavelength division multiplexing (or Wave division multiplexing) was introduced in Chapter 1, and has been mentioned several times thereafter. This chapter explains WDM in more detail, including examples of WDM bandwidth allocations, WDM components, and topologies of WDM networks. The chapter concludes with an example of how parts of the WDM spectrum are managed with a wavelength plan.

THE WDM OPERATION

WDM is based on a well-known concept called frequency division multiplexing or FDM. With this technology, the bandwidth of a channel (its frequency domain) is divided into multiple channels, and each channel occupies a part of the larger frequency spectrum. In WDM networks, each channel is called a *wavelength*. This name is used because each channel operates at a different frequency and a different optical wavelength (and the higher the frequency, the shorter the signal's wavelength).

In addition to the term wavelength, the terms frequency slot, lambda, and optical channel are also used to describe the optical WDM network channels. Recall that the term lambda is often noted with the Greek letter of λ. Notwithstanding all these terms, the idea of WDM is to use the optical channels (frequency slots) to carry user traffic.

Figure 7–1 shows a simple example of a WDM link. Four fibers are connected to a WDM multiplexer, which combines or multiplexes them onto one fiber. The opposite operation occurs at the receiving multiplexer, which separates (demultiplexes) the wavelengths and sends them to an appropriate output port, perhaps to other fibers.

As Figure 7–1 shows, each wavelength is separated by an unused spectrum to prevent the signals from interfering with each other. The ITU publishes standards on this spacing. The most common spacing is referred to as a 100 GHz spacing. Others are emerging that pack the wavelengths closer together at spacings of 50 GHz and 25 GHz. The 100 GHz spacing is sometimes cited as 0.8 nm, and the 50 GHz and 25 GHz are sometimes cited as 0.4 and 0.2 nm, respectively. These formulae can be used to determine the frequency of the wavelength and the wavelength spacings:

Frequency (Hz) = speed of light in a vacuum (in meters) / wavelength (in meters)

Wavelength separation = (frequency separation × wavelength^2) / Speed of light (in meters)

The range of frequencies (and, of course, wavelengths) carried in the fiber vary. A common set of wavelengths used today are those in the 1550 nm region; they are called the C band. Table 7–1 lists the WDM

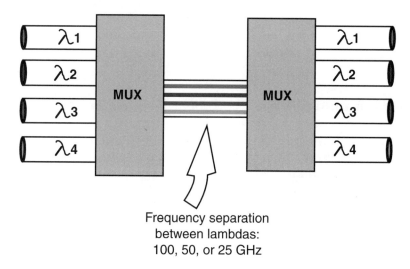

Figure 7–1   The WDM link.

Table 7–1   Examples of the C Band Wavelengths and Frequencies [LIGH01a]

Wavelength (nm)	Frequency (THz)	Wavelength (nm)	Frequency (THz)	Wavelength (nm)	Frequency (THz)
1539.766	194.7	1550.116	193.4	1560.606	192.1
1540.557	194.6	1550.918	193.3	1561.419	192.0
1541.349	194.5	1551.721	193.2	1562.233	191.0
1542.142	194.4	1552.524	193.1	1563.047	191.9
1542.936	194.3	1553.329	193.0	1563.900	191.8
1543.730	194.2	1554.134	192.9	1564.679	191.7
1544.526	194.1	1554.940	192.8	1565.496	191.6
1545.322	194.0	1555.747	192.7	1566.314	191.5
1546.119	193.9	1556.555	192.6	1567.133	191.4
1546.917	193.8	1557.363	192.5	1567.952	191.3
1547.715	193.7	1558.173	192.4	1568.773	191.2
1548.515	193.6	1558.983	192.3	1569.594	191.1
1549.315	193.5	1559.794	192.2	1570.416	190.9

wavelengths and associated frequencies ranging from 1539.766 nm to 1570.416 nm [LIGH01a]. Be aware that all vendors do not use all these wavelengths, and some vendors (and the ITU) define and use wavelengths on both sides of those shown in this table; that is, shorter and longer wavelengths. For example, the ITU G.692 Recommendation defines another band of frequencies in the L Band that operates above the C Band in the 1574.37 nm to 1608.33 nm range.

DENSE WAVE DIVISION MULTIPLEXING (DWDM)

DWDM systems allow the multiplexing of more than 160 wavelengths of 10 Gbit/s (1.6 Tbit/s per fiber with a 25 GHz spacing) by using both the C band and the L band spectra. Some vendors are proposing a spacing of 12.5 GHz. Consequently, it will be possible to transmit 320 wavelengths of 10 Gbit/s in a single fiber. A complementary method for increasing the effective capacity of a DWDM system is to include the 1480nm (S band) and 1650nm (U band) together with the deployment of fibers covering an ultra-wide waveband from 1460 to 1675nm (i.e., from the S band to the U band) [BELL01] for a total throughput of 3.2 Tbit/s per fiber.

TDM and WDM Topologies

Figure 7–2 shows the topology for a conventional optical TDM system and a WDM system. The WDM example is based on the Multiwavelength Optical NETworking (MONET) Consortium, funded partly by the Defense Advanced Research Projects Agency (DARPA) [JOHN99].

This example shows two layouts, each having a capacity of 40 Gbit/s. The optical terminals are OC-48 devices. An OC-48 link operates at 2,488.320 Mbit/s. In the TDM system, 16 fiber pairs operate at the OC-48 rate, each carrying one wavelength. In contrast, the WDM operates at the same capacity, using only a single fiber pair.

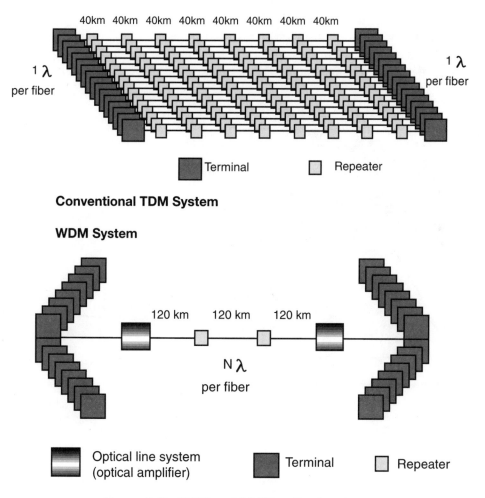

Figure 7–2   TDM and WDM optical systems.

The WDM system also needs fewer intermediate elements such as optical repeaters (also called amplifiers in the literature). Indeed, this figure illustrates a huge difference between TDM and WDM systems: the dramatic decrease in WDM networks in the number of fibers, and other components. In addition, the newer WDM technology does not need to space the amplifiers as closely together as in a TDM system.

RELATIONSHIP OF WDM TO SONET/SDH

Figure 7–3 shows the relationship of WDM to SONET and SDH [NORT98]. As previous discussions have emphasized, the idea of interworking WDM with SONET is to overlay SONET onto the photonic WDM layer.

There are parts of the network in which SONET frames are passed transparently and are not examined. One of these parts is at the multi-wavelength optical repeater (MOR). The decision to process (examine) the

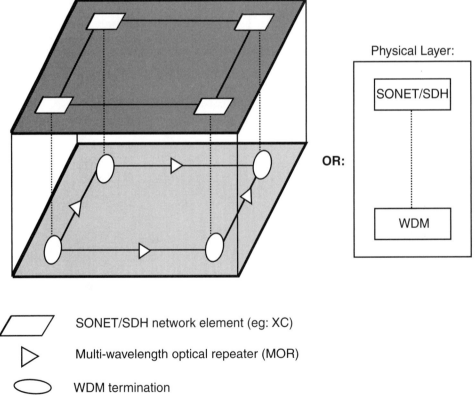

Physical Layer:

SONET/SDH

OR:

WDM

∠‾∠ SONET/SDH network element (eg: XC)

▷ Multi-wavelength optical repeater (MOR)

⬭ WDM termination

Figure 7–3   Relationship of SONET/SDH to WDM [NORT98].

SDH/SONET bits is based on the need to drop, add, or cross-connect payloads, and/or perform OAM operations, such as testing and diagnostics.

Any termination of WDM signals might remain transparent to SDH/SONET, or termination of WDM and SDH/SONET may occur at one site. This decision is based on the individual network topology and how customer payloads must be processed at each node.

Notice in Figure 7–3 that the SONET/SDH network element, such as a cross-connect, is situated at a WDM termination site. This arrangement makes good sense since an O/E/O operation at an optical node requires the termination of the optical signal. Also, the idea of these arrangements is shown in Figure 7–3 with the physical layer relationships: SDH/SONET layers operate over the WDM layer.

ERBIUM-DOPED FIBER (EDF)

With the advent of the erbium-doped fiber (EDF), the need for electronic circuitry in some of the optical components no longer exists. Moreover, EDF Amplifiers (EDFAs) are transparent to a data rate. They also provide high gain and experience low noise. The major attraction is that all the optical signal channels can be amplified simultaneously at the EDFA in a single fiber. Of course, this approach is the essence of WDM.

EDFAs play a big role in several parts of WDM optical networks. EDFAs can be found in amplifiers, optical cross-connects, wavelength add-drop multiplexers (ADM), and broadcast networks.

They are deployed as in-line amplifiers, in which they amplify an optical signal that has been attenuated by the fiber. They are used to boost optical power at the sending site as the signal enters the fiber (as well as at the receiver). They are found in optical cross-connects, and they are used to compensate for signal loss as well as wavelength ADMs for the same function. Lastly, they are now employed in optical broadcast systems to boost the power for the distribution system.

WDM AMPLIFIERS

One of the key components of WDM optical networks are optical fiber amplifiers. In the past, optical networks used optoelectronic regenerators between optical terminals. These devices converted optical signals to electrical signals and then back to optical signals. This approach required expensive high-speed electronic circuitry, and operated on one signal (one lightwave).

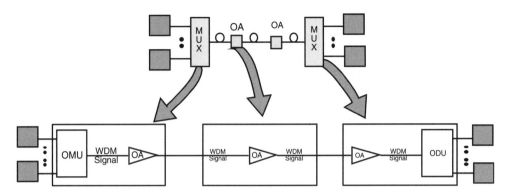

Figure 7–4   Optical amplifiers for WDM.

Figure 7–4 shows a typical schematic diagram for the use of optical amplifiers in a WDM transmission system (also called optical fiber amplifiers (OFAs)). At the sending end, multiple optical channels are combined in an optical multiplexer. This combined signal is amplified before it is launched into the first fiber span. At the receiving end, the opposite operations occur. The incoming WDM signals are amplified by a "preamplifier" and then they are demuxed and sent to their respective receivers.

As mentioned earlier, the optical amplifier is deployed as an in-line amplifier; it amplifies the optical signal that has been attenuated by the fiber. It also boosts optical power at the sending site (the optical multiplexing unit) and the receiving site (the optical demultiplexing unit).

The use of erbium-doped fiber for amplifiers in the late 1980s and early 1990s was a major milestone, leading to the development of a new generation of amplifiers for the 1500 nm wavelength window. The erbium-doped fiber amplifiers (EDFAs) are significantly less expensive than the optoelectronic regenerators. They are oblivious to the bit rate or the data format on the link, so any upgrades do not affect them. In addition, they can amplify multiple WDM wavelengths simultaneously.

Let's review once again three terms dealing with the physical signal: (a) 1R: signal is reamplified, (b) 2R: signal is reamplified and reshaped, (c) 3R: signal is reamplified, reshaped, and retimed. The OFA eliminates the need for 3R operations.

Gain Flatness

The WDM signal must be well-balanced throughout the entire fiber transmission. This means that each wavelength amplification should remain constant with respect to other wavelengths. To maintain this consistency, the optical amplifier is gain-flattened. One of the problems with conventional erbium-doped fiber amplifiers is that they amplify different wavelengths carried on the fiber. Under certain conditions, there can be a 3 to 4 dB of gain difference per amplifier within the 1530 to 1560 nm window. One approach to handle this problem is to use an equalization filter that controls peak attenuation, center wavelength, and signal width.

ADD-DROP MULTIPLEXERS

As the capacity of optical systems increases, opportunities are created for network service providers to provide more capacity to the systems' users. These users are located in many parts of a geographical region, including business sites, industrial parks, campuses, and stand-alone offices. These diverse sites require great flexibility in bandwidth management to the customers' requirements. In WDM networks, the service provider should be able to provision bandwidth in a fast, efficient, and cost-effective manner to these sites.

One of the key "tools" to support this environment is the wavelength add-drop multiplexer (WADM). Based on earlier TDM ADMs, these devices support the management of fiber capacity by the selective adding, inserting, and removal of WDM channels at intermediate points in the network; a general example of these operations is shown in Figure 7–5.

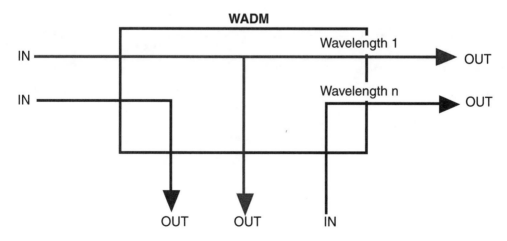

Figure 7–5   Generalized view of an optical ADM.

Metropolitan WDM networks are of keen interest in regards to WADM services. The requirements range from rearrangeable add-drop of 1–8 channels in a small business to 40 or more channels in an interoffice ring.

Due to the diverse customer mix, each WADM channel should be capable of carrying a different data rate and channel mix. The emerging WADMs support all the requirements described in this introduction.

Figure 7–5 shows a general example of an optical ADM. The machine has n inputs and a single mode fiber output with multiple wavelengths. The ADM must be able to demodulate each wavelength from the composite signal, and drop, pass through, or insert the wavelengths.

WADM Input and Output Ports

We continue the discussion of WADMs with a more detailed look at the ADM input and output ports. Figure 7–6 is a re-rendering of Figure 7–5. It shows four ways of managing a WDM channel at the ADM. The four notations are shown at the respective output port on the ADM.

- *Add:* An input channel is added to an output channel.
- *Drop:* These channels are the opposite of the adds. A channel coming into the ADM is dropped off to another node.
- *Through:* This channel is a straight pass-through the machine.
- *Drop-and-Continue or Bridge:* This channel is both a drop cross-connection and a through cross-connection from the same source. This configuration allows payload to be dropped off and also passed downstream.

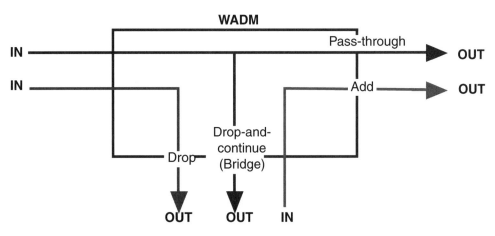

Figure 7–6   The WADM ports.

Figure 7–7 shows the WADM with in, out, add, and drop ports designated as 1–4 to later identify the relationships of the optical flows [GILE99]. The channel pathways are set up from the in and add ports to the out and drop ports. To manage these flows, a connection matrix is used, with rows corresponding to optical paths through the WADM and columns of 1s or 0s depicting the state of the flows for each WDM channel. An ideal WDM of N channels has at least 2^N possible connection states.

Figure 7–7 also shows two connection matrices for 16 WDM channels in a WADM. In the first matrix, channels 5-12 are through-channels, channels 1-4 are added, and channels 13-16 are dropped. In the second matrix, channels 2 and 11 are both dropped and added, and the other channels are passed-through the WADM.

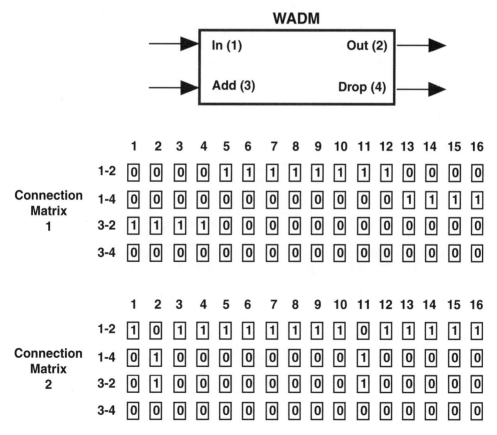

Figure 7–7   The WADM connection matrices [GILE99].

WDM CROSS-CONNECTS

The digital cross-connects (DCSs) are used to cross-connect optical links (point-to-point lines, and rings). One of their principal jobs is to map various types of input steams to output streams; in essence, they provide a central point for grooming and consolidation of user payload. The DCS can segregate high bandwidth traffic from low bandwidth traffic and send this traffic out to different ports. The DCS is also tasked with trouble isolation, loopback testing, and diagnostic requirements. It must respond to alarms and failure notifications.

The DCS may perform switching at the electrical level or (increasingly) at the optical level. The state-of-the-art optical cross-connects (OXCs) can convert an incoming signal of a specific wavelength to an outgoing signal of a different wavelength.

Figure 7–8 shows a functional diagram of an OXC. Four optical line systems (OLSs) are connected to the OXC [JACK99]. The WDM signals from two OLSs are demultiplexed and the resultant wavelengths are passed through wavelength converters. Each wavelength signal is cross-connected by the OXC, wavelength converted again, multiplexed, and sent out of a fiber interface.

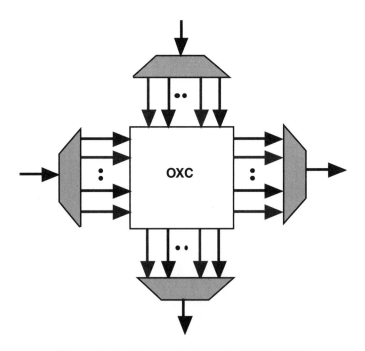

Figure 7–8   General view of a WDM OXC.

WAVELENGTH CONTINUITY PROPERTY

A WDM lightwave is said to satisfy the wavelength continuity property if it is transported over the same wavelength end-to-end. For optical nodes that do not have wavelength conversion features, this property is obviously in effect.

Nonetheless, as a wavelength is transported though multiple nodes, its properties will indeed change, a subject discussed in the last part of this chapter.

EXAMPLE OF DWDM WAVELENGTH PLAN

Vendors of optical equipment have their own methods of allowing the network operator to configure the wavelengths in the network. This section discusses one method used by Nortel Networks in several of their S/DMS TransportNodes™ [NORT98]. As shown in Table 7–2, this method supports up to 32 wavelengths (using NZDF fiber). The network operator can provision as few as two wavelengths, and add more (in increments of two) as traffic increases over time. The 32 wavelengths aggregate to 320 Gbit/s per fiber span. The wavelengths are divided into two bands, as shown in the table. Each band propagates in opposite directions on the fiber span. Table 7–2 also contains a column labeled "Order of Use." This entry provides guidance on the order in which the wavelengths are deployed. This plan is designed to provide the best performance for the span, as well as to assure that different nodes in the network are in agreement about which wavelengths are actually used.

Average Versus Maximum Span Loss and Chromatic Dispersion

In planning for DWDM deployment, it is important to know the signal loss over the span in relation to the number of wavelengths deployed, and the link speed. For example, using 32 wavelengths, the optical node supports the distances between DWDM repeaters, as shown in Table 7–3.

In addition, for the deployment of OC-192 on NDSF, the net chromatic dispersion must be limited to no more than 1400 ps.nm (using a measurement at 1557 nm) at the receiver. For OC-48 NDSF deployments, the system can tolerate up to 11,400 ps/nm for chromatic dispersion (corrected to an optical reach of over 700 km). An DWDM system will experience different amounts of chromatic dispersion in each wavelength on the band. To correct these different amounts of chromatic

Table 7–2 Example of a Wavelength Plan [NORT98]

Wavelength Grid (100 GHz spacing)	Order of Use	Band	Up to 32	Up to 24	Up to 16	Up to 8
1505.60		Red	Spare	Spare	Spare	Spare
1559.79	16	Red	√			
1558.98	6	Red	√	√	√	
1558.17	15	Red	√			
1557.36	1	Red	√	√	√	√
1556.55	10	Red	√	√		
1555.75	4	Red	√	√	√	√
1554.94	14	Red	√			
1554.13	8	Red	√	√	√	
1553.33	13	Red	√			
1552.52	2	Red	√	√	√	√
1551.72	9	Red	√	√		
1550.92	3	Red	√	√	√	√
1550.12	12	Red	√	√		
1549.32	7	Red	√	√	√	
1548.51	11	Red	√	√		
1547.72	5	Red	√	√	√	
1541.30		Blue	Spare	Spare	Spare	Spare
1540.56	16	Blue	√			
1539.77	5	Blue	√	√	√	
1538.98	15	Blue	√			
1538.19	6	Blue	√	√	√	
1537.40	14	Blue	√			
1536.61	7	Blue	√	√	√	
1535.82	13	Blue	√			
1535.04	1	Blue	√	√	√	√
1534.25	10	Blue	√	√		
1533.47	4	Blue	√	√	√	√
1532.68	12	Blue	√	√		
1531.90	8	Blue	√	√	√	
1531.12	11	Blue	√	√		
1530.33	2	Blue	√	√	√	√
1529.55	9	Blue	√	√		
1528.77	3	Blue	√	√	√	√

Table 7–3   Typical Optical Reach for 32 Wavelengths [NORT98]

Fiber Type	OC-48	OC-48 and OC-48/OC-192
NDSF	700km	500km
NZDSF	700km	500km

dispersion, Nortel Networks provides red and blue band compensation modules for use in several systems that span over 400 km in length.

Nortel Networks uses the following scheme to plan average and maximum span loss values. Let's use an OC-48, six-span, eight-wavelength application, with an average span loss value (budget) of up to 27 dB per span, where each of two spans introduce 29 dB of loss (or 2 dB in excess of the recommended budget). The total loss of 4 dB can be accommodated, providing that the total system loss budget is reduced to this formula:

Adjusted System Loss = Number of Spans × [Average Loss – Excess Loss Value]
Where: Excess Loss Value equals:
0 dB for total excess loss ≤ 2 dB,
1 dB for total excess loss > 2 dB and ≤ 4 dB

For this example, with an initial total system loss budget of 162 dB (6 spans × 27 dB per span), the adjusted system loss budget is:

6 spans × (27 dB – 1 dB) = 156 dB

HIGHER DISPERSION FOR DWDM

The subject of dispersion is explained in Chapter 3. If you would like to review the basic concepts of dispersion, see the section in Chapter 3 titled "Chromatic Dispersion." There has been considerable attention paid to channel spacing in DWDM systems, that is, the bandwidth between the wavelengths. Of course, it is desirable to reduce this spacing as much as possible, since the spacing represents unused bandwidth, and more channels can be placed in a single fiber. However, tight channel spacing can lead to interference between the wavelengths, and is evident on fibers with low dispersion levels, such as NZDF. Recall from Chapter 3 that

NZDF operates over a portion of the third wavelength window, with the chromatic dispersion small enough to support individual channel rates of 10 Gbit/s over distances of over 250 km.

A new type of fiber solves some of these problems. It is called Advanced NZDF (A-NZDF), and has been developed in conformance with the ITU G.655 Recommendation. This new class of fiber exhibits a maximum dispersion of 10 psec/nm-km at the far end of the C band. It tends to suppress the non-linealities that are introduced by the tighter channel spacing. It is expected that this improved DWDM operation will allow the dispersion to be high enough to minimize non-linearities and low enough to minimize the need for dispersion compensation. It will be an important tool in the deployment of 40 Gbit/s systems.

For the reader who wants more information on this new fiber class, you should read ITU G.655, and [RYAN01] provides an excellent explanation of the performance of A-NZDF, as well as some interesting cost comparisons of A-NZDF and other NZDF technologies.

TUNABLE DWDM LASERS

The WDM wavelengths are spaced very closely together to allow many wavelengths to be placed on one fiber. However, it is quite costly to build a system in which there is a dedicated laser for each wavelength. The solution is a tunable laser, one that can be tuned over a wide range of wavelengths. Thus, this laser can be modified to suit several wavelength channels.

SUMMARY

WDM represents a significant advance in optical fiber technology. It has allowed optical networks to increase their capacity by many orders of magnitude. WDM relies on a very old concept called frequency division multiplexing, but WDM deals with the optical spectrum.

With the progress made in the last few years with dense WDM, it is now possible to operate one optical fiber in the terabit per second range. With the advent of tunable lasers, and the emerging standards on dynamic wavelength configuration and spectrum management, optical networks will be deployed that support near-instantaneous "bandwidth on demand," as well as "QOS on demand."

8

Network Topologies and Protection Schemes

This chapter examines the way in which optical networks are put together, and the shape they take. The emphasis is on point-to-point, ring, and mesh topologies, which reflect the preferred methods for the network layout. The subject of protection is also discussed, which deals with how an optical network provider can exploit network topologies to give the network user robust connections, that is, protect the customer's traffic from link or node failures.

THE NON-NEGOTIABLE REQUIREMENT: ROBUST NETWORKS

In some of my writings, I have quoted the typical network manager dictum, "Whatever it costs, whatever the effort, keep the network up and running." Certainly those people who "foot the bill" must weigh the costs of building such a network. Nonetheless, some networks cannot afford to lose the ability to transport their customers' traffic. Optical networks are the backbone of most communications networks around the world, so it is critical that they be robust.

Of course, an optical network unto itself cannot offer any more fail-safe features than a copper-wire network. Optical fiber is inherently less error-prone, but it does not offer any more backup facilities than any other technology.

It does not matter if a network is copper- or fiber-based, any large backbone network must have ways to recover from problems and to keep these problems transparent to the network users. To gain a sense of how important this idea is, consider a telephone exchange in the metropolitan Boston area.

The telephone service provider supports over five million people in this particular area. In so doing, several powerful switches are employed to route the telephone calls to and from the calling parties and the called parties. Each switch has a backup switch in case one switch goes down. Each switch pair has ~500 communications links. Each link supports about 20 calls per second; therefore, $20 \times 60s \times 60min = 72,000$ calls per hour per link.

This particular exchange supports the following calls: 500 links × 4 switch pairs × 72,000 = 144,000,000 calls per hour or over 40,000 calls per second.

The failure of parts of this network will have very serious consequences, leading to a considerable amount of lost revenue, lost productivity, and psychological stress.

With these thoughts of "robustness" in mind, we can now explore how optical networks provide protection services to its customers.

DIVERSITY IN THE NETWORK: WHICH CONTROL PLANE?

In several IETF working papers, the term *diversity* refers to the relationship between lightpaths, such as fibers, or wavelengths on the fibers, called *optical links* in this discussion. Two optical links are said to be diverse if they have no single point of failure. Traditionally, this diversity has been implemented by the telephone and leased line service providers.

Data service providers (using IP and other data-oriented techniques) have not had to deal with this important issue; they have relied on the private line providers for these services. Thus, IP has operated over many different kinds of carrier transport networks, without concern about the activities of the diversity operations.

This relationship holds true for third generation networks, but the idea supported by many people in the industry is to bring IP (and MPLS) into the picture to assist in achieving link diversity, routing, and protection switching.

This "integration" must be approached with considerable care. It has not yet been demonstrated that the complex ID addressing scheme (with its many rules on address aggregation, OSPF/BGP routing, private address reuse, etc.) should be integrated with (or even make known to) the optical control plane. Indeed, I am not sure this IP addressing pox should be permeated down to yet another part of a network architecture.

My view is that the IP, MPLS, and optical control planes should be designed to allow their coupling together, or to allow them to operate independently. For a review of this idea, take a look at the section titled, "Management of the Planes" in Chapter 10, and more information is provided on this issue later in the book (see "Plane Coupling and Decoupling" in Chapter 12).

LINE AND PATH PROTECTION SWITCHING

We need to define some terms at the onset of this discussion. Two forms of protection switching are employed in an optical network: line protection switching and path protection switching. Line switching performs recovery on the entire optical link (the line). Path protection switching performs recovery on selected tributaries on the fiber.

For example, an STS-1 tributary on an OC-48 line that is carrying, say, ATM traffic from city A to city B might undergo recovery operations and not affect another STS-1 tributary that is carrying ATM traffic from city A to city C. Path protection switching provides more granularity of control than does line protection switching.

Path protection switching also works hand-in-hand with tributary provisioning (setting up and tearing down specific customer tributaries on the fiber), so it is a common mode of protection switching. Of course, if a fiber link is down, it makes no difference if line protection is used, so line protection switching is also quite common.

TYPES OF TOPOLOGIES

The next parts of this chapter explain in more detail the various types of topologies found in optical networks. To start this discussion, Table 8–1 shows the various choices for a topology. The basic topology can be a point-to-point, a ring arrangement, or a meshed layout. Within these three topologies, there can be two or four fibers connecting the optical nodes, the optical signals can flow in one or both directions, and the

Table 8–1   Network Topologies and Attributes

Topology	Fibers	Signal Direction	Role of Fiber	Protection Type
Point-to-point	2 or 4	Uni- or Bidirectional	Working or Protection	Line or Path
Ring	2 or 4	Uni- or Bidirectional	Working or Protection	Line or Path
Meshed	2 or 4	Uni- or Bidirectional	Working or Protection	Line or Path

method of recovery can be performed at a line or a path level. As the table reveals, all three topologies can provide the same kinds of protection attributes. These attributes of the topologies are explained next.

WORKING AND PROTECTION FIBERS

The term working fiber (or working copy) refers to a fiber (or a wavelength) that is carrying user payload. The term protection fiber (or protection copy) refers to a fiber (or a wavelength) that is acting as a backup to the working copy. A protection copy may also be carrying user payload, but in the event of problems, this payload (usually of a low priority) is removed from the protection copy, and the other (usually of a higher priority) payload is placed onto the protection copy.

Ideally, one would like to have the working and protection fiber in different paths (different feeders) between the network elements. This option is not always possible, but, as seen in Figure 8–1 (a), it may be possible to place two fiber cable sheaths in the same conduit structure and then separate them physically within the conduit.

Many systems and their conduits are laid out in a grid structure. It may be possible (as in Figure 8–1 (b)) to place the working and protection fibers in separate conduits for at least part of the feeder connection.

Yet another possible alternative (see Figure 8–1 (c)) is to use different feeders for the working and protection fibers. Finally, Figure 8–1 (d) shows another possible way to separate the cables. Since some feeder routes in densely populated areas may intersect or be situated close together, it may be feasible to use two dual paths to two separate central offices, and have the ring connected through these offices.

The list below should be helpful as you read this chapter:

- 1+1 unidirectional: A dedicated point-to-point link between nodes to provide line or path protection.

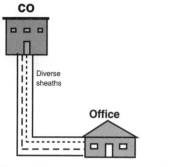

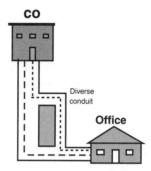

(a) Same CO, same feeder, diverse sheath   (b) Same CO, same feeder, diverse conduit

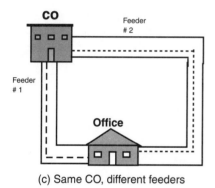

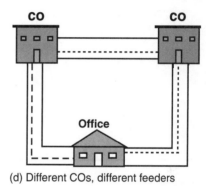

(c) Same CO, different feeders   (d) Different COs, different feeders

Figure 8–1   Topology diversity in the network.

- 1+1 bi-directional: A dedicated point-to-point link between nodes for line or path protection. Alarm information provided in SONET/SDH OAM bytes.
- 1:N: A protection link shared by N working links.
- 2 fiber bi-directional line switched ring (2F-BLSR): Provides line protection with one protection fiber.
- 4 fiber bi-directional line switched ring (4F-BLSR): Provides line protection with two protection fibers.
- Uni-directional path switched ring (UPSR): Provide path protection with an alternative fiber in the ring.

POINT-TO-POINT TOPOLOGY

The topology for the optical network chosen depends on the network manager's objectives pertaining to bandwidth availability, bandwidth efficiency, survivability/robustness, cost containment, and simplicity.

The point-to-point topology shown in Figure 8–2 is a common topology. The entire optical payload is terminated at each end of the fiber span between two access nodes. Two fibers connect the two optical access nodes. The term bi-directional fiber describes this arrangement: One fiber transports the signals in one direction and the other fiber transports the signals in the other direction. It is certainly possible to deploy a point-to-point system wherein only one fiber connects the nodes, but unidirectional point-to-point topologies provide no means to recover from errors on the fiber or fiber interfaces.

Point-to-point topologies are usually employed in a system that needs only a single system and single route solution. The topology is simple, but not designed to be completely survivable. The reliability of a

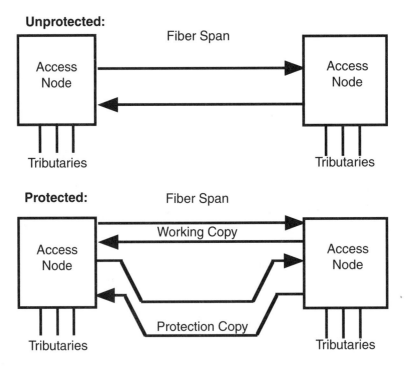

Figure 8–2   Point-to-point topology.

point-to-point system can be enhanced considerably through the user of a geographically diverse protection path, also shown in Figure 8–2. Since diverse routing may exceed the normal reach of the fiber, one or more regenerators or optical amplifiers can be employed on the span to reconstitute or boost the signal.

1:N Protection Channel Sharing

A common topology employed in many systems today is called the 1:N protection channel sharing, as shown in Figure 8–3. This topology employs multi-network elements (access nodes) in a point-to-point configuration. Its attraction is that it conserves fiber pairs by allowing multiple systems to share a common protection channel. In a network where there is rapidly growing traffic demand, the 1:N topology can either defer or avoid the deployment of new fiber cable.

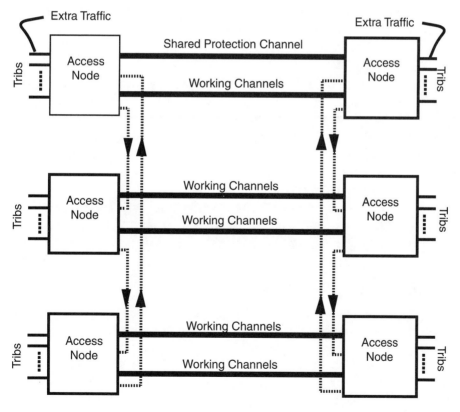

Figure 8–3   Point-to-point protection channel sharing.

If an error occurs on any of the working channels, the affected traffic on this channel is automatically diverted to the protection channel. The diversion operation occurs through the installment of inter-shelf protection loop line cards with a dedicated shelf at each end of the span.

Based on a customer's needs, the 1:N topology (which might be empty most of the time) can be used to carry extra traffic. Extra traffic is a term that refers to the exploitation of the normally idle protection fiber. While this bandwidth is available to ensure survivability, it is also capable of supporting ongoing user traffic. This approach also allows the introduction of new services without the costly implementation of additional fiber. Of course, the extra traffic is "unprotected," but additional measures may be undertaken to lessen or completely eliminate the impact of a switch to these protection facilities during an impairment to the system.

Three options can be implemented to protect the extra traffic:

- Diverse routing: The extra traffic can be protected by a redundant diverse route to prevent a single source of failure causing a service outage. The redundant route can also be provided via an extra traffic channel.
- Service discounting: The network service provider can offer an extra traffic-based service at a substantial discount with the understanding that service interruptions may occur.
- Degradable services: Multiple protected and unprotected service channels can be provisioned for certain data services. The data services would then be considered to be of lesser priority than other traffic. Due to the asynchronous nature of data traffic, the loss of a unprotected extra traffic channel will certainly result in degraded performance but may not result in a total service interruption.

Optical Channel Concatenation

Increasingly, as optical networks evolve, the legacy SONET/SDH equipment will probably be bypassed if these nodes cannot support the port speeds that are emerging today. To accommodate the high-speed optical links, a common practice is to cluster multiple backbone routers to meet the bandwidth demands. The resulting topology are many parallel links in a backbone network that are not protected with the conventional SONET/SDH ring protection operations.

Of course, one solution is to use protection channel sharing topology shown in Figure 8–3, and this is exactly what vendors are doing today. However, until recently, these schemes have been proprietary. Some use the K1 and K2 bytes of the SONET/SDH header to control the operations, some use the D bytes, and so on. Clearly, it will be beneficial to have a standardized scheme, and this section is devoted to this topic.

To give you an idea of some of the operations involved in this scheme, let's take a look at some work going on with [LEE01]. This IETF working group has set forth a scheme for managing parallel links, called optical channel concatenation. This operation uses a new framing method defined in [T1X1.501].

A new term is coined for this operation: the superchannel. It refers to a concatenation of multiple links, and perhaps wavelengths within the links. The superchannel can appear as one interface on a router, and thus be advertised as a single IP address by, say, OSPF. It is the job of the two nodes connecting the multiple parallel links to manage the individual subchannels (the ports and the wavelengths on the ports). Figure 8–4 shows how four parallel links are concatenated together, and treated as a superchannel by nodes A and B.

Figure 8–5 shows the messages that are sent between nodes A and B if all subchannels are operating without any problems. Each message is a bit map that reflects the state of each optical port. Alternatively, the bit

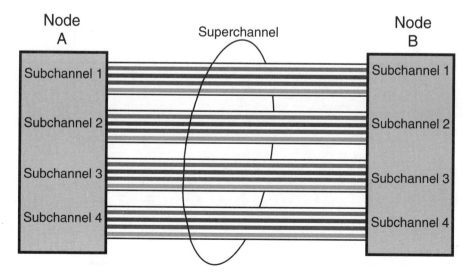

Figure 8–4 Concatenated optical channels.

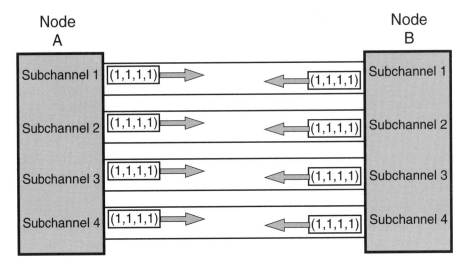

Figure 8–5   All subchannels are up and running.

map can reflect the state of the port interfaces as well as the state of each wavelength that is being received across each port. The four 1s in the message signify that all four subchannels are operating satisfactorily.

In the event that problems arise on one or more subchannels, the affected node uses the subchannels that are still operating to report on the problem. Figure 8–6 shows that subchannel 1 has failed. Both nodes

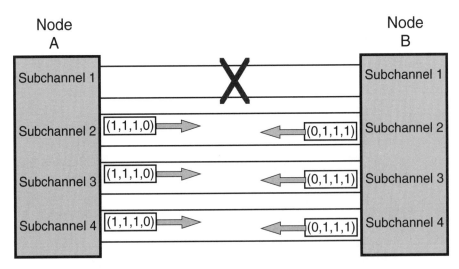

Figure 8–6   Reporting on faulty subchannels.

notice the failure, typically by not receiving any traffic from the partner node. In turn, the nodes alter the bit map in the message to identify the specific problem, in this example, at subchannel 1. The actions taken as a result of these alarms will vary, depending on the network provider's implementations. The nodes might place the user payload from subchannel 1 onto protection copies in the other subchannels, or the nodes might be configured to route this traffic to other nodes in the network. Whatever the action taken, the idea is to protect the user's traffic from these failures.

BI-DIRECTIONAL LINE-SWITCHED RING (BLSR)

The bi-directional line-switched ring (BLSR) connects adjacent nodes through a single pair of optical fibers. One fiber is used for the working copy (for user traffic) and the other fiber is used for protection. Many systems use more than two optical fibers, typically one pair for traffic, and the other pair for protection; this arrangement is covered later in the chapter.

This architecture provides a survivable closed loop architecture which can recover from either cable failure or node failure. As shown in Figure 8–7, the working traffic travels in one direction on the ring and the protection path is provided in the opposite direction. This approach is called BLSR 1:1 span protection switching: there is one protection copy for each working copy.

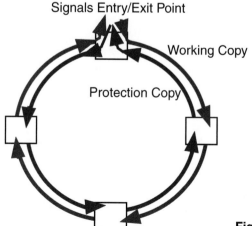

Signals Entry/Exit Point

Working Copy

Protection Copy

Figure 8–7   BLSR, two fibers.

Traffic may originate or terminate on the same BLSR or may be transferred to adjacent nodes into other rings. Each individual DS1, DS3, or STS1 signal travels around the ring in one direction. However, a duplicate signal passes in the opposite direction on the protection fiber. A path selector performs an ongoing monitoring function on the two fibers at each end of the path. In the event of a node failure or a fiber failure, the path selector automatically switches to the protection signal. The path selector is able to detect signal degradation as well as path failure and can transmit and receive: (a) path alarm indication signals (AIS), (b) path loss of pointer (LOP) signals, (c) signal degrade (SD) signals, and (d) excessive path layer bit interleaved parity (BIP) errors.

Figure 8–8 shows how the BLSR recovers from a fiber cut. The signal entry point is at node A and the exit point is at node B. Upon detecting the loss of a signal between nodes A and B, B sends an alarm signal to A on the working copy through nodes D and C (this operation is not shown in the figure).

This alarm alerts node A to the problem. Node A is already employing the protection path to send the traffic through the other nodes reaching the proper signal exit point at node B.

It should be emphasized that node B will notice a path failure because it receives no traffic on the working path between A and B; therefore, it does not have to rely on sending the alarm to A because it already has another signal from A on the protection path. The path selector simply selects the signal off the protection path at the signal exit point (node B).

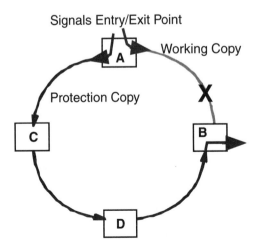

Figure 8–8   BLSR protection switching.

Notice the "cable cut" on the fiber between nodes A and B. It is now an easy task for node B to select the signal coming from node D. After all, node B is receiving nothing from node A.

Of course, the arrangement is very robust, and the recovery is instantaneous. The drawback to this topology is the consumption of resources to run the same traffic over duplicate fibers.

PROTECTION SWITCHING ON FOUR-FIBER BLSR

Figure 8–9 shows another common ring arrangement. There are four fibers in the ring, set up as two pairs. One pair is the working pair and the other is the protection pair. One fiber of the pair transmits in one direction, and the other fiber transmits in the other direction. The topology is used because it obviously provides for more capacity, and if the entire installation is performed at the same time, the benefits of the additional fibers and interfaces outweigh the costs.

Figure 8–10 shows how a four-fiber BLSR recovers from a loss of connectivity between two fiber nodes. The nodes that are affected directly (nodes A and B) can now divert (loop back; shown in the figure as LB) the traffic

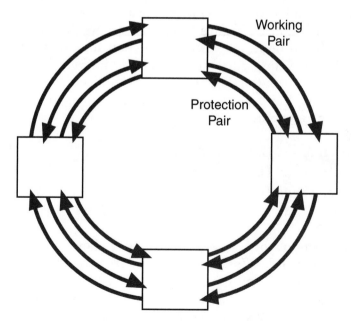

Figure 8–9   The four-fiber BLSR.

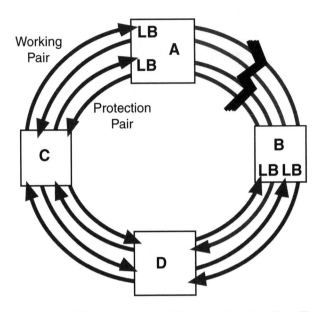

Figure 8–10   Fiber cut on working and protection fibers.

back to the other fibers in the working and protection pair. Nodes C and D are not involved in the protection switch operation, but they can be made aware of the problem by receiving diagnostic messages from nodes A and B.

The next example in Figure 8–11 shows how the ring topology can recover from a dual fault, one fault on one pair and another fault on the other pair. To keep the figure simple, the bi-directional arrows indicate that two fibers are sending the traffic in both directions on the ring. In this arrangement, the protection and working copies are utilized, based on where the errors occur:

- Between A and B: Use protection pair
- Between B and D: Use working pair
- Between C and D: Use protection pair
- Between C and A: Use working pair

The last example of ring fault recovery is shown in Figure 8–12. In this situation, node B has failed, which renders useless the links between B's neighbors, nodes A and D. These two nodes detect the failure by not receiving signals on their links to node B (or by not receiving responses to their link management protocol (LMP) hello messages, a topic for Chapter 11). In either case, nodes A and D perform the recovery by looping the signals back onto the mate of the protection and working copies.

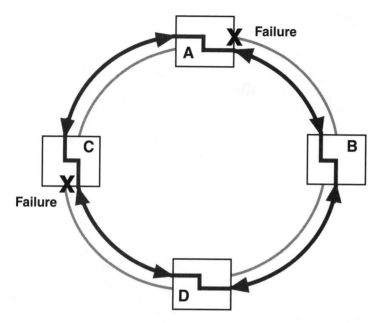

Figure 8–11   Example of a dual fault (bi-directional arrows denote two fibers).

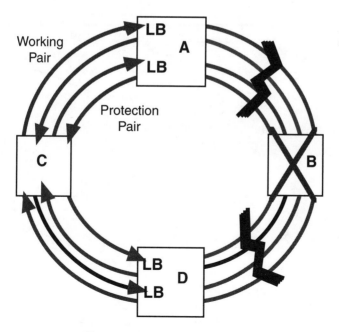

Figure 8–12   Node failure.

MESHED TOPOLOGIES

Optical rings are prevalent topologies in large-scale optical networks. But I would be remiss if meshed topologies are not discussed in this chapter, since they are a bedrock feature of Signaling System #7 (SS7), the control plane for the world's telephone system and many internets. Figure 8–13 shows a typical meshed topology. The user nodes (such as telephone central offices) are labeled A and F. The network nodes (B, C, D, and E) are called signaling transfer points (STPs), which are large switches that are responsible principally for keeping the backbone

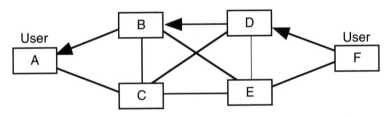

(a) Normal Traffic Flow from F to A

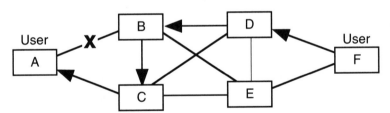

(b) Diverted Traffic Flow from F to A

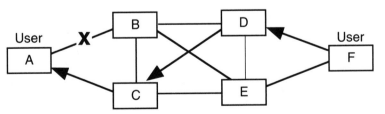

(c) STP B Informs STP D to Divert Traffic

Figure 8–13   Mesh topology.

network operational. The STPs in this example are fully connected, in that each node has a direct optical link with all other node. This topology is called a fully meshed network.

SS7 uses the term link set to define multiple links between two adjacent nodes. For optical networks, a link set could be separate fibers (most likely), or different wavelengths on the same fiber. In addition, SS7 uses a shorthand notation to describe the location of the link sets. For example, the notation link set A-B means a link set between nodes A and B.

During normal operations, routing traffic goes through the most direct route. In Figure 8–13 (a), the messages are sent across links between nodes F, D, B, and A. If a failure occurs between certain nodal pairs (B and C, for example), no routing change occurs. The reasons are that A can still reach its two switches (B and C). Also, under most conditions, upon receiving traffic from its attached switches (in this example, A) B would not send this traffic to C, but to a more direct route of B-D or B-E. Therefore, if link set B-C fails, only nodes B and C are aware of the failure. The B-C link set is always a lower priority than its alternatives.

It is possible for this topology to break down to such an extent that traffic is not routable for a particular STP. For example, at switch B, if link sets B-D, B-E and B-C are unavailable, B cannot relay traffic. But this topology provides 100% redundancy. Any single point of failure does not bring down the system, because the traffic can be diverted around the failure. So, even if B's links are down (or, for that matter, if B is down), traffic is diverted, and the network remains fully operational. Anyway, multiple link failures are rare; such an event would mean that all link sets and links within each link set would have failed.

In Figure 8–13 (a), traffic is routed between signaling points F and A through link sets FD-DB-BA. In Figure 8–13 (b), a failure occurs on the link (or link set) between B and A. These nodes take this link set out of operation and B diverts the traffic to C on link set B-C. However, a better route may exist between F and A. If the B-A failure persists for greater than a set period, B will send messages to D and E to inform them that traffic for A should be sent on link sets D-C and E-C, respectively. This new configuration is shown in Figure 8–13 (c), with link set D-C the primary link set from D.

For this next example, it is assumed that node D goes down, and/or all of D's link sets become unavailable. In Figure 8–14 (a), under normal conditions, traffic is moving from F to A through link sets F-D, D-B, B-A. In Figure 8–14 (b), node D goes down and any links that interface into D are unavailable. For traffic flowing from F to A, it is diverted to E,

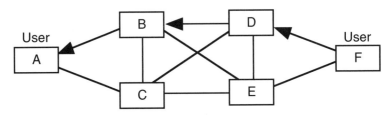

(a) Normal Traffic Flow from F to A

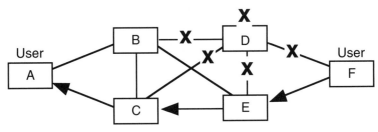

(b) Node D is Down

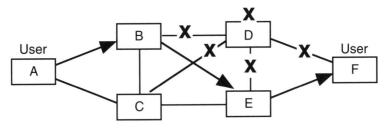

(c) Traffic in Other Direction

Figure 8–14   Node failure recovery.

through C, and then to A. In Figure 8–14 (c), for traffic flowing from A to F that was going through B, it is sent to B, through E, and then to F.

Once again, it is obvious how the meshed backbone topology provides for 100% recovery from any single point of failure. And some multiple points of failure are also recoverable. For example, assume that nodes B and E are declared unavailable. Traffic from A to F is diverted through link sets A-C, C-D, D-F, and traffic from F to A is diverted through link sets F-D, D-C, C-A.

It is evident that SS7 networks are highly reliable, but then they must be, since they are the control plane for the world's telephone networks.

PASSIVE OPTICAL NETWORKS (PONs)

We continue the discussion of optical network topologies with a look at passive optical networks (PONs). PONs are really not passive. They are actively sending and receiving optical signals. They are called passive because the outside plant has no electronics to power or maintain the components. As a consequence, PONs eliminate expensive power-based amplifiers, rectifiers, and, of course, batteries.

The active part of the PON is between the two ends. In most situations, these two ends are the service provider's node (say, a telephone central office), and the user node. The user node is typically a remote pedestal, often called a remote digital terminal (RDT).

Figure 8–15 shows a PON topology. The fiber can be forked out to multiple sites with the user of splitters. This approach saves a lot of money by multiplexing many user payloads on fewer fibers than in a conventional point-to-point topology. Of course, since multiple users must share the fiber, the multiplexing operation must be capable of efficient bandwidth management. The PON employs ATM for this important job.

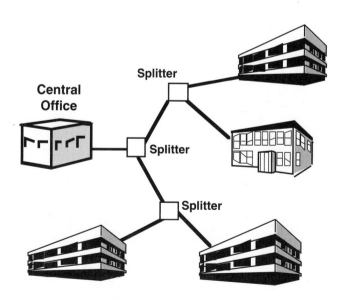

Figure 8–15   PONs.

OPTICAL ETHERNETS AND ETHERNET PONs

The use of Ethernet and the PON technology in the local loop reduces the cost substantially of providing high-capacity links to the customer. The reason is that expensive components such as SONET ADM, and ATM switches can be eliminated, and replaced with less expensive substitutes, as shown in Figure 8–16. At the customer premises, the SONET ADM is replaced with a simple and inexpensive optical network unit (ONU). At the Central Office (CO), the SONET ADM and the ATM switch(es) is(are) replaced with an optical line terminal (OLN). Of course, this arrangement does not offer the rich functionality of ATM and SONET, but that is precisely the point: Many user interfaces do not need all the powerful attributes of SONET and ATM.

Although Figure 8–16 shows a point-to-point topology, we learned earlier that the PON link can be split into multiple fibers with splitters or combined in a single link with splitters/couplers. Traffic is supported both upstream and downstream with the IEEE 802.3 (modified Ethernet) frame. The use of the Ethernet 1,518-byte frame makes better use of the link (compared to the ATM 53-byte cell).

Strictly speaking, the technology is not pure (original) Ethernet, in that the traffic upstream from the user to the CO uses dedicated TDM slots, and does not rely on the contention and collision detection aspects

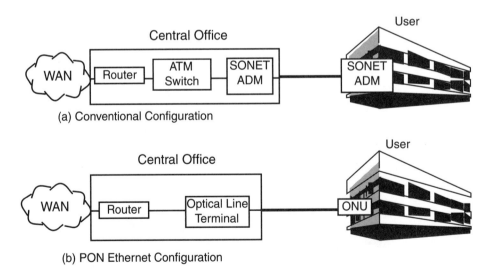

(a) Conventional Configuration

(b) PON Ethernet Configuration

Figure 8–16   Conventional ATM/SONET and ethernet PON configurations.

of 802.3. An enhanced Ethernet feature called rate limiting allows the
network operator to place transmission limits on each port on the link,
that is, on each subscriber. Thus, the shared media is managed in a
structured manner. In any case, the idea of the Ethernet PON is to use
switches to terminate the Ethernet collision domains.

ETHERNET IN THE WIDE AREA BACKBONE?

Ethernet in optical networks is a big issue and is becoming a big industry. But as of this writing, there is very little interest in deploying Ethernet in a wide area transport network due to the limited distances
resulting from Ethernet's collision window. If the CSMA/CD protocol is
not used, it is not Ethernet, as defined by IEEE 802.3. So, Ethernet over
optical is beyond the subject of this book, but if you want more information, I recommend [KOLE00] and [PODZ00].

METRO OPTICAL NETWORKING

Fiber optics has made remarkable progress in finding its way into the
local loops, also know as metro optical networking. Originally implemented within the network, it quickly proved itself as a cost-effective digital transport technology for the local access loop as well. Indeed, much of
its success is owed to those interfaces to the subscriber.

Optical networking plays a big role in residential broadband. It provides a robust, relatively inexpensive mechanism for deploying fiber in
the distribution plant. Its extensive operations, administration and
maintenance (OAM) capabilities make it an attractive technology for the
service providers.

Figure 8–17 shows how an optical network is being deployed to support the residential broadband technology. The most common approach is
to employ rings. These rings tie together the customers to the CO with
optical-based remote digital terminals (RDTs). The user payload can be
added or dropped off at the customer sites through conventional add-drop
operations. The optical signals are provisionable, allowing a wide range
of data rates. These "typical" rates are a function of the bandwidth requirements of the users attached to the ring.

These optical networks provide a variety of options to allow the service provider to adapt the residential broadband media to specific requirements. One of these requirements could be the use of rings, as

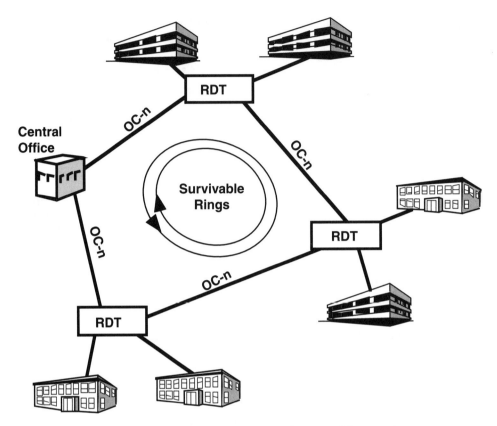

Figure 8–17   Metro optical networking.

illustrated in Figure 8–17, but other requirements may dictate other solutions, such as point-to-point topologies.

SUMMARY

There is no question that the use of backup links and backup nodes is an
expensive undertaking. Yet, for large-scale backbone networks such as
the telephone system or the Internet, there is no alternative. Downtime,
due to a link or nodal failure, is not only inconvenient to the network customers, it might be catastrophic. Thus, the deployment of redundant facilities on rings, point-to-point systems, or even meshed networks is
well-accepted and supported by both the network provider and the network customer.

9

MPLS and Optical Networks

Label switching and multiprotocol label switching (MPLS) are considered by many to be key components in third generation transport networks. Therefore, this chapter is devoted to these subjects and how they fit into optical networks. The major features of MPLS are explained with emphasis on the operations of label switching routers (LSRs), label assignments, and label swapping.

As a note to the introduction, this chapter is closely associated with several subsequent chapters in this book. For purposes of organization and clarity, it is necessary to break down the subject matter into different chapters. To lend continuity to the discussions, frequent references are made to related material in these chapters. You can ignore these references; I have written all material to be read serially from start to finish. Still, you might find it helpful to look ahead (or backwards) to the referenced material.

WHAT IS LABEL SWITCHING?

The basic concept of label switching is very simple. To show why, let's assume a user's traffic (say, an email message) is relayed from the user's computer to the recipient's computer. In traditional internets (those that do not use label switching), the method to relay this email is similar to postal mail: A destination address is examined by the relaying entity (for our work, a router; for the postal service, a mail person). This address determines how the router or mail person forwards the data packet or the mail envelope to the final recipient.

Label switching is different. Instead of using a destination address to make the routing decision, a number (a label) is associated with the packet. In the postal service analogy, a label value is placed on the envelope and is thereafter used in place of the postal address to route the mail to the recipient.

In computer networks, a label is placed in a label header in the packet and is used in place of an address (an Internet Protocol [IP] address, usually). The label is used by the router to direct the traffic to its destination.

Reasons for Using Label Switching

Let's look at the reasons label switching is of such keen interest in the industry. They can be summarized as follows:

- Speed, delay, and jitter: Label switching is considerably faster than traditional IP forwarding. This speed translates into less delay in transporting traffic through the network. It also translates into less variable delay (jitter), an important consideration for applications that cannot tolerate a lot of jitter, such as voice and video.
- Scalability: MPLS allows a large number of IP addresses to be associated with one or a few labels. This approach reduces further the size of address (actually label) tables, and allows a router to support more users; that is, to scale to a large user population.
- Resource consumption: Label switching networks do not need a lot of the network's resources to execute the control mechanisms to establish label switching paths (LSPs) for users' traffic.
- Route control: Most IP-based networks use the concept of destination-based routing, wherein the destination IP address in the IP datagram determines the route through a network. Destination-routing is not always an efficient operation, and MPLS offers methods to use more efficient route control techniques, thus providing a higher level of service to the user.
- Traffic engineering: As part of route control, many of the MPLS operations are designed to allow the network provider to engineer

the links and nodes in the network to support different kinds of traffic, as well as constrain the traffic to specific parts of the network. This idea is important in optimizing expensive network resources.

- Labels and Lambdas: If label switching is used in optical networks, it is possible to correlate (map) a label (or labels) to wavelengths, then use a PXC O/O/O switch for forwarding the traffic, thus reducing further the delay and jitter of user payload processing.

THE FORWARDING EQUIVALENCE CLASS (FEC)

The term FEC is applied to label switching operations. FEC is used to describe an association of discrete packets with a destination address, usually the final recipient of the traffic, such as a host machine. FEC implementations may also associate an FEC value with the destination address and a class of traffic. The class of traffic is associated (typically) with a destination TCP/UDP port number, and/or the protocol ID (PID) field in the IP datagram header.

Why is FEC used? First, it allows the grouping of packets into classes. From this grouping, the FEC value in a packet can be used to set priorities for the handling of the packets, giving higher priority to certain FECs. FECs can be used to support efficient QOS operations. For example, FECs can be associated with high-priority, real-time voice traffic, or low-priority newsgroup traffic, and so on.

Scalability and Granularity: Labels and Wavelengths

The network administrator has control over how big the MPLS forwarding tables become by implementing FEC coarse granularity. If only the IP destination address is used for the FEC, the tables can probably be kept to a manageable size. Yet this "coarse granularity" does not provide a way to support classes of traffic and QOS operations. On the other hand, a network supporting "fine granularity" by using port numbers and PIDs will have more traffic classifications, more FECs, more labels, and a larger forwarding table. This network will not scale as easily to a large user base. Fortunately, label switching networks need not be one or the other. A combination of coarse and fine granularity FECs is permissible.

Nonetheless, the issue is important in relation to how many labels are correlated to optical wavelengths, a topic discussed later in this chapter, and in Chapter 10 (see "Considerations for Interworking Layer 1 Lambdas and Layer 2 Labels"), and Chapter 12 (see "Granularity of Labels vs. Wavelength Support").

TYPES OF MPLS NODES

Figure 9–1 shows the three types of MPLS nodes. They perform the following functions:

- Ingress LSR: Receives native-mode user traffic (for example, IP datagrams), and classifies it into an FEC. It then generates an MPLS header and assigns it an initial label. The IP datagram is encapsulated into the MPLS packet, with the MPLS header attached to the datagram. If it is integrated with a QOS operation (say, DiffServ), the ingress LSR will condition the traffic (such as using different queues for different priorities of the traffic) in accordance with the DiffServ rules.
- Transit, interior, or core LSR: Receives the packet and uses the MPLS header to make forwarding decisions. It will also perform label swapping (exchanging label values). It is not concerned with processing the IP header, only the label header.
- Egress LSR: Performs the decapsulation operations (i.e., it removes the MPLS header).

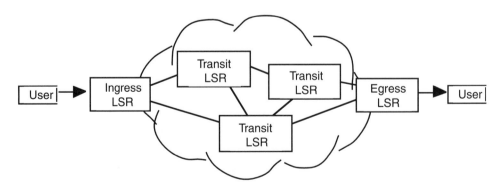

Figure 9–1   The MPLS nodes.

LABEL DISTRIBUTION AND BINDING

To use labels between the LSRs, MPLS executes a control plane to perform (a) the advertising of a range of label values that an LSR wants to use, (b) the advertising of associated IP addresses that are to be associated with the labels, and (c) perhaps the advertising of QOS performance parameters and suggested routes for the user's label switching path through the network. The process of agreeing to these parameters, and then building label switching tables in the LSRs, is called binding.

Methods for Label Distribution

MPLS does not stipulate a specific label distribution protocol.[1] Since several protocols are currently in operation that can support label distribution, it makes sense to use what is available. Nevertheless, the IETF has developed a specific label distribution protocol to complement MPLS that is called the label distribution protocol (LDP).

Another protocol, the constraint-based LDP (CR-LDP), is an extension to LDP. It allows the network manager to set up explicitly routed Label Switched Paths (LSPs). CR-LDP operates independently of any IGP. It is used for delay-sensitive traffic and emulates a circuit-switched network. CR-LDP is also designed to support traffic engineering operations by allowing the network administrator to dictate how and where the users' label switched paths flow through the network.

RSVP can also be used for label distribution; this extension is called RSVP-TE. By using the RSVP PATH and RESV messages (with extensions), it supports label binding and distribution operations. Extensions to BGP are yet another method for advertising and distributing labels. Most of the attention in the industry is focused on extended LDP and extended RSVP for label distribution.

Additionally, an extension to MPLS, called generalized MPLS (GMPLS), has been published that provides information on using MPLS (and extended RSVP or extended LDP) for optical networks. GMPLS is discussed later in this chapter. The other protocols are explained in the companion book to this series on MPLS [BLAC02].

---

[1]Some papers call a label distribution protocol a signaling protocol. If this term is used, be aware that it does not refer to conventional signaling protocols, such as ISDN's Q.931 and SS7's ISUP.

LABEL SWAPPING AND TRAFFIC FORWARDING

In Figure 9–2, nodes A, B, G, and H are user machines and are not configured with MPLS. Node C is the ingress LSR, nodes D and E are transit (interior) LSRs, and node F is the egress LSR.

The example in Figure 9–2 uses generic addresses. For example, the address for node G is "G," which could be an IP address or some other address, such as IPX, a telephone number, etc.

LSR C receives an IP datagram from user node A on interface a. This datagram is destined for node G. LSR C analyzes the FEC fields, correlates the FEC with label 80, encapsulates the datagram behind a label header, and sends the packet to output interface c. The OUT entry in LSR C's table directs it to place label 80 onto the label header in the packet. This operation at LSR C is called a label push.

Hereafter, LSRs D and E process only the label header, and their swapping tables are used to (at LSR D) swap label 80 for label 76, and (at LSR E) swap label 76 for label 44. Notice that the swapping tables use the ingress and egress interfaces at each LSR to correlate the labels to the ingress and egress communications links. Egress LSR F is configured to recognize label 44 on interface b as its own local label; that is, there are no more hops, and the end of the LSP has been reached. Notice that the OUT entry in F's table directs LSR F to send this datagram to G on interface d; this implies removing the label from the packet. This label removal is part of an operation called a label pop.

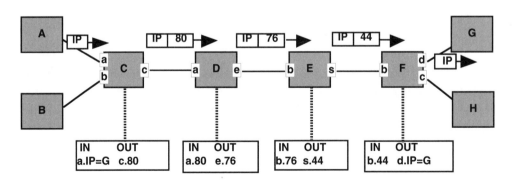

Notes: Nodes A, B, G, and H are not aware of MPLS in this example. Nodes C, D, E, and F are MPLS-aware.

Figure 9–2   Label swapping and forwarding.

MPLS SUPPORT OF VIRTUAL PRIVATE NETWORKS (VPNs)

Before proceeding with more examples of label operations, the subject of label switching and virtual private networks (VPNs) is discussed. Figure 9–3 shows how MPLS could be used to support a large base of VPN customers with a very simple arrangement.

Certain assumptions must be made for this operation to work well. First, the customers are at the same ends of the MPLS end-to-end path (the label switching path, or LSP). Second, they have the same QOS requirements, and FEC parameters. But these two requirements should not be unusual. For example, many customers may be running VoIP, or Web retrievals, and so forth, from one site to another.

This example shows the idea of label stacking: the placing of more than one label in the MPLS header. Three sets of customers are supported by the VPN in this example (A-D, B-E, and C-F), but there could be hundreds or even thousands or customers. Label stacking allows designated LSRs to exchange information with each other and act as ingress and egress nodes to a large domain of networks and other LSRs. This concept allows certain labels to be processed by a node while others are ignored. The point is that, by label stacking, the VPN backbone can accommodate all the traffic with one set of labels for the LSP in the backbone. The customers' labels are pushed down and are not examined through the MPLS tunnel.

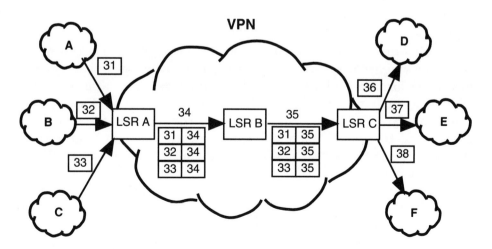

Figure 9–3   Label stacking in a VPN.

For example, labels 31, 32, and 33 from users A, B, and C, respectively, are pushed down into the label header, and label 34 is used between the network LSR A and LSR B to process the packets. LSR B swaps label 34 for label 35, but does not examine labels 31, 32, and 33. When the packets arrive at LSR C, its label switching table reveals that label 35 represents the end of the label switching path. So, LSR C pops label 35, thus revealing labels 31, 32, and 33. Upon examination of these labels, LSR C knows (a) to swap them for labels 36, 37, and 38, respectively, and (b) to pass the packets to end users on networks D, E, and F.

MPLS TRAFFIC ENGINEERING (TE)

As noted, traffic engineering (TE) deals with the performance of a network in supporting the network's customers and their QOS needs. The focus of TE for MPLS networks is (a) the measurement of traffic and (b) the control of traffic. The latter operation deals with operations to ensure the network has the resources to support the users' QOS requirements.

An Internet working group has published RFC 2702. This informational RFC defines in a general way the requirements for traffic engineering over MPLS [AWDU99]. The next part of this chapter provides a summary of [AWDU99], with my comments added to the discussion.

Traffic Oriented or Resource Oriented Performance

Traffic engineering in an MPLS environment establishes objectives with regard to two performance functions: (a) traffic oriented objectives and (b) resource oriented objectives.

Traffic oriented performance supports the QOS operations of user traffic. In a single class, best effort Internet service model, the key traffic oriented performance objectives include: minimizing traffic loss, minimizing delay, maximizing of throughput, and enforcement of service level agreements (SLAs). Resource-oriented performance objectives deal with the network resources, such as communications links, routers, and servers—those entities that contribute to the realization of traffic oriented objectives.

Efficient management of these resources is vital to the attainment of resource oriented performance objectives. Available bandwidth is the bottom line; without bandwidth, any number of TE operations is worthless, and the efficient management of the available bandwidth is the essence of TE.

Traffic Trunks, Traffic Flows, and Label Switched Paths

An important aspect of MPLS TE is the distinctions between traffic trunks, traffic flows, and label switched paths (LSPs). A traffic trunk is an aggregation of traffic flows of the same class which are placed inside an LSP. A traffic trunk can have characteristics associated with it (addresses, port numbers). A traffic trunk can be routed, because it is an aspect of the LSP. Therefore, the path through which the traffic trunk flows can be changed.

MPLS TE concerns itself with mapping traffic trunks onto the physical links of a network through label switched paths. As explained in Chapters 10 and 12, third generation transport networks extend the MPLS traffic engineering of label switched paths to optical switched paths (OSPs) by correlating labels to wavelengths (If you want to look ahead, see "Interworking the Three Control Planes" in Chapter 10, and "Correlating the Wavelength OSP with the MPLS LSP" in Chapter 12).

LDP, CR-LDP, RSVP-TE, and OSPF (Extensions) for TE Support

Four protocols have been developed or extended to provide the signaling capabilities for MPLS. Some of them were introduced earlier in this chapter. They are explained in detail in a companion book to this series [BLAC02], and are summarized here:

- LDP: Designed specifically for MPLS label advertising and distribution operations.
- CR-LDP: An enhanced LDP that supports the building of defined (constrained) LSPs in an MPLS network.
- RSVP-TE: To RSVP that permit the negotiation and establishment of LSPs.
- OSPF (several extensions): Several extensions to OSPF for discovery of LSPs based on network-specific criteria.

MULTIPROTOCOL LAMBDA SWITCHING (MPλS)

The framework for interworking optical networks and MPLS is called MPλS, and is defined in [AWDU01]. As noted in the introduction to this chapter, MPLS and optical networks are a good match, but it is important that this effort has a standardized approach. Both technologies have control mechanisms (a control plane) to manage the user traffic.

These control planes (introduced here and covered in more detail in Chapters 10 and 12), are shown in a general way in Figure 9–4. The MPLS control plane is concerned with label distribution and binding an end-to-end LSP. The optical control plane is concerned with setting up wavelengths, optical coding schemes (SDH/SONET), transfer rates (in bit/s), and protection switching options (1:1, 1:N, etc.) on an OSP between two adjacent nodes.

The [AWDU01] authors hold that it is not a good idea to have different control planes when two technologies must interwork. They cite IP over ATM, with IP using OSPF, BGP, and IS-IS for its control plane and ATM using PNNI (and, to some extent, Q.2931) for its control plane.

I understand [AWDU01]'s points, but some interworking of the MPLS and optical control planes is not only necessary, but desirable (and suggested by the vertical arrows between these planes in Figure 9–4). The reasons for this statement are presented later in this chapter and in Chapters 10, 12, and 13.

For this immediate discussion, [AWDU01] describes the framework for adapting the MPLS TE control plane for optical cross-connects. It is a useful document because it sets up a model for an MPLS-based optical Internet, including an analysis of the similarities and differences between MPLS and optical network control operations.

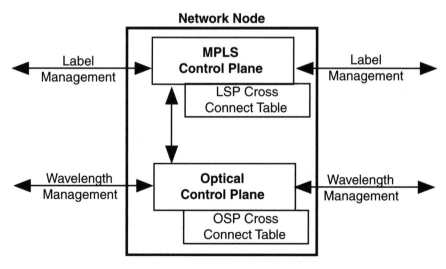

Figure 9–4   The MPLS and optical control planes.

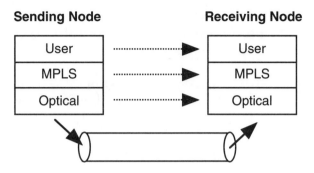

Figure 9–5   MPλS.

Relationships of OXC and MPLS Operations

A convenient way to view the relationship of MPLS and optical networking is through the layered model, as shown in Figure 9–5. The optical operations occur in layer 1; the MPLS operations occur in a combination of layers 2 and 3.[2]

The data plane of an LSR uses the label swapping operation to transfer a labeled packet from an input port to an output port. The data plane of an OXC uses a switching matrix to connect an optical channel trail from an input port to an output port. Recall that an optical trail is an optical connection between two nodes, such as an LSR or an OXC.

Traffic from the control plane of an upper layer can be sent to either the data or control plane of the adjacent lower layer on the transmit side, with a reverse operation occurring on the receive side. In fact, such an approach is common. For example, an LSR may send a control message to an adjacent LSR that sets up some timers for label management operations. This control message could go over either an optical data channel or an optical control channel.

An LSR performs label switching by first establishing a relation between an input port and an input label, and an output port and an output label. Likewise, an OXC provisions an optical channel by first establishing a relation between an input port and an input optical channel (and/or wavelength), and an output port and an output optical channel (and/or wavelength). In the LSR, the next hop label forwarding entry (NHLFE) maintains the input–output relations.

---

[2]Some of the new protocols' operations span layers 2 and 3. ATM is one example; MPLS is cited in some literature as another. Strictly speaking, MPLS is a layer 3 protocol in that it does not define the critical function of layer 2 frame delineation.

In the OXC, the switch controller reconfigures the internal interconnection fabric (called an optical switching path [OSP] cross-connect table or a wavelength forwarding information base [WFIB]) to establish the relationships.

The functions of the control plane include resource discovery, distributed routing control, and connection management. In particular, the control plane of the LSR is used to discover, distribute, and maintain relevant state information associated with the MPLS network, and to manage label switched paths (LSPs).

The control plane of the OXC is used to discover, distribute, and maintain relevant state information associated with the OTN, and to establish and maintain optical channel trails under various optical internetworking traffic engineering rules and policies.

A significant difference between current LSRs and OXCs is that, with LSRs, the forwarding information is carried explicitly as part of the labels appended to data packets, while, with OXCs, the switching information is implied from the wavelength or optical channel. The label is used by the LSP cross-connect table (the NHLFE), and the wavelength is used by the OSP cross-connect table.

MPLS and Optical Wavelength Correlation

A key aspect of MPLS and optical network interworking is to correlate an MPLS label value with an optical wavelength. This operation is introduced in this chapter and explained in more detail in Chapters 10 and 12. In Figure 9–6, the user sends traffic to the network (the definition on page 17 might be helpful). At the ingress node (now noted as an LSR/OXC)

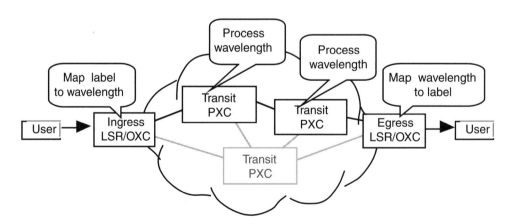

Figure 9–6   Processing the user traffic.

the MPLS label is correlated to an appropriate wavelength; that is, an appropriate channel into the network and out of the network to reach the destination user. The transit nodes, now labeled as transit PXCs, have been configured to process the wavelength to make the routing decisions.

The MPLS label is not examined at the transit PXCs. For this example, it is assumed that the user payload is to be sent through the network from the ingress LSR/OXC to the egress LSR/OXC. Thus, it is not necessary to know about the MPLS label, as long as all nodes know the relationship of the wavelength that is associated with the label, and its final destination.

An explicit LSP is one whose route is defined at its origination node, or by a control protocol such as OSPF (that discovers and sets up a path through the network). However the path is defined, once it is set up, it remains stable, unless problems occur at a node or on an optical trail. Explicit LSPs and optical channel trails exhibit certain commonalties. They are both uni-directional, point-to-point relationships. An explicit LSP provides a packet forwarding path (traffic-trunk) between an ingress LSR and an egress LSR. An optical channel trail provides an optical channel between two endpoints for the transport of user traffic.

The payload carried by both LSPs and optical trails is transparent to intermediate nodes along their respective paths. Both LSPs and optical trails can be configured to stipulate their performance and protection requirements.

Label Merging and Label Stacking. In the MPLS networks, it is possible to merge and stack labels. Label stacking was explained earlier in this chapter. Label merging is the replacement of multiple incoming labels for a particular FEC with a single outgoing label. This operation can reduce the number of labels processed by an LSR.

There are commonalties in the allocation of labels to LSPs and the allocation of wavelengths to optical trails. Two different LSPs that traverse through a given LSR port or interface cannot be allocated the same label. The exception is for LSP aggregation using label merge or label stacking. Similarly, two different optical trails that traverse through a given OXC port cannot be allocated the same wavelength.

Failure of the Optical Connection

In the event of a fiber failure or a fiber node failure, there must be a method to find a backup route. This subject is discussed in Chapter 8 regarding how optical networks use backup fibers and protection switching to recover from failures.

In an MPλS network, there must be very close coordination between the optical and label control planes, if they are indeed different software processes in the nodes. For example, if an optical connection is lost, the optical control plane must be able to inform the MPλS control plane so that neighbor LSRs can be informed of the problem. As the MPLS and the optical layers mature, it is likely that this coordination will be aided by a data link layer especially designed for this purpose; this is the subject of Chapter 11.

MPLS AND OPTICAL TE SIMILARITIES

RFC 2702 establishes the major requirements for TE support in an MPLS network. This part of the chapter summarizes this part of RFC 2702 as well as associated ideas from [AWDU01]. In reading this summary, it will be helpful to visualize the relationship of the optical layer to MPLS by substituting the MPLS term *traffic trunk* with the optical layer term *optical channel trail*.

A traffic trunk is an aggregation of traffic belonging to the same FEC which is forwarded through a common path. It is used in MPLS to allow certain attributes of the traffic transported through LSPs to be configured based on TE parameters, such as delay and throughput. The attributes that can be associated with traffic trunks include:

- Traffic parameters: Indicate the bandwidth requirements of the traffic trunk.
- Adaptivity attributes: Specify the sensitivity of the traffic trunk to changes in the state of the network, with the possibility of rerouting the traffic trunk to a different part of the network.
- Priority attributes: Impose a partial order on the set of traffic trunks and allow path selection and path placement operations to be prioritized.
- Preemption attributes: Indicate whether a traffic trunk can preempt an existing traffic-trunk from its path.
- Resilience attributes: Stipulate the survivability requirements of the traffic trunk and, in particular, the response of the system to faults that impact the path of the traffic trunk.
- Resource class affinity attributes: Further restrict route selection to specific subsets of resources. Allow inclusion and exclusion policies to be implemented.

POSSIBILITIES FOR THE MPλS NETWORK

Additional work remains to be done on a complete MPλS network, but [AWDU01] has established a coherent framework for further efforts. In concluding this chapter, we review several ideas from this IETF working draft, and my thoughts about its suppositions. As noted, other examples of the interworking of labels and wavelengths are provided in Chapters 10, 11, and 13.

If the XC is a wavelength routing switch (a PXC), then the physical fiber between a pair of PXCs can represent a single link in the OTN network topology. Individual wavelengths or channels can be analogous to labels. If there are multiple fibers between a pair of PXCs, then, as an option, these multiple fibers could be logically grouped together through a process called bundling and represented as a single link in the OTN network topology. This concept is supported in the emerging optical link management protocol, discussed in Chapter 11.

If a fiber terminates on a device that functions as both an OXC and an IP router, then the following situations may be possible:

- A subset of optical channels within the fiber may be uncommitted. That is, they are not currently in use and hence are available for allocation.
- A second subset of channels may already be committed for transit purposes. That is, they are already cross-connected by the PXC element to other out-bound optical channels and thus are not immediately available for allocation.
- Another subset of optical channels (within the same fiber) could be in use as terminal channels. That is, they are already allocated but terminate on the local PXC/router device, for example, as SONET interfaces.

In the above scenario, one way to represent the fiber in the OTN network topology is to depict it is as several links, where one of these links would represent the set of uncommitted channels that constitute the residual capacity of the fiber, while each terminal channel that terminates on the PXC/router could be represented as an individual link.

IS-IS or OSPF and possibly additional optical network specific extensions would be used to distribute information about the optical transport network topology, about available bandwidth and available channels per fiber, as well as other OTN network topology state data. This information is then used to compute explicit routes for optical channel trails. An MPLS signaling protocol, such as RSVP extensions, is used to instantiate the optical channel trails. Using the RSVP extensions, for example, the wavelength information and/or optical fiber information can be carried in the LABEL object, which will be used to control and reconfigure the PXCs.

The use of a uniform control plane technology for both LSRs and PXCs introduces a number of interesting architectural possibilities. One such possibility is that a single MPLS traffic engineering control plane can span both routers and PXCs. In such an environment, a label switched path can traverse an intermix of routers and PXCs, or can span just routers, or just PXCs. This concept offers the potential for real bandwidth-on-demand networking, in which an IP router may dynamically request bandwidth services (a part of the bandwidth of a wavelength, for example) from the optical transport network.

Another possibility cited by [AWDU01] is that PXCs and LSRs may run different instances of the control plane which are decoupled with little or no interaction between the control plane instances. I am not convinced that the decoupling of the MPLS and optical control planes will be the best approach, and I will explain my reasons for this statement as we proceed though the remainder of this book. For now, take a look at footnote 3 for a brief explanation.[3]

To configure the mapping and switching functions, PXCs must be able to exchange control information. The favored method that is emerging in the industry is to preconfigure a dedicated control wavelength between each pair of adjacent PXCs, or between a PXC and a router, and to use this wavelength as a supervisory channel for exchange of signaling and OAM traffic. This idea is examined in Chapters 10, 11, and 12.

In the proposed control plane approach, a PXC maintains a wavelength forwarding information base (WFIB), also called an OSP cross-connect table per interface (or per fiber). This approach is used because lambdas and/or channels (labels) are specific to a particular interface (fiber), and the same lambda and/or channel (label) could be used concurrently on multiple interfaces (fibers).

---

[3]As I explain in Chapter 10, I favor using an integrated control plane, one in which MPLS labels and optical wavelengths are correlated. This approach facilitates the interworking for MPLS and lambdas for protection switching. It appears to me to be difficult to implement de-coupled label and optical control planes. But then, we are in uncharted waters here, and I would welcome your views after you read my thoughts about this matter in Chapters 10, 12, and 14.

If the bandwidth associated with an LSP is small relative to the capacity of an optical channel trail, then inefficient utilization of network resources might result if only one LSP is mapped onto a given optical channel trail. To improve utilization of resources, therefore, it is necessary to be able to map several low bandwidth LSPs onto a relatively high-capacity optical channel. Note that since a PXC cannot perform label push/pop operations, the start/end of a nested LSP must be on a router (as nesting requires label push/pop).

Control and Data Planes Interworking

My thoughts about this aspect of [AWDU01] (and looking to the future) is that it is not desirable to have a PXC O/O/O node involved in label management; otherwise, it becomes an O/E/O node. Fine, but the questions then remain of how the PXC is going to be able to (a) interwork labels with wavelengths, and (especially) (b) how protection switching performed on fibers and/or wavelengths can be correlated to the labels that are running on the label/wavelength. To illustrate, if an optical channel fails, and it destroys a label channel, the label layer must be aware of this failure (if the optical layer cannot recover).

The key to interworking effectively the MPLS and optical planes is to carefully distinguish the interactions between not only the control planes but also between the data planes and the control planes. The subsequent chapters will lay out the procedures to accomplish these operations.

SUMMARY

The use of MPLS in the emerging 3G transport network is certainly not a given. Traffic engineering and some other features of label switching can be achieved by other means. For example, constrained routing can be set up at either layer 3 or layer 1, or both. But MPLS is gaining a lot of momentum, at least for networks that will be deployed in the future, and many vendors intend to build products that combine and/or interwork the L3, L2, and L1 control planes. In the meantime, stay tuned to tried-and-true ATM over optical.

10

Architecture of IP and MPLS-based Optical Transport Networks

One of the central issues arising in Internet and optical networks is how best to interwork the two sets of technologies. Clearly, IP is not going to go away for the foreseeable future; it is heavily embedded into PCs, palm devices, Web servers, and so on. Optical transport networks are here to stay for a while as well, and so are label switching networks using MPLS.

This chapter picks up on the introductory information on control planes in Chapters 6 and 9, and discusses one approach to the efficient and graceful interworking of IP and optical networks. In addition, the role of MPLS is explained as well. Three control planes of IP, MPLS, and the optical layer are examined, and we show how these planes can interwork to exploit all the features of IP, MPLS, and optical networks.

The chapter concludes with an explanation of generalized MPLS (GMPLS), and its use in optical networks in general and specifically in the G.709 –based OTN, discussed in Chapter 6. As noted in earlier discussions, in some circles the interworking of GMPLS in third generation optical transport networks is called MPλS.

IP, MPLS, AND OPTICAL CONTROL PLANES

This part of the chapter extends the introduction of control planes made in Chapter 9, and describes in more detail a control plane model for third generation transport networks that encompasses three control planes:

(a) IP, (b) MPLS, and (c) optical. Also, it might prove helpful to review the material in Chapter 6 (see Figure 6–2) that introduces the concepts of the control and data planes.

The Internet Control and Data Planes

The Internet control and data planes are well-understood in the industry. But until recently, these two planes have not been so named in most Internet RFCs. As shown in Figure 10–1, they have usually been named the routing layer (for the control plane) and the forwarding layer (for the data plane).

The control plane is comprised of the Internet and ISO routing protocols, shown in Figure 10–1 as OSPF, IS-IS, and BGP. The data plane is comprised of the forwarding protocol, IP.

In order to connect networks together so that they may exchange information, and in order to move traffic through these networks efficiently, a method is needed whereby a specific path (a route) is found among the many nodes (routers, servers, workstations) and routes that connect two or more network users together. The identification of a route entails a route discovery operation, which is called routing, and fits into the control plane of the Internet layered model. In its simplest terms, route discovery in the Internet control plane is the process of finding the best route between two or more nodes in a network or in multiple networks.

The MPLS Control and Data Planes

MPLS also operates with control and data planes, as depicted in Figure 10–2. The job of the control plane is to advertise labels and

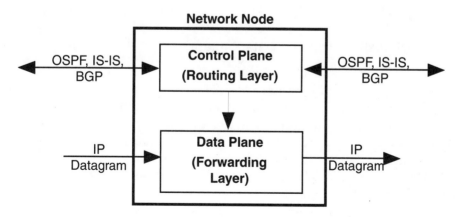

Figure 10–1   The Internet control and data planes.

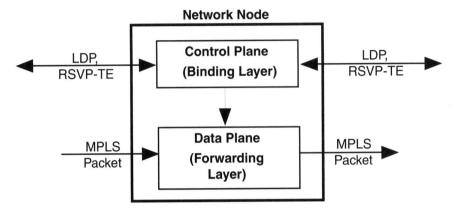

Figure 10–2   MPLS control and data planes.

addresses and to correlate them; that is, to bind labels to addresses. This idea is explained in more detail in Chapter 9.

There is more than one protocol operating at the MPLS control plane. Extensions to RSVP have been made to allow the use of this protocol to advertise, distribute, and bind labels to IP addresses. This extension is called RSVP-TE. LDP is yet another option for executing the MPLS control plane.

After MPLS nodes have exchanged labels and IP addresses, they bind the labels to addresses. Thereafter, the MPLS data plane forwards all traffic by examining the label in the MPLS label. The IP address is not examined until the traffic is delivered across the network (or networks) to the receiving user node. The label is then removed, and the IP address is used by the IP data plane to deliver the traffic to the end user.

The Optical Control and Data Planes

Figure 10–3 shows the optical control and data planes for a third generation optical transport network. The control plane (which I call the λ mapping layer) can be executed with LMP or GMPLS or a combination of the two. Whatever the specific implementation may be, the optical control plane is used to coordinate the use of wavelengths between adjacent optical nodes, as well as to insure the nodes are up and running. As explained later in this chapter, the optical control plane is also responsible for configuring optical nodes to accept different kinds of traffic, such as SDH or SONET formatted frames. It also is used to negotiate the bit transfer rate that is used between nodes.

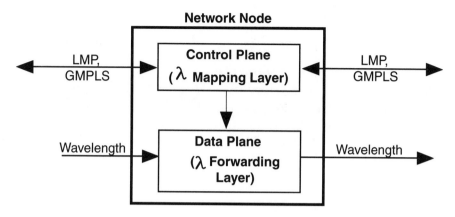

Figure 10–3   The optical control and data planes.

Thereafter, the control plane is invoked only for ongoing management operations, diagnostics, recovery, and so on. User traffic is processed in the data plane (the λ forwarding layer).

Requirements of the Optical Control Plane.   The IP optical networking group defines the requirements for the optical control plane [FREE00] and has established that this plane must be able to support the following types of connections:

- A permanent optical channel set up by the network management system via network management protocols.
- A soft permanent optical channel set up by the network management system, using network-generated signaling and routing protocols to establish connections.
- A switched optical channel, which can be set up by the customer on demand using signaling and routing protocols.

INTERWORKING THE THREE CONTROL PLANES

The separate operations of the IP, MPLS, and optical control planes should be coordinated in order to take advantage of (a) the route discovery capabilities of the IP control plane, (b) the traffic engineering capabilities of the MPLS control plane, and (c) the forwarding (switching) speed of the optical data plane. Figure 10–4 illustrates how this interworking can be accomplished, from the author's perspective.

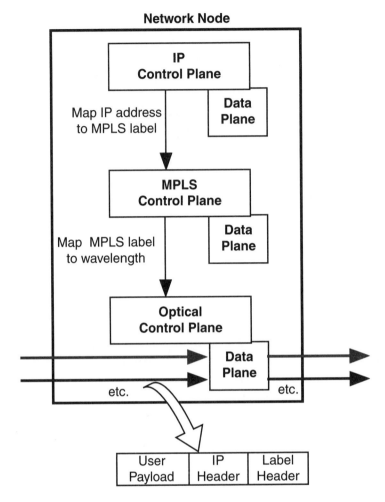

Figure 10–4   Interworking the three control planes.

Using Figure 10–4 for reference, the following three events must take place to exploit the powerful capabilities of all three control planes:

1. The IP routing protocols advertise and discover addresses as well as the routes to the nodes that are identified by the addresses.
2. The MPLS label distribution protocols distribute labels associated with the IP addresses, so that the cumbersome IP addresses do not have to be used in the network. Remember that this idea is called binding; it maps certain addressees to certain labels.

3. The MPLS labels can be mapped to specific wavelengths between adjacent optical nodes so that the nodes can resort to PXC-based O/O/O operations and not be concerned with MPLS label swapping and cumbersome O/E/O operations. Ideally, the same wavelength is used on each OSP segment of the end-to-end LSP.

Events 1 and 2 are beyond the subject of this book; they are covered extensively in other books in this series. Event 3 is certainly a relevant topic for this book and is explained in the next part of this chapter and in Chapters 12 and 14.

MANAGEMENT OF THE PLANES

While some literature suggests that the three control planes should not be coupled, this author strongly disagrees, and several IETF working groups are defining a model for the control plane interworkings. The basic idea is to implement yet another layer, as shown in Figure 10–5. This idea is not new, as networks such as ATM have used this idea for years, and revisions to SS7 also define a management plane. The function of the management plane is to coordinate the interactions of the other planes, or equally important, allow the control planes to operate independently of each other. In most implementations, such as ATM, the interactions are defined by OSI-based primitive calls, which are used by software programmers to write function calls or system calls between the

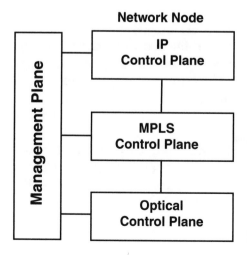

Figure 10–5   The management plane.

management plane and the control planes. For 3G transport networks, these calls have not yet been defined.

Diverse Views on Control Planes' Interworkings

At this stage in the evolution of the optical Internet, there is no common agreement on the exact manner in which the control planes will interact with each other. Consequently, there is no wide-spread agreement on how the many operations in OSPF (extensions), IS-IS, BGP (extensions), RSVP-TE, CR-LDP, LMP, GMPLS, or the OIF UNI and NNI will be executed. Indeed, there are different views on this issue. In the remainder of this chapter, and in Chapters 12 and 14, we will examine the main aspects of these issues, and I will present my views and those of several IETF working groups.

To get this exercise started, the next section provides an overview of two key Internet drafts on the subject; I recommend these papers to you if you are going to be involved in this aspect of 3G transport networks.

A FRAMEWORK FOR IP OVER OPTICAL NETWORKS

[RAJA02] sets forth, in a general way, the issues of operating IP over optical networks. The authors state that there is general consensus in the industry that the optical network control plane should utilize IP-based protocols for dynamic provisioning and restoration of lightpaths within and across optical sub-networks. This opinion is based on the view that signaling and routing mechanisms developed for IP traffic engineering applications could be re-used in optical networks. I agree in general with [RAJA02], but there is no consensus, and I refer you to [FREE00] for an opposing view. I think revisions to current IP-based protocols, and the addition of GMPLS, LMP, and the OIF UNI and NNI procedures will work, and this book uses this model, but [FREE00] provides some balanced, opposing views on the issue. Later, we will take a look at the main arguments for the [FREE00] working group.

Regarding the use of revisions to existing protocols, two major issues are discussed. The first is the adaptation and reuse of IP control plane protocols within the optical network control plane, irrespective of the types of clients that utilize the optical network. The second is the transport of IP traffic through an optical network together with the control and coordination issues that arise therein.

Two General Models

Two general models are discussed in [RAJA02]. I expect that, in future commercial implementations, these models will be merged because a combination of the two will provide the best alternative. Below is a summary of these models (I will refer you to my descriptions of these models in other parts of this book).

Domain Services Model

Under the domain services model, the optical network primarily offers high bandwidth connectivity in the form of lightpaths. Standardized signaling across the UNI is used to invoke the following four services, which are covered in this book in Chapter 13:

- Lightpath creation: This service allows a lightpath with the specified attributes to be created between a pair of termination points in the optical network, perhaps based on network administration decisions, such as security.
- Lightpath deletion: This service allows an existing lightpath to be deleted.
- Lightpath modification: This service allows certain (and limited) parameters of the lightpath to be modified.
- Lightpath status enquiry: This service allows the status of certain parameters of the lightpath to be queried by the router that created the lightpath.

A service discovery procedure may be employed as a precursor to obtaining UNI services. Service discovery allows a client to determine the static parameters of the interconnection with the optical network, including the UNI signaling protocols supported. The protocols for neighbor and service discovery are different from the UNI signaling protocol itself; for example, see LMP in Chapter 11.

Because a small set of well-defined services is offered across the UNI, the signaling protocol requirements are minimal. As you read Chapter 13, you will notice that the UNI message set is relatively sparse. Specifically, the signaling protocol is required to convey a few messages with certain attributes in a point-to-point manner between the router and the optical network. Such a protocol may be based on RSVP-TE or LDP, for example.

The optical domain services model does not deal with the type and nature of routing protocols within and across the optical network. The ODS model results in the establishment of a lightpath topology between routers at the edge of the optical network.

Unified Service Model

With the united service model, the IP and optical networks are treated as a single integrated network from a control plane view. The XCs are treated just like any other router in regard to control plane operations. Thus, in principle, there is no distinction between the UNI, NNIs and any other router-to-router interface from a routing and signaling point of view. It is assumed that this control plane is MPLS-based, as described in Chapter 9 and in the last section of this chapter.

The optical network services are obtained implicitly during end-to-end MPLS signaling. An edge router can create a lightpath with specified attributes, or delete and modify lightpaths as it creates MPLS LSPs. In this regard, the services obtained from the optical network are similar to the domain services model. These services, however, may be invoked in a more seamless manner as compared to the domain services model. For instance, when routers are attached to a single optical network, a remote router could compute an end-to-end path across the optical internetwork.

It can then establish an LSP across the optical internetwork. But the edge routers must still recognize that an LSP across the optical internetwork is a lightpath, or a conduit for multiple LSPs. The concept of "forwarding adjacency" can be used to specify virtual links across optical internetworks in routing protocols such as OSPF. In essence, once a lightpath is established across an optical internetwork between two edge routers, it can be advertised as a forwarding adjacency (a virtual link) between these routers. Thus, from a data plane point of view, the lightpaths result in a virtual overlay between edge routers. The decisions as to when to create such lightpaths, and the bandwidth management for these lightpaths, are identical in both the domain services model and the unified service model.

Interconnections for IP over Optical

Given that IP/MPLS over optical can use the models described above, the transport of the IP datagrams over an optical network can occur though three kinds of interconnections: (a) peer, (b) overlay, and (c) augmented.

Peer.   Under the peer model, the IP/MPLS layers act as peers of the optical transport network, so that a single control plane runs over both the IP/MPLS and the optical domains. When there is a single optical network involved, presumably a common routing protocol such as OSPF or IS-IS, with appropriate extensions, can be used to distribute topology information over the integrated IP-optical network. In the case of OSPF, opaque LSAs can be used to advertise topology state information. In the case of IS-IS, extended TLVs can be defined to propagate topology state information.

Overlay.   Under the overlay model (supported by the optical domain service interconnect (ODSI)), the IP/MPLS routing, topology distribution, and signaling protocols are independent of the routing, topology distribution, and signaling protocols at the optical layer. Topology distribution, path computation, and signaling protocols are defined for the optical domain. Interactions between signaling and routing are accomplished through UNI-defined procedures.

Augmented.   Under the augmented model, there are actually separate routing instances in the IP and optical domains, but information from one routing instance is passed through the other routing instance. For example, external IP addresses could be carried within the optical routing protocols to allow reachability information to be passed to IP clients.

AN OPPOSING VIEW

As noted, [FREE00] takes a different view from [RAJA02]. Here are the main arguments quoted from the [FREE00] working group:

> User plane connections are separable entities from the control plane in the OTN. In particular, user plane and control plane traffic need not be congruently routed. This is one distinguishing feature that does not apply to traditional IP connectionless (CNLS) networks. More importantly, however, the user-plane is transparent, connection-oriented (CO), and has no practical buffering. In essence, the OTN user-plane is completely agnostic regarding the type of traffic it carries (indeed, this is also true of other layer 1 technologies such as SDH/SONET, which can support ATM, IP, PDH, etc. encapsulated within fixed length frames).
>
> A key feature of a layer 1 user plane is its ability to accommodate large administrative bandwidth entities and have the flexibility to accommodate new

client layer networks as they are introduced. These client layer networks may or may not be customer application interfacing.

Given the CO and client-agnostic nature of the OTN, one cannot logically draw the conclusion that a set of control-plane protocols which were originally developed to suit a CNLS environment are the right choice for the control plane of an OTN. Indeed, the only valid justification for this is the re-use of an existing set of protocols, which can save development effort. Based on this argument, one would then have to ask why other control plane protocols developed for a CO environment should not be used.

We have not seen any evidence that such an analysis has been carried out.

Which Approaches to Use?

Once again, it is certainly possible that combinations of all the approaches cited in [RAJA02] and [FREE00] will see implementations. At this juncture, I favor the approaches cited in [RAJA02]. Let's now take a more detailed look at some of the general thoughts of these study groups. We start here with GMPLS and then continue the discussion in the remainder of this book.

GENERALIZED MPLS (GMPLS) USE IN OPTICAL NETWORKS

As noted earlier in this book, the method of distributing and binding labels between LSRs can vary. The LDP can be used, and so can extensions to RSVP. GMPLS has been developed to support MPLS operations in optical networks with the ability to use such optical technologies as time-division (e.g., SONET ADMs), wavelengths, and spatial switching (e.g., incoming port or fiber to outgoing port or fiber) [ASHW01]. This part of the chapter describes those parts of GMPLS that pertain to optical networks.

MPLS assumes that LSRs have a forwarding protocol that is capable of processing and routing signals that have packet, frame, or cell boundaries. LSRs are assumed to be OXCs (O/E/O devices). In contrast, GMPLS assumes that LSRs are PXCs (O/O/O devices) that recognize neither packet nor cell boundaries. Thus, the forwarding decision is based on time slots, wavelengths, or physical ports.

We must pause a moment here to clarify some terms used in GMPLS. Recall that this book uses the term OXC to identify an O/E/O device, the term PXC to identify an O/O/O device, and XC as a generic term to identify either an OXC or a PXC. GMPLS uses the following terms (the remainder of this chapter adopts the GMPLS terminology):

- Packet-switched capable (PXC): Processes traffic based on packet/cell/frame boundaries.
- Time-division multiplex capable (TDM): Processes traffic based on a TDM boundary, such as a SONET/SDH node.
- Lambda-switch capable (LSC): Processes traffic based on the optical wavelength.
- Fiber-switch capable (FSC): Processes traffic based on the physical interface, such as an optical fiber.

Therefore, our term of OXC describes the GMPLS PXC and TDM. Our term of PXC describes the GMPLS LSC.

Traditional MPLS LSPs are uni-directional, but GMPLS supports the establishment of bi-directional LSPs. Bi-directional LSPs have the benefit of lower setup latency and the requirement for fewer messages to support a setup operation.

Considerations for Interworking Layer 1 Lambdas and Layer 2 Labels

In Chapter 2 (see "Considerations for Interworking Layer 1 and Layer 2 Networks"), five points were made about the relationships of layer 1 circuit-switched and layer 2 label-switched networks. Recall that optical switching is considered a layer 1 switching function. To set the stage for the remainder of this chapter, we revisit the five points and modify them in relation to MPLS generally, and to GMPLS specifically.

1. Circuit-switched nodes may have thousands of physical links (ports). A key issue for optical/MPLS networks is the configuration and management of these ports, and the wavelengths on the ports. Insofar as possible, it is desirable not to execute O/E/O functions in the core network in the data plane. Therefore, the ideal lightpath through the network would have use of the same wavelength end-to-end. This is not a trivial task, since it requires all nodes in one or more networks to be able to agree on the specific wavelength. Nevertheless, GMPLS permits the negotiation of these wavelengths.

   Note: At this writing, it is not clear whether or not the optical switches are going to need switching matrices that support these thousands of ports. It appears the MEMS technology is being pushed into the future, and very large photonic cross-connects have not reached a point of high demand.

2. The layer 1 switch ports do not have IP addresses. It is the intent to use IP addresses for all nodes and the nodes' interfaces. This requirement adds a significant task to the 3G transport network.

3. Layer 1 neighbor nodes do not need to know about their neighbor's internal port number ID; they need to know the channel ID on the port in order to recognize each piece of traffic. This condition still holds when MPLS is added to the mix, and I recommend a per-interface label assignment (as opposed to a per-platform (per-switch) arrangement) in order to more easily meld with current layer 1 practices. Examples that follow in later chapters all use a per-interface label assignment scheme.

4. Many of the circuit-switches' features are configured manually, and the operations remain static (fixed slots, etc.). This practice cannot continue if the network resources are to be dynamically and adaptively utilized. Therefore, the 3G transport network adopts a new concept: The network no longer consists of fixed pipes; it is now dynamically changing. A good analogy is offered by [XU01]: The transport network can be conceived as a large circuit switch with a dynamically-configurable backplane. Thus, the layer 1 operations must be amenable to the same kinds of bandwidth and OAM manipulation as the upper layers (such as ATM and MPLS at layer 2).

5. The switching technology on circuit-switches is based on a very fast hardware-oriented cross-connect fabric, wherein the input and output ports are very tightly synchronized. In an optical/MPLS node, the next hop should be set up by binding the MPLS label in the cross-connect fabric to the output port to that next node. Furthermore, label distribution, say with LDP, is analogous to say SS7 (ISUP) setting up connections at layer 1.

Examples of GMPLS Operations

This part of the chapter explains the GMPLS messages used in an optical network. The message that conveys this information can be sent to an XC via a variety of protocols, such as the extensions to RSVP and LDP. Consequently, we do not need to delve into the specific formats (bit positions, and so on) here, but will confine ourselves to understanding the functions of the fields in the message.

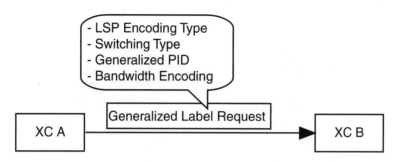

Figure 10–6   The generalized label request.

Generalized Label Request.   Figure 10–6 shows one example of how GMPLS is employed. XC A sends a GMPLS message to XC B. This message contains a control label called a Generalized Label Request and its intent is to provide an XC B with sufficient information to set up resources for the connection of an LSP with XC A. As depicted in Figure 10–6, there are three required and one optional fields in this message. These fields perform the following functions:

The first field is the LSP encoding type. It identifies the encoding (format) type that is to be used with the data associated with the LSP. This field tells the receiving node about the specific framing format. Thus far, twelve types have been stipulated, as shown in Table 10–1. Note that

Table 10–1   LSP Encoding Type

Value	Type of Encoding (Format of Traffic)
1	Packet (conventional IP formats)
2	Ethernet V2
3	ANSI PDH (DS1, etc., payloads)
4	ETSI PSH (E1, etc., payloads)
5	SDH ITU-T G.707 (1996)
6	SONET ANSI T1.105 (1995)
7	Digital Wrapper
8	Lambda (photonic)
9	Fiber
10	Ethernet IEEE 802.3
11	SDH ITU-T G.707 (2000)
12	SONET ANSI T1.105 (2000)

Table 10–2   Generalized PID (G-PID)

Value	Type	Technology
0	Unknown	All
1	DS1 SF (Superframe)	ANSI-PDH
2	DS1 ESF (Extended Superframe)	ANSI-PDH
3	DS3 M23	ASNI-PDH
4	DE3 C-Bit Parity	ANSI-PDH
5	Asynchronous mapping of E4	SDH
6	Asynchronous mapping of DS3/T3	SDH
7	Asynchronous mapping of E3	SDH
8	Bit synchronous mapping of E3	SDH
9	Byte synchronous mapping of E3	SDH
10	Asynchronous mapping of DS2/T2	SDH
11	Bit synchronous mapping of DS2/T2	SDH
12	Byte synchronous mapping of DS2/T2	SDH
13	Asynchronous mapping of E1	SDH
14	Byte synchronous mapping of E1	SDH
15	Byte synchronous mapping of 31 * DS0	SDH
16	Asynchronous mapping of DS1/T1	SDH
17	Bit synchronous mapping of DS1/T1	SDH
18	Byte synchronous mapping of DS1/T1	SDH
19	Same as 12, but in a VC-12	SDH
20	Same as 13, but in a VC-12	SDH
21	Same as 14, but in a VC-12	SDH
22	DS1 SF asynchronous	SONET
23	DS1 ESF asynchronous	SONET
24	DS3 M23 asynchronous	SONET
25	DS3 C-bit parity asynchronous	SONET
26	VT	SONET
27	STS	SONET
28	POS – no scrambling, 16 bit CRC	SONET
29	POS – no scrambling, 32 bit CRC	SONET
30	POS – scrambling, 16 bit CRC	SONET
31	POS – scrambling, 32 bit CRC	SONET
32	ATM mapping	SONET/SDH
33	Ethernet	Lambda, Fiber
34	Ethernet	Lambda, Fiber
35	SONET	Lambda, Fiber
36	Digital wrapper	Lambda, Fiber
37	Lambda	Fiber

the Lambda (photonic) encoding type identifies wavelength switching (needing the services of an LSC module). The fiber encoding type identifies an FSC-capable module.

The second field is the switching type, and it informs the XC about the type of switching that is to be perfumed on a particular link. The switching capabilities are defined as (a) several variations for PSC, (b) layer-2 switching capable (for example, ATM and Frame Relay), (c) TDM switching capable, LSC switching capable, or FSC switching capable. The multiple options for PSC allow the network operator to stipulate more than one packet-switched operation.

The third field is the generalized protocol ID (G-PID), and it identifies the payload that is carried by an LSP; that is, the traffic from the client for the specific LSP. This field uses the standard Ethertype values as well as the values shown in Table 10–2.

The fourth field is a bandwidth encoding value. It defines the bandwidth for the LSP. Table 10–3 shows the recommended values for this field.

Table 10–3   Bandwidth Values

Signal Type	Bit Rate
DS0	0.064 Mbit/s
DS1	1.544 Mbit/s
E1	2.048 Mbit/s
DS2	6.312 Mbit/s
E2	8.448 Mbit/s
Ethernet	10.00 Mbit/s
E3	44.736 Mbit/s
DS3	44.736 Mbit/s
STS-1	51.84 Mbit/s
Fast Ethernet	100.00 Mbit/s
E4	139.264 Mbit/s
OC-3/STM-1	155.52 Mbit/s
OC-12/STM-4	622.08 Mbit/s
Gigabit Ethernet	1000.00 Mbit/s
OC-48/STM-1	2488.32 Mbit/s
OC-192-STM-64	9953.28 Mbit/s
10 G-Ethernet - LAN	1000.00 Mbit/s
OC-768/STM-256	39812.12 Mbit/s

Generalized Label. The generalized label request can be extended to identify not only the labels for the packets, but (a) a single wavelength within a waveband or fiber, (b) a single fiber in a bundle of fibers, (c) a single waveband within a fiber, or (d) a set of time slots within a fiber or a waveband. This extension can also identify conventional ATM or Frame Relay labels.

Port and Wavelength Labels. As Chapter 11 explains in more detail, the FSC and PSC may use multiple channels/links that are controlled by a single control channel. If so, the port/wavelength label identifies the port, fiber, or lambda that is used for this purpose.

Wavelength Label. This label groups contiguous wavelengths and identifies them with a unique waveband ID. Its function is to provide a tool for the switch to cross-connect multiple wavelengths as one unit. This label contains three fields:

- Waveband ID: The unique ID (selected by the sending node) of the wavelengths, to be used on all subsequent, related messages.
- Start label: The lowest value wavelength in the waveband.
- End label: The highest value wavelength in the waveband.

Suggested Labels for the Wavelengths

GMPLS can be used to configure the PXC's hardware. One method is called *suggested labels* and is used by an upstream PXC to notify its neighbor downstream of a label that is to be used (suggested) for a wavelength, or a set of wavelengths. Chapter 12 shows this operation in conjunction with the configuration of a PXCs MEMS's hardware.

For this discussion, the GMPLS specification defines the use of a label set to limit the label choices made between adjacent GMPLS nodes. Label sets are useful when an optical node is restricted to a set of wavelengths; obviously, not all optical nodes have the same capabilities. The other helpful aspect of negotiating labels in regards to wavelengths is that some optical nodes are O/E/O capable, and others are O/O/O capable, and this aspect of the node will necessarily dictate wavelength capabilities.

BI-DIRECTIONAL LSPs IN OPTICAL NETWORKS

GMPLS defines the use of bi-directional LSPs that have the same traffic engineering requirements in each direction.[1] First, to establish a bi-directional LSP when using RSVP-TE or CR-LDP, two uni-directional paths between peer LSRs must be independently established. The principal disadvantage to this approach is the time it takes to set up this bi-directional relationship. Second, setting up two uni-directional LSPs requires more messages to be exchanged than with the setting up of one symmetrical bi-directional LSP. Third, independent LSPs for a user's traffic profile can lead to different routes taken through the network for the two LSPs. This situation may not be a problem, but it does make for more complex resource allocation schemes.

Of course, since either optical node can initiate label allocations, it is possible for two peer nodes that are in conflict with each other to suggest labels at about the same time. Examples are the same label values for different fibers, or the same labels for different wavelengths on a fiber. This is not a major issue. Contention resolution of potentially conflicting virtual circuit or label bindings is well-studied, and GMPLS defines the procedures for resolving these label contention conflicts.

Link Protection

Another attractive feature of GMPLS is the provision for link protection information, including what kind of protection is needed. The following types of link protection are defined in GMPLS:

- Enhanced: Indicates that a protection scheme that is more reliable than dedicated 1+1 should be used (e.g., 4-fiber).
- Dedicated 1+1: Indicates a dedicated link layer protection scheme.

---

[1]My clients and I have long favored the simultaneous setting up of bi-directional virtual circuits in X.25, Frame Relay, ATM, and for MPLS: LSPs. It is good news to us that GMPLS adapts this approach for the reasons cited in the text of this chapter. Of course, one idea behind two uni-directional connections/LSPs for a user's traffic is the understanding that many users' traffic flows are asymmetric, with more traffic flow in one direction than the other. The idea is to find the bandwidth, wherever it is in the network, to support this asymmetric flow. Fine, but a multi-gigabit, fiber network makes the argument for independent uni-directional traffic paths even less tenable.

- Dedicated 1:1: Indicates that a dedicated link layer protection scheme, i.e., 1:1 protection, should be used to support the LSP.
- Shared: Indicates that a shared link layer protection scheme, such as 1:N protection, should be used to support the LSP.
- Unprotected: Indicates that the LSP should not use any link layer protection.
- Extra Traffic: Indicates that the LSP should use links that are protecting other higher priority traffic. Such LSPs may be pre-empted when the links carrying the higher priority traffic being protected fail.

THE NEXT HORIZON: GMPLS EXTENSIONS FOR G.709

G.709 establishes the framework for new-generation optical networks; this was explained in Chapter 6. [BELL01] sets forth the guidelines for interworking GMPLS with G.709. This part of the chapter highlights [BELL01], and I recommend this working draft to you if you need more details on the G.709/MPLS (otherwise, this part of the chapter probably contains too much detail for the casual reader).

Also, as noted earlier, it is important to repeat that the IETF working drafts are subject to change, so you should frequently go to www.ietf.org to make certain that you have the latest version.

Adapting GMPLS to control G.709 can be achieved by considering that G.709 defines two transport hierarchies: a digital hierarchy (also known as the digital wrapper) and an optical transport hierarchy. First, within the digital hierarchy (the previously defined digital wrapper), a digital path layer is defined. Then, within the optical transport hierarchy, an optical channel layer or optical path layer, including a digital OTM overhead signal (OOS; i.e., a non-associated overhead) is defined.

The generalized label request includes a technology independent part and a technology dependent part (i.e., the traffic parameters).

Technology Independent Part

The GMPLS LSP encoding type and the generalized protocol identifier (G-PID) constitute the technology independent part. Since G.709 defines two networking layers (ODUk layers and OCh layer), the LSP encoding type can reflect these two layers or can be considered as a common layer.

If an LSP encoding type is specified per networking layer or, more precisely, per group of functional networking layer (i.e., ODUk and OCh), then the signal type must not reflect these layers. This means that two LSP encoding types have to be defined: (a) one reflecting the digital hierarchy (the digital wrapper layer) through the definition of the digital path layer (i.e., the ODUk layers) and (b) the other reflecting the optical transport hierarchy through the definition of the optical path layer (i.e., the OCh layer).

The G-PID identifies the payload carried by an LSP. The G-PID, which defines the client layer of that LSP, is used by the G.709 endpoints of the LSP. The G-PID could take one of the following values at the digital path layer, in addition to the payload identifiers already defined in GMPLS:

- CBRa: asynchronous constant bit rate (i.e., STM-16/OC-48, STM-64/OC-192 and STM-256/OC-768)
- CBRb: bit synchronous constant bit rate (i.e., STM-16/OC-48, STM-64/OC-192 and STM-256/OC-768)
- ATM: constant bit rate at 2.5, 10, and 40 Gbit/s
- BSOT: non-specific client bit stream with octet timing at 2.5, 10, and 40 Gbit/s
- BSNT: non-specific client bit stream without octet timing at 2.5, 10, and 40 Gbit/s

The G-PID defined in GMPLS are then used when the client payloads are encapsulated through the GFP mapping procedure: Ethernet, ATM mapping and IP packets.

Backward Compatibility.   In order to include pre-OTN developments, the G-PID at the optical channel layer can, in addition to the G.709 digital path layer (at 2.5 Gbit/s for ODU1, 10 Gbit/s for ODU2, and 40 Gbit/s for ODU3), take one of these values: (a) SDH: STM-16, STM-64, and STM-256, (b) SONET: OC-48, OC-192, and OC-768, and (c) Ethernet: 1 Gbit/s and 10 Gbit/s.

Technology Dependent Part

The technology dependent of the generalized label request (also referred to as traffic-parameters) must reflect the following G.709 features: (a) ODUk mapping, (b) ODUk multiplexing, (c) OCh multiplexing,

(d) OTM overhead signal (OOS), and (e) transparency (only for pre-OTN). As defined in GMPLS, the traffic-parameters must include the technology-specific G.709 networking signal types (i.e., the signals processed by the GMPLS control-plane). The corresponding identifiers reflect the signal types requested during the LSP setup. The following signal types must be considered: ODU1, ODU2, ODU3, and (at least one) OCh.

A second field must indicate the type of multiplexing being requested for ODUk LSP or OCh LSP. Two kinds of multiplexing are currently defined: flexible multiplexing (or simply multiplexing) and inverse multiplexing.

At the ODUk layer (i.e., digital path layer), flexible multiplexing refers to the mapping of an ODU2 into four arbitrary OPU3 tributary slots (i.e., each slot containing one ODU1) arbitrarily selected. Inverse multiplexing currently under definition at ITU-T should also be considered. The requested multiplexing type must include a default value indicating that neither ODUk flexible multiplexing nor ODUk inverse multiplexing is requested.

At the Och layer, flexible multiplexing is not defined today while inverse multiplexing means that the requested composed signal constitutes a waveband (i.e., an optical channel multiplex). A waveband, denoted as OCh[j.k] (j >= 1), is defined as a non-contiguous set of identical optical channels j x OCh, each of them associated with an OTM-x.m (x = nr or n) sub-interface signal. The bit rate of each OCh constituting the waveband (i.e., the composed L-LSP) must be identical; k is unique per OCh multiplex.

Consequently, since the number of identical components included in an ODU multiplex or an OCh multiplex is arbitrary, a dedicated field indicating the requested number of components must also be defined in order to reflect individual signals constituting the requested LSP.

OTM Overhead Signal (OOS)

A dedicated field should support the following options:

- With OTM-0r.m and OTM-nr.m interfaces (reduced functionality stack), OTM overhead signal (OOS) is not supported. Therefore, with these types of interface signals, non-associated OTM overhead indication is not required.
- With OTM-n.m interfaces (full functionality stack), the OOS is supported and mapped into the Optical Supervisory Channel (OSC), which is multiplexed into the OTM-n.m using wavelength division multiplexing.

- With OTM-n.m interfaces or even with OTM-0.m and OTM-nr.m interfaces, non-standard OOS can be defined to allow for instance interoperability with pre-OTN based devices or with any optical devices that do not support G.709 OOS specification. This specific OOS enables the use of any proprietary monitoring signal exchange through any kind of supervisory channel (it can be transported by using any kind of IP-based control channel).

Transparency

Transparency is defined only for pre-OTN developments since, by definition, any signal transported over an OTN is fully transparent. This feature is used to request a pre-OTN LSP (i.e., a non-standard lambda-LSP) including transparency support. It may also be used to set up the transparency process to be applied in each intermediate LSR.

As is commonly the case today with pre-OTN capable interfaces, three kinds of transparency levels are currently defined:

- SONET/SDH Pre-OTN interfaces with RS/Section and MS/Line overhead transparency: The pre-OTN network is capable of transporting transparently STM-N/OC-N signals.
- SONET/SDH Pre-OTN interfaces terminating RS/Section overhead with MS/Line overhead transparency: The pre-OTN network is capable of transporting transparently MSn signals.
- SONET/SDH Pre-OTN interfaces terminating RS/Section and MS/Line overhead: The pre-OTN network is capable of transporting transparently HOVC/STS-SPE signals.

For pre-OTN optical channels a specific field (in the generalized label request) must indicate the transparency level requested during the L-LSP setup. However, this field is relevant only when the LSP encoding type value corresponds to the on-standard lambda layer.

G.709 Label Space

The G.709 label space must include two sub-spaces: the first reflecting the digital path layer (i.e., the ODUk layers) and the second, the optical path layer (i.e., the OCh layer).

ODUk Label Space. As noted in Chapter 6, the digital path layer (i.e., ODUk layers), G.709 defines three different client payload bit rates. An optical data unit (ODU) frame has been defined for each of these bit rates. Recall that ODUk refers to the frame at bit rate k, where k = 1 (for 2.5 Gbit/s), 2 (for 10 Gbit/s), or 3 (for 40 Gbit/s).

In addition to the support of ODUk mapping into OTUk, the G.709 label space must support the sub-levels of ODUk flexible multiplexing (or simply ODUk multiplexing):

- ODU2 multiplexing: The mapping of an ODU2 into four arbitrary OPU3 tributary slots selected arbitrarily (i.e., each slot containing one ODU1).
- ODU3 multiplexing: Not applicable today since higher order OPU tributary slots are not defined in the current G.709 recommendation.

Also recall that the value space of the k1, k2, and k3 fields are defined as follows:

- k1: indicates a particular ODU1 in one ODU2 (k1 = 1,..,4), ODU3 (k1 = 5,..,20); k1 values from 21 to 84 are reserved for future use.
- k2: indicates a particular ODU2 in one ODU3 (k2 = 1,..,4); k2 values from 5 to 20 are reserved for future use.
- k3: k3 values (k3 = 1,..,4) are reserved for future use.

If k1, k2, and k3 values are equal to zero, the corresponding ODUk are not structured; that is, k[i]=0 (i=1,2,3) indicates that the ODU[I] is not structured and the ODU[i] is simply mapped into the OTU[I].

If k1 and k2 values are equal to zero, a particular ODUk is not structured; that is, ki=0 indicates that the ODUi is not structured. Here are some examples:

- k2=0, k1=0 indicates a full ODU3 (full 40 Gbit/s).
- k2=0, k1=3 indicates the third unstructured ODU1 in the ODU2.
- k2=2, k1=0 indicates the second unstructured ODU2 in the ODU3.
- k2=0, k1=8 indicates the fourth unstructured ODU1 in the ODU3.
- k2=4, k1=2 indicates the second ODU1 of the fourth ODU2 in the ODU3.

OCh Label Space

The OCh label space should be consistently defined as a flat value space whose values reflect the local assignment of OCh identifiers corresponding to the OTM-x.m sub-interface signals (m = 1, 2, or 3 and x = 0r, nr, or n). The OCh identifiers could be defined as specified in [GMPLS-SIG] either with absolute values (e.g., channel identifiers [channel ID]), also referred to as wavelength identifiers or relative values (e.g., channel spacing), also referred to as inter-wavelength spacing. The latter is strictly confined to a per-port label space while the latter could be defined as a local or a global label space. Such an OCh label space is applicable to the OTN optical channel and the pre-OTN optical channel layer.

Applications

GMPLS extensions for G.709 must support the following applications:

- When one ODU1 (ODU2 or ODU3) non-structured signal is transported into one OTU1 (OTU2 or OTU3) payload, the upstream node requests in a non-structured ODU1 (ODU2 or ODU3) signal. In such conditions, the downstream node has to return a unique label since the ODU1 (ODU2 or ODU3) is directly mapped into the corresponding OTU1 (OTU2 or OTU3). When a single ODUk signal is requested, the downstream node has to return a single ODUk label.
- When one ODU2 signal is transported into an ODU3 payload, which is sub-divided into 16 ODU1 tributary slots, the ODU1 tributary slots (here, denoted A, B, C, and D with A < B < C < D) can be arbitrary selected. For instance, one ODU2 can be transported in ODU1 tributary slots 5, 12, 13, and 18. Therefore, when the upstream node requests in such conditions a composed ODU2 signal, the downstream node returns four labels, each of them representing a pointer to an ODU1 tributary slot.
- When a single OCh signal of 40Gbps is requested, the downstream node has to return a single wavelength label to the requestor node.
- When a composed OCh[4.2] signal is requested (i.e., a waveband or optical channel multiplex composed by four bit-rate identical Och signal of 10Gbps), the downstream node has to return four wavelength labels to the requesting upstream node since the optical channels constituting the optical multiplex are not necessarily contiguously multiplexed.

ODUk General Communication Channel (GCC)

As defined in the ITUT-G.709 recommendation, two fields of two bytes are allocated in the ODUk overhead to support two general communications channels between any two network elements with access to the ODUk frame structure (i.e., at 3-R regeneration points). The bytes for GCC(1) are located in row 4, columns 1 and 2, and the bytes for GCC(2) are located in row 4, columns 3 and 4 of the ODUk overhead.

These bytes are defined as clear channels so that the format specification and their content can be defined for the purpose of in-fiber/in-band signaling transport mechanism.

A MORE IMMEDIATE HORIZON: GMPLS WITH SONET AND SDH

As explained in earlier parts of this book, the 3G transport network is now just beginning to emerge, and optical internets using 3G standards, and GMPLS are also in their infancy. For the more immediate future, a number of vendors and network providers think that the use of an extended GMPLS with the 2nd generation SONET and SDH transport networks can be of benefit to customers and service providers. To that end, an IETF working group has defined GMPLS extensions for use in SONET and SDH networks [MANN01]. This part of the chapter highlights the major aspects of this specification.

Traffic Parameters

The GMPLS parameters for SONET/SDH are carried in the GMPLS generalized label request within the RSVP-TE or CR-LDP packets and within the SONET/SDH payload or headers. Six fields are coded in this label request:

- Signal type (ST): This field indicates the type of elementary signal that comprises the requested LSP. Several transforms can be applied successively on the elementary signal to build the final signal being requested for the LSP. The permissible values for the signal type field are listed in Table 10–4.
- Requested contiguous concatenation (RCC): This field is used to request and negotiate the optional SONET/SDH contiguous concatenation of the elementary signal. The field allows an upstream node to indicate to a downstream node the different types of contiguous concatenation that it supports.
- Number of contiguous components (NCC): This field indicates the number of identical SONET/SDH SPEs/VCs that are requested to be concatenated, as specified in the RCC field.

Table 10–4   Signal Type Values

Value	Type
1	VT1.5 SPE / VC-11
2	VT2 SPE / VC-12
3	VT3 SPE
4	VT6 SPE / VC-2
5	STS-1 SPE / VC-3
6	STS-3c SPE / VC-4
7	STS-1/STM-0 (only when requesting transparency)
8	STS-3/STM-1 (only when requesting transparency)
9	STS-12/STM-4 (only when requesting transparency)
10	STS-48/STM-16 (only when requesting transparency)
11	STS-192/STM-64 (only when requesting transparency)
12	STS-768/STM-256 (only when requesting transparency)
13	VTG /TUG-2
14	TUG-3
15	STSG-3 /AUG-1
16	STSG-12 / AUG-4
17	STSG-48 /AUG-16
18	STSG-192/AUG-64
19	STSG-768/AUG-256
20	"VC-3 via AU-3 at the end"

- Number of virtual components (NVC): This field indicates the number of signals that are requested to be virtually concatenated.
- Multiplier (MT): This field indicates the number of identical signals that are requested for the LSP (i.e., that form the final signal). These signals can be either identical elementary signals, or identical contiguously concatenated signals, or identical virtually concatenated signals. Note that all these signals therefore belong to the same LSP.
- Transparency (T): This field indicates the type of transparency being requested. Transparency as defined from the point of view of this signaling specification is applicable only to the fields in the SONET/SDH frame overheads. In the SONET case, these are the fields in the section overhead (SOH), and the line overhead (LOH). In the SDH case, these are the fields in the regenerator section

overhead (RSOH), the multiplex section overhead (MSOH), and the pointer fields between the two. With SONET, the pointer fields are part of the LOH. Transparency is applicable only when using the following signal types: STM-0, STM-1, STM-4, STM-16, STM-64, STM-256, STS-1, STS-3, STS-12, STS-48, STS-192, and STS-768. At least one transparency type must be specified when requesting such a signal type.

SUMMARY

After reading Chapter 10, it is evident that third transport networks are intended to contain extensive MPLS operations. Other chapters have discussed the advantages of using MPLS in general, and the last two chapters have made the case for applying it in optical networks in order to exploit its TE and constrained routing capabilities. The remainder of this book brings in more information on optical networks, MPLS, and their joint contributions toward the creation of an optical Internet.

11

The Link Management Protocol (LMP)

The first part of this chapter explains the basic operations of the Link Management Protocol (LMP), including the motivation for creating the protocol. The major operations of LMP are described, as well as the messages that are exchanged between optical nodes. The second part of the chapter discusses enhancements to LMP for fault detection and recovery of optical links that run between PXCs and optical line systems (OLSs).

KEEP THE OPTICAL LINK UP AND RUNNING

Link reliability between switches and other network components has always been an important priority for the network manager. After all, if a link is inoperable, user payload cannot be sent across the link. The result is the loss of revenue and possibly the good will of the customer. The need for link reliability in an optical network is magnified by the fact that a failed link can affect many more users than if a failure occurs on a link of lesser capacity, say, a copper-wire link.

To emphasize how great the problem is, WDM systems are available in which one fiber can operate at the terabit/s rate. As noted in Chapter 1, this rate is 1,000,000,000,000, or 10^{12} bit/s. Another system multiplexes 160 wavelengths of 10 Gbit/s each for a 1.6 Tbit/s rate. Some vendors are suggesting a system that supports 320 wavelengths in a single fiber, yielding a throughput of 3.2 Tbit/s per fiber.

With these systems, a fiber failure has the potential to affect scores of millions of user connections. Therefore, there have been concerted efforts in the industry to develop link management procedures that ensure optical links stay up, and, if problems occur, to provide mechanisms for speedy recovery. One such effort, sponsored by the IETF, is called the link management protocol (LMP) [LANG01] and [BROR01]. Let's take a look at this protocol and some of its associated operations.

WHAT IS MANAGED

LMP can manage different components of the link, as shown in Figure 11–1. It can manage a data link carrying user payload, as well as control links. The term link means an optical fiber, a wavelength on the fiber, or a group of wavelengths on the fiber. LMP does not require that the control channel (or channels) be on the same physical medium as the data-bearing links; the control channel can be on a separate fiber. This common-sense approach means that the health of the data-bearing channels need to be correlated with the health of the control channel.

LMP operates on the links between optical nodes and is used for link provisioning and fault isolation. LMP is capable of handling whatever the granularity of the link may be: wavelength, waveband, or fiber. LMP operates as part of the Internet and Ethernet standards. Therefore, if it runs over Ethernet, it is identified with an Ethertype field; if it runs over PPP, it is identified with a PPP protocol ID field.

As noted, and to emphasize, a control channel is used to manage the connections between the two optical nodes. The control channel can be both in-band (part of a bundle) and out-of-band (a separate fiber).

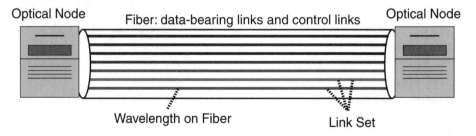

Figure 11–1   Managed components.

DATA-BEARING LINKS

An important distinction of LMP is categorizing a data-bearing link as a port or a component link. Component links are multiplex-capable, and port links are not.

LMP draws this distinction because the management of such links is different based on their multiplexing capability. For example, a SONET cross-connect with OC-192 interfaces may be able to demultiplex the OC-192 stream into four OC-48 streams. If multiple interfaces are grouped together into a single TE link using link bundling, then the link resources must be identified using three levels: TE link id, component interface id, and timeslot label. Resource allocation occurs at the lowest level (timeslots), but physical connectivity occurs at the component link level.

As another example, consider the case where a PXC transparently switches OC-192 lightpaths. If multiple interfaces are once again grouped together into a single TE link, then link bundling is not required and only two levels of identification are required: TE link id and port id. Both resource allocation and physical connectivity happen at the lowest level (i.e., port level).

LMP is designed to support the aggregation of one or more data-bearing links into a TE link (either ports into TE links, or component links into TE links).

CLARIFICATION OF TERMS

Before proceeding into a more detailed analysis of LMP, several terms used in the LMP specifications need to be clarified, and I will use LMP's terms in this chapter. The term OXC refers to all categories of optical cross-connects, irrespective of the internal switching fabric. LMP distinguishes between cross-connects that require opto-electronic conversion, called digital cross-connects (DXCs), and those that are all-optical, called photonic switches or photonic cross-connects (PXCs), also referred to as pure cross-connects. In addition, LMP refers to optical line systems (OLSs) as regenerators that are placed on long-haul links between PXCs. Even though the PXC is all-optical, long-haul OLSs typically terminate channels electrically and regenerate them optically (at least within the context of the LMP specifications), which presents an opportunity to monitor the health of a channel between PXCs [BROR01].

Because of the transparent nature of PXCs, there are new restrictions for monitoring and managing the data channels. LMP, however, can be used for any type of node.

We have learned that an all-optical node does not translate the wavelength to electrical signals, and this signal is declared by LMP to be *transparent*, and is not terminated in the node. A component link is *opaque* if it can be terminated. LMP is able to isolate faults in both opaque and transparent networks, independent of the encoding scheme used for the component links.

BASIC FUNCTIONS OF LMP

LMP is designed to provide four major functions between adjacent optical nodes: (a) control channel management, (b) link connectivity, (c) link property correlation, and (d) fault management (fault isolation). These functions are described in the following sections of this chapter.

Tables 11–1, 11–2, and 11–3 are key tools for the remainder of this chapter. The messages and fields in the messages are described in these tables, and I make frequent reference to LMP messages and fields in the following discussions.

LMP messages are "IP encoded"; that is, they use the same encoding procedure as IP. Thus, the messages can be fragmented if they are too large to meet the MTU size on the physical link by using IPv4 (or IPv6) fragmentation procedures.

LMP Messages

Table 11–1 provides a summary of the LMP messages that are exchanged between the optical nodes. The first column is the message number that resides in the message header; it identifies the message type, shown in the second column. The third column provides a short description of the function of the message.

LMP Message Header

Every LMP message contains a header, followed by the fields in the message. This header is short and simple; it contains the following fields:

- Version of LMP, which is version 1.
- Flags, which provide information on the status of the control channel, if a node is rebooting, the type of node sending the message, and if authentication fields are attached to the message.

Table 11–1   LMP Messages

Message Number	Message Type	Message Function
1	Config	Used in negotiation phase
2	ConfigAck	Acks the Config and indicates agreement on all parameters
3	ConfigNak	Indicates disagreement on Config message non-negotiable parameters
4	Hello	Sent to adjacent node to keep LMP connection alive
5	BeginVerify	Initiates the link verification process
6	BeginVerifyAck	Acks the BeginVerify message; node is ready for Test messages
7	BeginVerifyNak	Node is unwilling or unable to begin verification procedure
8	EndVerify	Terminates the link verification process
9	EndVerifyAck	Acks the EndVerify message
10	Test	Verifies the data link physical connectivity
11	TestStatusSuccess	Transmits mapping between local and remote Interface id
12	TestStatusFailure	Indicates Test message was not received
13	TestStatsAck	Acks receipt of TestStatusSuccess or TestStatusFailure
14	LinkSummary	Synchronizes Interface ids and correlates properties of the link
15	LinkSummaryAck	Acks the LinkSummary message
16	LinkSummaryNak	Naks the LinkSummary message
17	ChannelFail	Notifies a neighbor if a data link failure is detected
18	ChannelFailAck	Indicates extent of channel failure(s) in relation to received ChannelFail message
19	ChannelFailNak	Indicates that reported failures are CLEAR in upstream node (failure is isolated between two nodes)
20	ChannelActive	Indicates data link is now carrying user traffic
21	ChannelActiveAck	Acks the ChannelActive message

- The message type, as shown in column 1 of Table 11–1.
- Total length of the message, including all fields following the header.
- A checksum field to check for bit damage during the transmission.
- Local control channel id (CCid), which identifies the control channel being used for the transport of the message.

Table 11–2   Fields Residing in the LMP Messages

TLV Name	YLV Function
HelloConfig	Establishes timer values for sending Hello messages
LMP Capability	Indicates which extended LMP procedures are supported
TE Link	Indicates type of protection on the link, and its multiplexing capabilities
Data Link	Indicates if data link is a port or component link, its encoding type, and its Interface id
Failed Channel	Identifies Interface id of the failed data link(s)
Active Channel	Identifies Interface id of a data link that has become active

LMP TLVs

Like many Internet-sponsored protocols, LMP describes the formats of parts of the message with a type-length-value format (TLV). This term refers to a standard way of coding parts of the message that have variable lengths, depending on the specific message sent by an optical node to its neighbor. The TLVs follow the header, and contain: (a) type field: the specific TLV, (b) length: the length of the value field, and (c) the value field, which is the actual content of the TLV. The value field is also called the TLV object. LMP also defines one more very important field in the TLV; it is a one-bit field that indicates if a TLV object is negotiable or non-negotiable. Table 11–2 provides a summary of the TLVs currently defined in LMP.

These TLVs are explained in later parts of this chapter, but here are a few comments about some of them that should prove helpful. The LMP capability TLV is used between nodes to indicate that they are willing to execute some extra (extended) operations. The operations are: (a) the link verification procedure, (b) fault management procedure, and (c) the LMP-DWDM procedure.

The Fields in the LMP Messages

Finally, Table 11–3 provides a summary of the fields that reside in the LMP messages. Some of these fields are coded in TLVs, and others are coded as separate fields. Please note that I do not include all the fields, such as some flags that are not instrumental in understanding LMP. I refer you to [LANG01] for these details.

Table 11–3   Fields Residing in the LMP Messages

Field Name	Field Function
node id	Unique identifier for the optical node
BitRate	Rate (in bit/s) at which Test messages are sent
EncType	Optical link encoding syntaxes, such as SONET, SDH, etc.
HelloDeadInterval	How long to wait for receipt of a Hello before declaring control channel has failed
HelloInterval	How frequently Hello messages are sent
TELinkid	Id of link (local or remote)
Local Control Channel id (CCid)	Identifies control channel of the sender of the message
Message id	A unique identifier for each message, used with CCid
RcvSeqNum	Used to ack or nak Hello messages
Received Linkid	Linkid in a received message
TxSeqNum	Current sequence number in Hello message
Verify Interval	Interval at which Test messages are sent
Wavelength	Specific wavelength, measured in nanometers (nm)
LinkDown	A flag, set to 1, indicates link is down
Authentication	Several fields using MD5 for authenticating the message
Capability Flags	Indicates if link verification and fault management procedures are to be used
RemoteTELinkid	Id of TE link of remote node
VerifyTransport Mechanism	Defines transport mechanism for Test messages: (a) JO bytes, (b) DCC bytes, (c) POS, (d) GigE, (e) 10GigE
VerifyDeadInterval	If Test message not received within this value, node sends TestStatusFailure message
Verifyid	Used to differentiate Test messages from different TE links and/or LMP peers
interface id	Id of data link (port or component link)
ProtectionType	Type of link protection, such as unprotected, dedicated, shared, etc.

CONTROL CHANNEL MANAGEMENT

Control channel management is used to establish and maintain link connectivity between adjacent (neighbor) nodes. This action is accomplished using Hello messages that act as a fast keep-alive mechanism between the nodes. Before an optical link is used between two nodes, a bi-directional primary control channel must first be configured. The control channel can be used in a variety of ways, not necessarily restricted to the manner in which LMP defines its use. For example, it can be used to exchange MPLS control-plane information such as link provisioning and fault isolation information, or path management and label distribution information using RSVP-TE, or CR-LDP. It can also be used to distribute topology and state distribution information using traffic engineering extensions to protocols such as OSPF and IS-IS.

LMP is organized along two major sets of operations: (a) control channel management is used to establish and maintain control channel connectivity between neighbor optical nodes, (b) link property correlation is used to synchronize the optical link properties between the nodes.

LMP requires that the control channel be assigned a 32-bit integer control channel identifier (CCid) to each direction of the control channel. At least one active bi-directional control channel must operate between a pair of nodes. Secondary (backup) control channels can be defined as well, and LMP provides considerable flexibility in how the secondary channels are outfitted. For example, a data-bearing channel can be preempted to become a control channel. As another example, secondary channels become active only when the primary channel is lost.

The link property correlation function aggregates multiple ports or component links into a TE link, and synchronizes the properties of the TE link between the optical nodes. As part of the link property correlation function, a LinkSummary message exchange is defined. The LinkSummary message includes the local and remote TE Link id, a list of all ports or component links that comprise the TE link, and various link properties, such as the wavelengths on the link.

All LMP messages except for the Test message are exchanged over the control channel. The Test message is sent over the data link that is being verified. Data links are tested in the transmit direction because they are uni-directional, and as such, it may be possible for both nodes to exchange the Test messages simultaneously.

Parameter Negotiation

During the control channel management operations, Config, Config-Ack, and ConfigNak messages are exchanged, and the fields in these messages are used to begin the LMP procedures. Figure 11–2 shows these procedures.

The Config message is periodically transmitted until its parameters are synchronized between the peer nodes or until one node simply

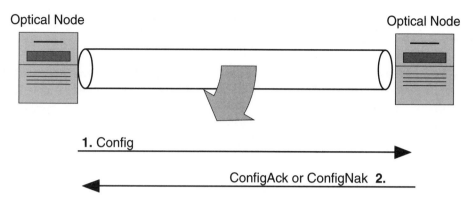

Optical Node   Optical Node

1. Config

ConfigAck or ConfigNak **2.**

Figure 11–2   The configuration operations.

refuses to participate. The ConfigAck message is used to acknowledge receipt of the Config message and express agreement on all the configured parameters (both negotiable and non-negotiable). The ConfigNak message is used to acknowledge receipt of the Config message, to indicate which (if any) non-negotiable parameters are unacceptable, and to propose alternate values for the negotiable parameters. The Config message includes the LMP Capability TLV and the HelloConfig TLV.

The Hello Protocol

After a control channel has been established with vendor-specific configuration/crafting tools, the Hello protocol is invoked to establish and maintain connectivity between the nodes and to detect control channel failures. It is designed to react very quickly to problems so that routing protocols, such as OSPF, do not remove the adjacency status between the two nodes.

Like many Hello protocols, the LMP Hello consists of two phases: (a) the negotiation phase that establishes several operating parameters for the link, and (b) the keep-alive phase, in which the two nodes make sure that each is up and running and all is well.

Negotiation Phase.   During the negotiation phase, the local and remote CCids are exchanged, and the two nodes agree on the values for the HelloInterval and HelloDeadInterval to be used on this specific control channel. These fields are encoded into the Config message. The ConfigAck message acknowledges and accepts the HelloInterval and HelloDeadInterval parameters. The ConfigNak message suggests other values for these two parameters.

Fast Keep-Alive.   Assuming that all these operations are agreed upon by the two nodes, Hello messages are then exchanged. These messages contain two sequence numbers. The TxSeqNum is the sequence number for this Hello message and the second sequence number (RcvSeqNum) is the sequence number of the last Hello message received from the neighbor node.

Each node increments its sequence number when it sees its current sequence number reflected in Hellos received from its peer, as shown in Figure 11–3. The sequence numbers are 32 bits in length; they start at 1

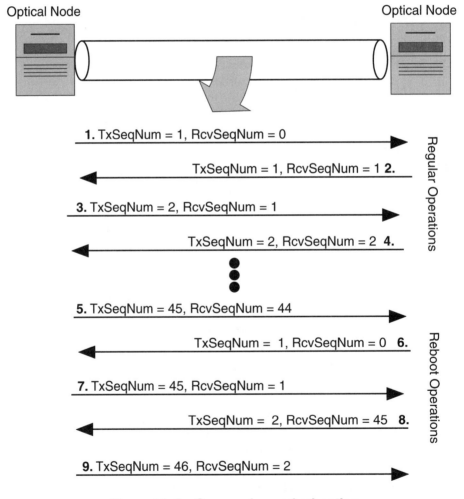

Figure 11–3   Sequencing and rebooting.

and wrap around back to 2; as shown at the bottom of Figure 11–3, 0 is used in the RcvSeqNum to indicate that a Hello has not yet been seen and 1 is used to indicate a node boot/reboot.

Under normal operations, the difference between the RcvSeqNum in a Hello message that is received and the local TxSeqNum that is generated will be, at most, 1. There are two cases where this difference can be more than 1: when a control channel reboots and when switching over to a backup control channel.

Having sequence numbers in the Hello messages allows each node to verify that its peer is receiving its Hello messages. This feature ensures that the remote node will detect that a node has rebooted if TxSeqNum=1. If this event occurs, the remote node will indicate its knowledge of the reboot by setting RcvSeqNum=1 in its Hello messages. Also, by including the RcvSeqNum in Hello packets, the local node will know which Hello packets the remote node has received, an important aspect in coordinating control-channel switchover due to a control channel failure.

Down and Degraded States.   Links may be taken down for administrative or maintenance purposes. They are not taken down if component links are in use. In addition, the control channel can go down, yet the component links may be in operation. In this situation, the fiber does not have the same level of service, and it cannot accept new connections, and to bring it back up, the Config messages must be exchanged. However, if the data links are in operation, they are not taken down, but obviously they are not guaranteed the same level of service if the control channel were operable.

LINK PROPERTY CORRELATION

Link property correlation operations use the link summary messages (LinkSummary, LinkSummaryAck, and LinkSummaryNak) (a) to aggregate multiple data links (ports or component links) into a TE link, (b) to exchange interface ids, (c) to indicate the type of link protection, such as shared (M:N), dedicated (1:1), dedicated (1+1), etc. and (d) to establish the local and remote TE link id.

The LinkSummary message contains data link TLVs, and therefore might be quite large.

LINK CONNECTIVITY VERIFICATION

LMP provides an option that may be used to verify the physical connectivity of the data-bearing links (either ports or component links). Recall that in an all-optical PXC, the data-bearing links are not terminated at the PXC, but instead are passed through the switch transparently. Therefore, to ensure proper verification of data link connectivity, LMP requires that until the links are allocated, they must be opaque; that is, the bytes in them must be available for examination. To support various degrees of opaqueness of the test messages, a verify transport mechanism is included in the BeginVerify and BeginVerifyAck messages.

To interconnect two nodes, a TE link is added between them, and, at a minimum, there is at least one active control channel between the nodes. A TE link must include at least one data link (else, why bother with the exercise? . . .). The next section provides a summary of Section 5 of [LANG01].

Once a control channel has been established between the two nodes, data link connectivity can be verified by exchanging test messages over each of the data links specified in the bundled link.

To initiate the link verification process, the local node sends a BeginVerify message over the control channel. The BeginVerify message contains the number of data links that are to be verified, the interval (the VerifyInterval field) at which the test messages will be sent, the encoding scheme, the transport mechanisms that are supported, and data rate for test messages. When data links correspond to fibers, the wavelength over which the test messages will be transmitted is also included.

The BeginVerify message is periodically transmitted until (a) node A receives either a BeginVerifyAck or BeginVerifyNack message to accept or reject the verify process or (b) a timeout expires and no BeginVerifyAck or BeginVerifyNack message has been received.

If the remote node receives a BeginVerify message and it is ready to process test messages, it sends a BeginVerifyAck message back to the local node specifying the desired transport mechanism for the test messages. The remote node includes a 32-bit node unique Verifyid in the BeginVerifyAck message. The Verifyid is then used in all corresponding test messages to differentiate them from different LMP peers and/or parallel test procedures.

When the local node receives a BeginVerifyAck message from the remote node, it may begin testing the data links by transmitting periodic test messages over each data link. The test message includes the Verify id and the local Interface id for the associated data link. The remote node then sends either a TestStatusSuccess or a TestStatusFailure message in response for each data link.

Message correlation is accomplished using message identifiers and the Verify id; this approach supports the parallel verification of data links belonging to different link bundles or LMP sessions.

When the test message is detected at a node, the received Interface id (used in GMPLS as either a Port id or Component Interface id, depending on the configuration) is recorded and mapped to the local Interface Id for that channel. The receipt of a TestStatusSuccess message indicates that the test message was detected at the remote node and the physical connectivity of the data link has been verified. The TestStatusSuccess message includes the local Interface id and the remote Interface id (received in the test message), along with the Verifyid received in the test message. When the TestStatusSuccess message is received, the local node marks the data link as UP, sends a TestStatusAck message to the remote node, and begins testing the next data link.

If the test message is not detected at the remote node within an observation period (specified by the VerifyDeadInterval field), the remote node will send a TestStatusFailure message over the control channel indicating that the verification of the physical connectivity of the data link has failed. When the local node receives a TestStatusFailure message, it will mark the data link as failed, send a TestStatusAck message to the remote node, and begin testing the next data link.

When all the data links on the list have been tested, the local node sends an EndVerify message to indicate that testing has been completed on this link. The EndVerify message is periodically transmitted until an EndVerifyAck message has been received.

Figure 11–4 shows an example of the link verification scenario that is executed when a link between PXC A and PXC B is added. The verification process is as follows:

- Event 1: PXC A sends a BeginVerify message over the control channel to PXC B, indicating that it will begin verifying the ports.
- Event 2: PXC B receives the BeginVerify message and returns the BeginVerifyAck message over the control channel to PXC A.
- Event 3: PXC A begins transmitting periodic test messages over the first port (Interface id=1).
- Event 4: PXC B receives the test messages and maps the received Interface id to its own local Interface id = 10.

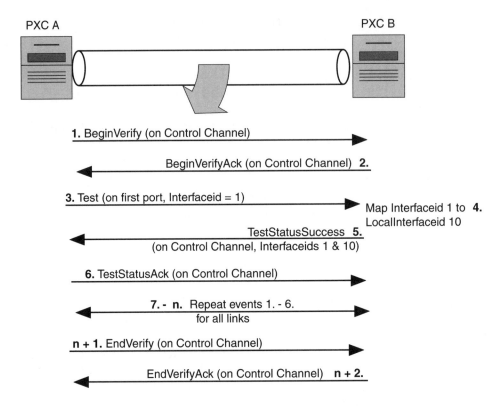

Figure 11–4   Verifying link connectivity.

- Event 5: PXC B transmits a TestStatusSuccess message over the control channel back to PXC A. The TestStatusSuccess message includes both the local and received Interface ids for the port.
- Event 6: PXC A sends a TestStatusAck message over the control channel back to PXC B, indicating that it received the TestStatus-Success message.
- Events 7 – n: The process is repeated until all of the ports are verified.
- Event n+1: Consequently, PXC A sends an EndVerify message over the control channel to PXC B to indicate that testing is complete.
- Event n + 2: PXC B responds by sending an EndVerifyAck message over the control channel back to PXC A.

FAULT MANAGEMENT

Fault isolation is used to localize failures in both opaque and transparent networks. In the situation where the nodes are O/O/O PXCs, the conventional layer 2 methods for link monitoring (framing, FCS checks, etc.) are not appropriate, and the fault detection must occur at layer 1 with the analysis of the light signals, such as the loss of light (LOL). When a failure is detected, the downstream node sends a ChannelFail message to the upstream node, which identifies all the failed component links and the associated ports.

In order to isolate the failure, the following procedures take place. An upstream node that receives the ChannelFail message will correlate the failure to see if there is a failure on the corresponding input and output ports. If there is also a failure on the input port(s) of the upstream node, the node will return a ChannelFailAck message to the downstream node (bundling together the notification of all the component links), indicating that it too has detected a failure. If, however, the fault is CLEAR in the upstream node (e.g., there is no LOL on the corresponding input channels), then the upstream node will have localized the failure and will return a ChannelFailNack message to the downstream node. Once the failure has been localized, the signaling protocols can be used to initiate span or path protection/restoration procedures.

Figure 11–5 shows three examples taken from Section 7.3 of [LANG01] of how fault isolation occurs. In scenario 1, there is a failure on a single component link between PXC2 and PXC3. Both PXC3 and PXC4 will detect the failure and each node will send a ChannelFail message to the corresponding upstream node (PXC3 will send a message to PXC2 and PXC4 will send a message to PXC3). When PXC3 receives the ChannelFail message from PXC4, it will correlate the failure and return a ChannelFailAck message back to PXC4. Upon receipt of the Channel FailAck message, PXC4 will move the associated ports into a standby state. When PXC2 receives the ChannelFail message from PXC3, it will correlate the failure, verify that it is CLEAR, localize the failure to the component link between PXC2 and PXC3, and send a ChannelFailNack message back to PXC3.

In scenario 2, three component links fail between PXC3 and PXC4. It is the job of PXC4 to correlate the failures and send a bundled ChannelFail message for the three failures to PXC3. In turn, PXC3 will correlate the failures, localize them to the channels between PXC3 and PXC4, and return a bundled ChannelFailNack message back to PXC4.

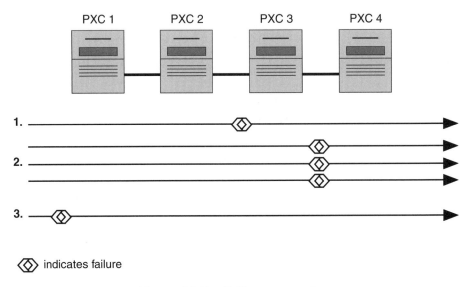

Figure 11–5   Failure scenarios.

In scenario 3, there is a failure on the tributary link of the ingress node (PXC1) to the network. Each downstream node will detect the failure on the corresponding input and send a ChannelFail message to the upstream neighboring node. When PXC2 receives the message from PXC3, it will correlate the ChannelFail message and return a ChannelFailAck message to PXC3 (PXC3 and PXC4 will also act accordingly). Since PXC1 is the ingress node to the optical network, it will correlate the failure and localize the failure to the component link between itself and the network element outside the optical network.

EXTENDING LMP OPERATIONS FOR OPTICAL LINK SYSTEMS (OLSS)

The focus of LMP is to manage the optical links between the optical switches, such as PXCs. The Internet standards groups have also recognized the need to manage links between the optical link systems (OLSs) that are installed between the switches and these OLSs. The revised editions of LMP do provide sufficient rules to implement link management at OLSs. This section of the chapter explains an extension to LMP to support OLSs and highlights the salient parts of [BROR01]. The situation is illustrated in Figure 11–6. As discussed thus far in this chapter, LMP

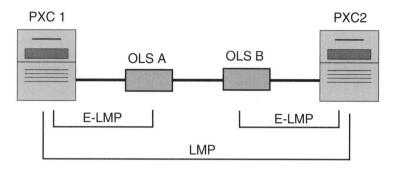

Figure 11–6   Extended LMP (E-LMP).

has been designed to operate between PXCs, or other types of optical switches. Extended LMP operates between the switch and the OLS.

The idea for extending LMP to the OLS is to use the information the OLS has on the activity on the links between the switches. Providing this information to the control plane via LMP can improve network usability by further reducing required manual configuration and also greatly enhancing fault detection and recovery. Even though the PXC is all-optical, long-haul OLSs may terminate channels electrically and regenerate them optically (although this situation will change), which presents an opportunity to monitor the health of a channel between PXCs.

However, extended LMP is not confined to the PXC/OLS operation. It can be applied to any optical link that exhibits opaqueness. I think the authors should retitle their IETF draft, because the limited title does not do justification to the specification.

Because extended LMP is based on LMP, the best approach is to refer to the major LMP functions discussed earlier in this chapter and look at how extended LMP uses them. You may want to refer back to the LMP material during this discussion.

- Control channel management: Extended LMP uses the same rules as LMP.
- Link verification: Extended LMP uses the same test procedures as LMP.
- Link summarization: Extended LMP defines additional TLVs and fields (this is explained later).
- Fault management: Extended LMP is the same as LMP, except that additional messages and procedures are defined (and explained later).
- Trace monitoring: This feature is new and is not defined in LMP.

Link Summarization

As noted, additional TLVs and fields are defined in extended LMP to provide more details about link characteristics. Following is a summary of this information:

- Link group id. Identifies a group of data links. It allows the sending of one message (instead of perhaps many) for each member of a group. For example, a link group can be created for each laser on a node or for each fiber. A failure to the laser and/or the fiber can affect many data links, and they can be identified with the link group id.
- Link descriptor. Specifies the minimum and maximum reservable bandwidth for a data link, and the encoding type for the link (SDH, SONET, etc.).
- Shared risk link group identifier (SRLG). This id is used to define the link's membership in a group of data links.
- Bit error rate (BER) estimate. Used to gauge the quality of the data link, such as 10^{12}, 10^{13}, and so on.
- Optical protection: Specifies how (if) the OLS protects the data link, with the schemes listed in Table 11–4.
- Span length: Explains the distance of the OLS fiber, expressed in meters.
- Administrative group (color): Specifies the administrative group (or color) to which the data link belongs.

Table 11–4   OLS Protection Schemes [ASHW01]

Enhanced:	A protection scheme that is more reliable than Dedicated 1+1 should be used, e.g., 4-fiber.
Dedicated 1+1:	A dedicated link layer protection scheme, i.e., 1+1 protection, should be used to support the LSP.
Dedicated 1:1:	A dedicated link layer protection scheme, i.e., 1:1 protection, should be used to support the LSP.
Shared:	Indicates that a shared link layer protection scheme, such as 1:N protection, should be used to support the LSP.
Unprotected:	The LSP should not use any link layer protection.
Extra Traffic:	The LSP should use links that are protecting other (primary) traffic. Such LSPs may be preempted when the links carrying the (primary) traffic being protected fail.

Fault Management

The overall fault management operations between LMP and extended LMP are similar. The main differences are that the OLS can initiate upstream and downstream testing, and it does not participate in end-to-end fault localization that LMP performs. Since OLS has more detailed information about an optical link, it can more concisely identify faults, say, of amplifiers on the optical span.

Extended LMP uses several ChannelStatus messages (requests, responses, Acks, Naks) on the control channel to report the status of the data link. It must be sent each time the status of a channel changes. The message contains a condition field that is coded to reveal the following condition of the data link:

- Signal OK: Data link is operational.
- Signal degrade: BER has exceeded a threshold, typically in the range of 10^{-5} to 10^{-9}.
- Signal fail: Indication of a SONET/SDH-defined hard failure, such as LOS, LOF, Line AIS, or a BIP exceeding a threshold.

Trace Monitoring

This extended LMP capability is used to request an OLS to monitor one or more data links for a specific event. It uses several TraceMonitor messages (requests responses, Acks, Naks) to define the type of trace and, of course, to respond to the request for the trace type. The trace types defined thus far are:

SONET section trace (J0 byte)
SONET path trace (J1 byte)
SDH section trace (J0 byte)
SDH path trace (J1 byte)

SUMMARY

Scores of link management protocols have been invented during the past few decades. All are concerned with managing the communications links between nodes such as servers, routers, and host computers. The LMP is yet another example of a link management protocol, and it is tailored to operate on and support optical links. It is capable of managing the link itself, as well as the wavelengths on the link.

Library Resource Center
Renton Technical College
3000 N.E. 4th St.
Renton, WA 98056

12

Optical Routers: Switching in Optical Internets

This chapter discusses how optical routers forward IP packets through the optical network. The term router is used in more than one context. It can be a conventional IP-based node, a label switching router (LSR), an O/E/O node, an O/O/O node, or a combination of any of these attributes. The specific role the router plays depends on its position and responsibility in the network, and this role will be identified as appropriate.

We also look at the relationships between a label switching path (LSP) and an optical switched path (OSP), the architecture of a Micro-Electro Mechanical System (MEMS), and the role of MPLS and optical cross-connect tables in switching and protection switching operations.

THE STATE OF THE ART IN OPTICAL SWITCHING

Parts of this chapter look to the future. First, optical switches are far from mature, and the demand for them at this time is limited. Second, 3rd generation transport internets using PXCs are not yet implemented. Third, work is not complete on specifications for IP, MPLS, and lambda control plane interworkings, not to mention that there are no implementations other than in labs. Nonetheless, this book is part of the series titled Advanced Communications Technologies, so, to that end, let's examine how the optical Internet can evolve with regard to switching operations.

ORDER OF PREFERENCES IN SWITCHING IMPLEMENTATIONS

Throughout this chapter, it will be a goal to resort to layer 1 switching, called lambda switching. Pure lambda switching is not yet possible unless the switched wavelength remains the same through the switch. As of the writing of this book, the prevalent photonic switch in the industry is opaque and must use transponders for O/E/O operations. However, we will see that this restriction need not preclude the use of O/O/O data plane operations for certain paths and traffic.

As a general guideline, the preferences (from least desirable to most desirable) are listed below, and the evolving networks will use combinations of these methods:

1. O/E/O with IP forwarding
2. O/E/O with label switching
3. O/E/O with λ switching (and wavelength conversion)
4. O/O/O with λ switching (and no wavelength conversion)

CLARIFICATION OF KEY TERMS

To make certain two key terms are understood, this part of the chapter re-emphasizes these terms:[1]

- Label switched path (LSP): The end-to-end path between two MPLS users, including all nodes and links that are on the path between these two users. An LSP segment between two adjacent nodes represents one physical path of the logical LSP. LSP segments are concatenated together to form the end-to-end LSP.
- Optical switched path (OSP): The node-to-node paths between the users of the optical link. The OSP is not an end-to-end path between the users; it exists only between two adjacent MPLS/optical nodes. The OSP begins at one node and terminates at a neighbor node that is directly adjacent to the originating node. It is the job of an MPLS-optical network to be able to concatenate each OSP segment to that of an MPLS segment, and, ultimately, to an

---

[1]A small point of calrification about these terms: Some literature uses the term switching instead of switched. Both terms are acceptable.

end-to-end LSP. In this chapter, we will see how this operation is accomplished.

- OSP cross-connect table: The literature on optical networks uses the terms wavelength forwarding information base (WFIB), switching fabric, and optical routing table to describe this component in an optical switch. I prefer OSP cross-connect table, since this term conveys the idea of correlating an input OSP to an output OSP.

ONE AFTERMATH OF SEPTEMBER 11: INCREASING LOAD ON THE TRANSPORT NETWORKS

It was noted in Chapter 1 that the transport backbone has more bandwidth than is currently needed. Nonetheless, most predictions state that Internet traffic alone will as least double by 2003. Other predictions are even higher.

In my view, there is no question that the tragic events of September 11, the Anthrax threats, and other likely future happenings will push even more mail and correspondence onto the Internet.

Our nation's physical infrastructures are porous and fragile; such are the underpinnings of an open society. But the telecommunications infrastructure is far more immune to electronic viruses than the other infrastructures' almost helpless defenses against biological and chemical attacks. It follows that organizations and individuals will move more to electronic mail and electronic commerce. This sudden event has not yet been absorbed by the industry (I am writing this passage shortly after the September 11 tragedy).

The point of my discussion here today is that it is even more important that the transport networks have the capacity and robustness to support what I believe will be a huge increase in electronic mail, faxes, legal documents, etc.

EVOLUTION OF SWITCHING TECHNOLOGIES

One of the areas of interest in high-speed networks is how fast these networks can relay traffic from node to node. Figure 12–1 provides a summary of the evolution of switching technologies. Since the inception of

	Circuit Switching	Message Switching	IP-based Packet Forwarding	Frame Relay (Switching)	Cell Relay (Switching)	Label Switching	Optical Switching
Relay Technique	Direct connect	Store & forward	Hold & forward	Hold & forward	Hold & forward	Hold & forward	Direct connect
Size of PDU	DS0	Variable, large to small	Variable, large to small	Variable, large to small	Fixed, very small	Variable, large to small	Variable, large
Delay	Very fast	Slow	Slow	Fast	Very fast	Very fast	Very, very fast
Supports	Voice	Data	Data	Data	Voice, video, data	Voice, video, data	Voice, video, data

Figure 12–1   Evolution of switching/routing systems.

circuit switching in telephone networks, there has been a migration away from some of the circuit-switching concepts, principally from the reliance on the fixed TDM DS0 channel. This migration led to message switching in the 1960s, packet switching in the 1970s, and frame and cell switching in the 1980s and 1990s. Most of these technologies (except cell relay) allow the protocol data unit (PDU)[2] to be of variable length. In addition, IP packet switching introduced the idea of a connectionless network, one in which there were no circuits set up (physical or virtual), and the packets were completely self-contained with a source and destination

---

[2]The term protocol data unit, or PDU, was invented by the ITU-T to describe any "piece" of traffic that is transmitted across a communications link. It can refer to any layer's traffic, thus it is a convenient (and generic) term.

address in each packet. This approach allowed networks to use adaptive, dynamic relaying techniques, with the result that traffic from one user session might take different paths through the network, and arrive out of order.

The attraction of circuit switching (its low delay) has come back into vogue, but its fixed-size unit has not. In addition, it is recognized that the use of IP destination-based forwarding, as well as dynamic routing (route discovery) is not a preferred approach for modern networks. Therefore, we see an evolution toward a synthesis of some of these forwarding and relaying technologies:

- Keeping the delay through the network as low as possible.
- Keeping jitter (variable and accumulated delay) consistent.
- Allowing the use of variable data units.
- Relying on MPLS label switching to replace IP destination-based routing.

But as suggested by the right-most entry in Figure 12–1, label switching is not the end of the story. The current label switching routers (LSRs) use electronics to make their switching decisions. While these machines are very fast, they suffer from the fact that they use the O/E/O processing introduced in Chapter 1. They must convert the optical signal to an electrical counterpart, make the switching decision with electronics (and software) and then convert the outgoing signal (and packet) back to an optical signal for transferral across the next optical fiber link.

THE SPEEDS OF ELECTRONICS AND PHOTONICS

The basic problem is that the performance (in speed) of photonics is outpacing electronics—the so-called electronic bottleneck. The optoelectronic conversions create too many delay points in the network. The solution is obvious. The O/E/O switch must be redesigned to be an O/O/O switch, also called a photonic switch, or a photonic cross-connect (PXC). A vast effort is underway in the industry to invent this technology, and another part of this chapter describes these emerging switches. But for now (and the current marketplace), let's take a look at the optical router, a machine that performs O/E/O operations.

AN OPTICAL ROUTER

Figure 12–2 shows a functional diagram of a router that is capable of processing optical packets [BLUM01]. The major functions of the router are:

- Demux and mux: Separates and combines wavelengths.
- Optical splitter: Sends copies of packet to control element and/or label eraser.
- Label eraser: Removes label header.
- Label writer: Places a new label on the packet.
- Wavelength converter: Places packet onto one of several wavelengths.
- Buffer: Holds packet until mux is ready to process it (work is underway to develop techniques to support this difficult requirement).
- Control element: Controls the operations of the label writer, the wavelength converter, and the buffer.

The Control Element

It is very difficult to build an all-optical logic circuit in which light controls light. Lab experiments have demonstrated that it is possible, but for the immediate future (the early part of this decade), the optical router will have some of its control elements made of electronics.

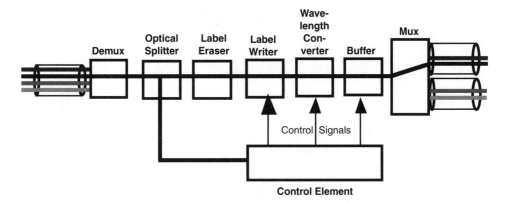

Figure 12–2   Functional view of the optical router [BLUM01].

Figure 12–3 shows two implementations of the control element in the router. The first relies on electronics. The incoming packet has some of its energy diverted to the control element. The photodetector converts the optical signal to an electronic signal and is processed by the control electronics. The incoming label in the packet header is matched to a routing table and an outgoing label is chosen. The control element instructs the switch as to which wavelength is to carry this packet. The payload is not processed by the control element; thus the optical-to-electronic conversion is performed on a very small set of bits (probably 20 bits, the size of an MPLS label).

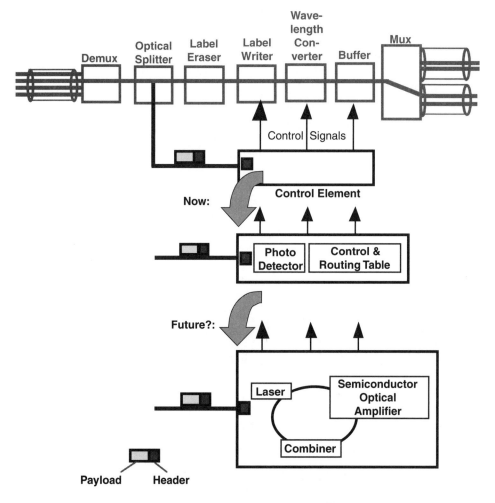

Figure 12–3   The control element [BLUM01].

The challenge (and problem) is the slow speed of electronics in relation to the amount of optical traffic that must be processed by the switch. It is recognized that the transfer of the packet from one fiber to another must eventually occur in less than one nanosecond. Several prototypes have been developed to deal with this problem. One such device is a semiconductor-amplifier, shown at the bottom of Figure 12–3. It forms a optical bridge between the appropriate input and output fibers. When the packet reaches the bridge, a control signal (an electric current) injects electrons and holes (absence of electrons) into the amplifier. When light enters the amplifier, it causes the holes and electrons to combine, giving off photons. These photons are the exact copy of the optical packet that is going to pass through the bridge. After reaching a certain power threshold, the signal moves from one side of the bridge to the other. Of course, the control of this system is with electrical signals, but the photonic packets need not be converted to electronic packets.

We continue the examination of the optical router by examining each of its other components in more detail. Figure 12–4 shows a packet arriving at the router on λ2. The packet is composed of the header, which contains the label, and the payload, which contains traffic (user traffic or control traffic).

The demux (demultiplexer) separates the wavelengths into different pathways, and the optical splitter sends the packet to the control element and the label eraser.

The demux and the optical splitter do not process the packet's contents. They simply send the packet, in its entirety, to the next components. Also, the packet at this point is still associated with a specific optical channel (in this example, the λ2 channel).

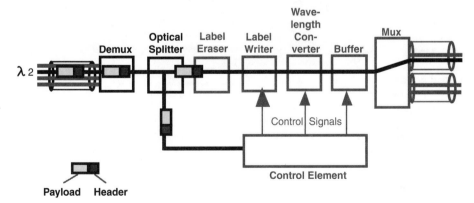

Figure 12–4 Operations at the demux and the optical splitter [BLUM01].

It was noted earlier that the control element controls the label writing operations. Figure 12–5 shows the operations of the label eraser and the label writer in conjunction with the control element. The label eraser (without interacting with the control element) removes the header from the packet, and the label writer inserts a new header. The header contains either an IP address or a label. (It would be very inefficient to use an address.)

The control element thus contains the label swapping information. This information has been loaded into the control element based on the execution of:

- IP address and discovery operations using OSPF, IS-IS, or BGP.
- Binding the discovered address to a label at this router, both for the incoming label and the outgoing label (the label that was inserted in Figure 12–5).

Again, under the direction of the control element, the wavelength converter sends the packet from one wavelength (λ2) to another (λ3), as depicted in Figure 12–6. Although not shown in this figure, the same operations are occurring with the other three input wavelengths.

Conceptually, the optical buffer holds a packet until the control element instructs it to send the packet to the output multiplexer. This

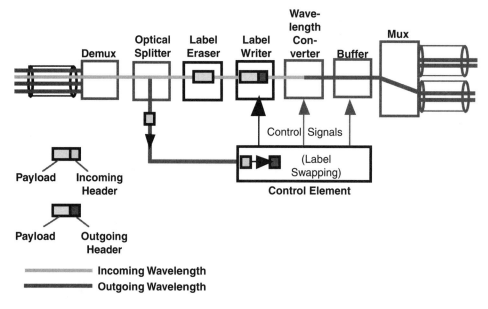

Figure 12–5   Operations of the label eraser and the label writer [BLUM01].

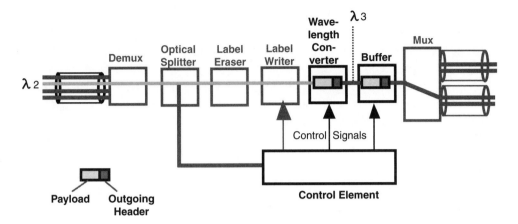

Figure 12–6   Operations at the wavelength converter and buffer.

operation is more easily described than implemented. An electronic buffer uses dynamic random-access memory (DRAM) to hold the packets until they are sent out onto the link. Photons cannot be stored like electrons. Therefore, an optical buffer may (a) "corral" the light pulses into a holding area (something like an automobile traffic circle), or (b) synchronize the time it takes to move the pulses through the switch to that of the processing time at the switch so that both end their respective movements and tasks at the same time.

The last operation at the optical router occurs at the output mux, shown in Figure 12–7. This element sends the packet on to the appropriate wavelength and the appropriate fiber.

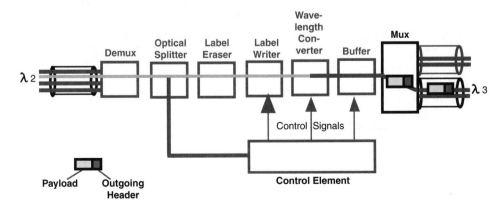

Figure 12–7   Operations at the output multiplexer.

OPTICAL SWITCHING TECHNOLOGIES

As noted earlier in this chapter, the volume of traffic in networks today, and the real-time requirements of this traffic, are creating a demand for an O/O/O (PXC) switch. The basic concept is simple: User traffic is modulated and multiplexed on to a wavelength, perhaps at the edge router of the network to an optical backbone network. Thereafter, the wavelength is transferred through the switch, dropped off, or imprinted onto a different wavelength, perhaps onto a different output fiber. At the terminating edge router (leaving the network), the wavelength is converted to electronics, and the user's traffic is taken through the conventional routing processes to deliver it to the final recipient. The next part of the chapter provides an overview of an emerging technique for optical switching [BISH01].

OPTICAL RESOURCES

For the remainder of this chapter, it is important to keep in mind that the deployment of optical networks that provision and perhaps switch high-capacity bandwidths (say OC-192) must be managed quite carefully. A single OC-192 link across a wide area is very expensive, and its efficient use and resilience is quite important. The nailing-up, switching, and tearing-down of these links can certainly be accomplished with a well-designed hardware and software platform (as will be demonstrated in the remainder of this book), but this platform must be applied judiciously.

As of this writing, it is too soon to know, but it seems likely that long-haul optical networks that integrate IP and MPLS will be designed to aggregate very large communities of users at major POPs (playing the role of ingress nodes to the long-haul backbone) into a small number of labels and wavelengths for transport across the backbone across wavelengths that tend to stay nailed up for a long time.

With these thoughts in mind, the next section examines optical switches.

MicroElectroMechanical Systems (MEMS)

MEMS is a technique used in the fabrication of the optical switch. It involves building a very small set of mirrors that are positioned to be illuminated by one or more wavelengths. In effect, the incoming wavelength is reflected by the mirror to an outgoing wavelength, as shown in Figure 12–8.

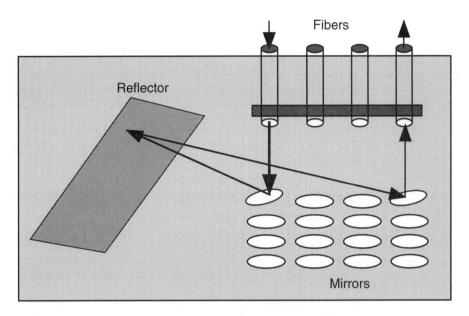

Figure 12–8   MEMS [BISH01].

The MEMS is constructed in a manner similar to the making of integrated circuits by using photolithographic and etching operations. However, in place of transistors, the lithographic process builds very small devices that move (tilt) when directed by an electric current. In effect, these devices are tiny mirrors about .5 millimeter in diameter (about the size of a pin head). The mirror is illuminated by the optic wavelengths coming from a fiber. Based on how the mirror is tilted, the wavelength can be reflected from N input fibers to M output fibers. The tilting of the mirrors is controlled by software.

One manufacturer of a MEMS switch has 256 mirrors deposited on a 2.5 centimeter-square piece of silicon. The mirrors are one millimeter apart, which translates into a switch that is 32 times more dense than an electronic switch. The switch performs a complete switching operation in a few milliseconds. Moreover, since the optoelectronic conversion is not needed, the MEMS switch provides up to a 100-fold reduction in power needs.

In an extraordinary example of the versatility and power of silicon-based technology, the MEMS technology takes advantage of how amino acids arrange themselves into three-dimensional shapes. During the final stages of the fabrication process, small springs on the surface of the silicon lift each mirror above the silicon surface to allow them to move (tilt), all under the control of software.

[BISH01] describes Lucent's LambdaRouter, the first large-scale MEMS switch announced in the industry. It operates at 10 terabits-per-second speed, which is almost 10 times the traffic sent over the most heavily used link of the Internet. This switch is a 256 X 256 device (256 input channels and 256 output channels). Each channel supports speeds of 320 Gbit/s.

Controlling the Mirrors with GMPLS.   Ideally, a network operator would like to control the mirrors in order to affect the routing of traffic though an O/O/O PXC. One method being considered in the industry to accomplish this feature is to use GMPLS at the optical control plane to configure the PXC's hardware. This idea is called suggested labels and is shown in Figure 12–9 with the following events:

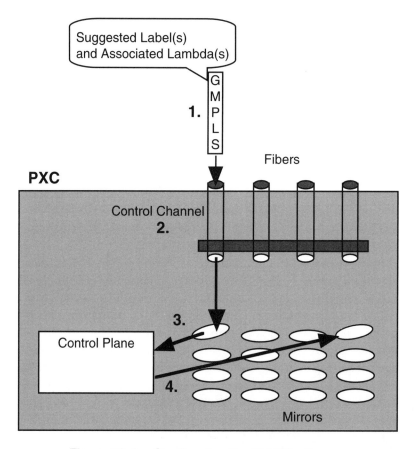

Figure 12–9   Configuring the MEMS mirrors.

- Event 1: The GMPLS message contains a suggested label for one or more wavelengths.
- Event 2: This message arrives over a designated control channel, as established with the Link Management Protocol (Chapter 11).
- Event 3: The message is sent to the control plane where software acts on the GMPLS information (such as assigning a label to a wavelength).
- Event 4: The PXC is configured with the control plane altering a mirror to change its reflecting angle, and thus its output characteristics, say, to another fiber.

You might be wondering why the term "suggested label" is used. As a general rule, MPLS stipulates that the downstream node is to specify the label. In this example, the PXC is indeed a downstream node, but it is accepting a label suggested by the upstream node (not shown in the figure). GMPLS recognizes that the suggested label by the upstream PXC allows the upstream PXC to begin its configuration as soon as it sends the suggested label to the downstream node. In this manner, the upstream node can begin early configuration of its hardware to reduce configuration delays. However, in keeping with the basic MPLS approach, if the downstream PXC passes a different label to this peer upstream node, the upstream node must use it.

If you would like to read more about MEMS, both its potential and its problems, I recommend [FERN00].

PROTECTING THE LABEL SWITCHED PATH

In the event that a link or node fails, a robust network must provide protection to the customer's traffic that is traversing the part of the network that encounters problems. We introduced this idea in Chapter 8. In this section, we extend the information in Chapter 8 with examples of how a partnership between MPLS and an optical switch can help protect the user's payloads. The analysis begins with a typical MPLS protection scenario.

MPLS supports the concept of protection switching and backup routes. An MPLS network can be set up to assure that a link for node failure will not create a situation where the user traffic is not delivered. Figure 12–10 shows the operations to recover from a failure.

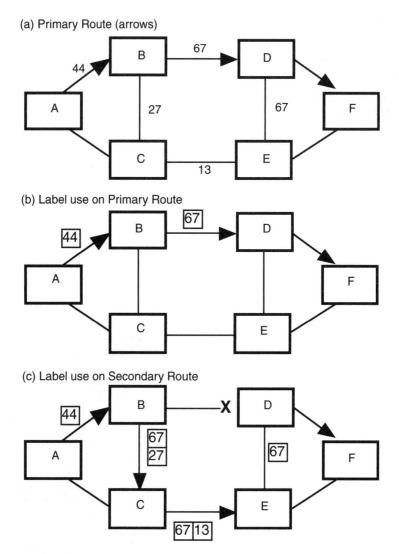

Figure 12–10   MPLS protection switching and backup routing.

In Figure 12–10 (a), the traffic is forwarded across the primary LSP from LSR A to LSR F, through LSRs B and D. The other labels shown in Figure 12–10 (a) are the labels for the backup path, and they will be explained shortly.

As shown in Figure 12–10 (b), labels 44 and 67 are used for this LSP, and at LSR D, a label pop terminates the MPLS tunnel.

In Figure 12–10 (c), the link between LSR B and D fails, or perhaps node D goes down. LSR B detects this failure (by not receiving an acknowledgment to its Hello messages from LSR D). By prior arrangement (by using, say, OSPF), LSR B knows the backup path for this LSP is to LSR C, and that the label for this part of the tunnel is 27. LSR B is configured to push label 67 into the stack behind label 27. Recall that label 67 was to be used at LSR D.

A label swap occurs at LSR C (13 for 27). Label 67 is not examined, since it is not at the top of the stack. At LSR E, label 13 is popped, leaving label 67 as the only label that arrives at LSR D. LSR D is configured to know that this label is associated with the same LSP as the one with the same label number emanating from LSR B. Thus, the LSP is protected by configuring alternate paths through the MPLS network.

PROTECTION OF THE OPTICAL SWITCHED PATH (OSP)

In order to take advantage of the speed and efficiency of optical switching, as well as the traffic engineering aspects of MPLS, it is possible to correlate the MPLS label with the optical channel, specifically a wavelength on the fiber. Using the previous example, Figure 12–11 shows how node B performs the correlation. One entry in node B's LSP cross-connect table has been provisioned for label 44 on interface c. The primary path

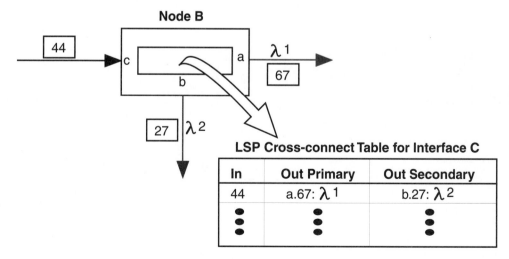

LSP Cross-connect Table for Interface C

In	Out Primary	Out Secondary
44	a.67: $\lambda 1$	b.27: $\lambda 2$

Figure 12–11   Correlating MPLS labels and optical wavelengths: The O/E/O OXC.

out of the node is through interface a. The label value of 44 is mapped to label 67 for this interface. The traffic associated with label 44 (as well as the label header of 67) is then placed on λ1 at interface a for transmission to the next node. The secondary (backup) route has also been set up, with a mapping of label 44 to label 27, and a cross-connect to λ2 on interface b. Similar cross-connect tables are configured for all the optical nodes that are part of the LSP.

The example in Figure 12–11 represents an O/E/O optical/electrical cross-connect (OXC), probably situated as an edge router to a routing domain (the ingress node to a backbone optical network). The optical signals are converted to electrical signals in order to execute hardware and software in the node for making the cross-connect and mapping decisions. Obviously, the O/E/O operations must take place at some of the nodes in the network, but it is desirable to avoid the signal conversions.

The next example in Figure 12–12 shows how a O/E/O cross-connect operating in the core (in the backbone) of the optical network would handle a relaying operation.

In this operation, node B is playing the role of an O/E/O XC but does not examine the bits on the wavelength. Instead, the wavelengths themselves provide the information to make a cross-connect switching decision. The optical switch is configured to reflect *and convert* incoming λ3

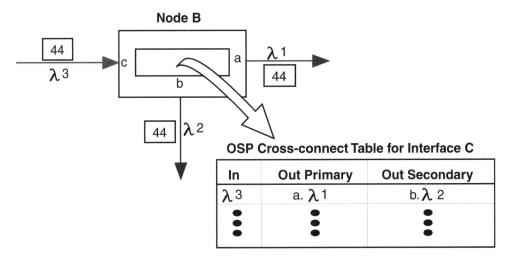

Figure 12–12   The O/E/O OXC.

on interface c to either $\lambda 1$ on interface a, or $\lambda 2$ on interface b. The conversion (at this stage of the practice) requires electrical intervention.

Thus, the optical cross-connect table is configured to support an optical switching path (OSP). Recall that the OSP is the optical path between two adjacent nodes.

Figure 12–13 shows the switch operating as an O/O/O node. Two aspects of this node are of interest here: (a) MPLS labels are passed transparently through the node and (b) the same wavelengths are used on the three interfaces. For this scenario, the physical signal is amplified and reflected through the amplification and switching components, perhaps with a MEMS architecture.

Obviously, this operation is the fastest of the systems examined in this section of the chapter. However, there are restrictions on how many O/O/O spans the optical signal can traverse. Recall from Chapter 3 that the network designer must be concerned with the ASE, PMD, crosstalk, and chromatic dispersion performance of the link and link nodes.

Also, Figure 12–13 shows the operations taking place with use a "table." The operations can be performed in amplifiers and MEMS components; the table is for illustrative purposes.

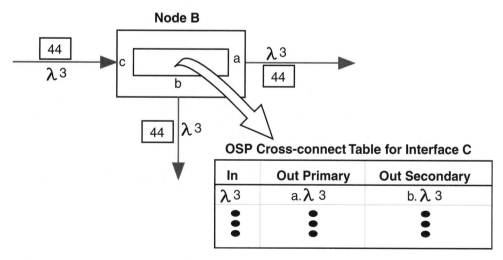

Figure 12–13 The O/O/O PXC.

CORRELATING THE WAVELENGTH OSP WITH THE MPLS LSP

Mapping a label to a wavelength at an optical node is not a difficult technical job, and photonic switching is now viewed as not only feasible, but also desirable. The task for this part of the chapter is to resolve how an optical node can exploit the traffic engineering capabilities of MPLS, as well as the fast switching capabilities of photonic switching. In explaining one approach to this issue, keep in mind that I am offering my own views on the matter, and, in some aspects, they may differ from some of my clients' views. With others we are in agreement. I welcome your views as well, since the issues in this matter are not yet settled.

Figure 12–14 illustrates a simple topology of four XCs. They are capable of both O/E/O and O/O/O operations. The central idea is to use an O/E/O control plane to set up both the wavelength OSPs and the MPLS LSPs, then execute an O/O/O data plane to relay the traffic through the interior XCs in the core part of the network for nodes that use the same λ on the end-to-end lightpath, and an O/E/O data plane for nodes using different wavelengths.

Three subchannels (wavelengths) will be set up between the four nodes, named G, H, I, and J. The wavelengths are λ1, λ2, and λ4. The three wavelengths between the nodes represent four OSPs; two of the OSPs use the same wavelength (λ1). Furthermore, two MPLS LSPs are set up between nodes H and J. Since MPLS allows label binding between

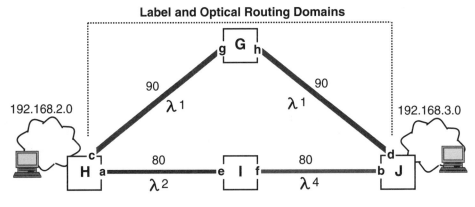

LSP 80: H and J, through I
LSP 90: H and J, through G

Figure 12–14   Optical switching paths (OSPs) and label switching paths (LSPs).

nonadjacent nodes, it is not necessary for nodes G and I to participate in the MPLS label binding operations between nodes H and J. Certainly, nodes G and I must pass the binding messages back and forth between H and J. But that is the point: Nodes G and I are pass-through nodes with regards to label distribution and binding.

Nodes H and J are designated as edge routers for this switching domain. In this role, they must be capable of executing both the MPLS and optical control and data planes. Furthermore, they must be able to map IP addresses to MPLS labels.

Nodes G and I are core routers. In this example, these nodes do not become involved in the MPLS data plane. Their main job is to perform photonic switching using the OSP cross-connect table.

Prior to the OSP and LSP operations, a routing protocol such as OSPF has been used to inform node H that IP address 192.168.3.0 can be reached through node I. When a user at network 192.168.2.0 sends traffic to the user at address 192.168.3.0, the four nodes use the data (forwarding) plane to relay the traffic. In order to accomplish this transfer, the operations take place as described in the next section.

Setting up the OSPs and LSPs Between Nodes H, I, and J

The following events can occur between nodes H, I and J to set up optical switching paths between nodes H, I, and J, and label switching paths between nodes H and J. These events do not have to occur in the exact order described here. For example, event 2 can precede event 1.

- Event 1: Node H knows it can reach node J (and 192.168.3.0) via node I because of IS-IS, OSPF, or BGP. (Note: Node H must have the complete topology map of the other nodes.)
- Event 2. Node I sets up its OSP cross-connect table to correlate (map) λ2 on interface e and λ4 on interface f to node H and node J, respectively.
- Event 3: Node I uses GMPLS, LMP or some other optical control plane protocol to configure λ2 and λ4 between nodes H and J, respectively. Consequently, node H knows it can reach node I on λ2 at interface a. Node H does not care (or know) about the OSP relationship of interface f, λ4 that node I has with node J.
- Event 4: Nodes H and J bind label 80 for all traffic with address 192.168.3.0 between them on their respective interfaces of a and b. This operation may begin at Node J because it is the downstream node (the next hop) to address 192.168.3.0. Node I merely acts

as a pass-through node for this label distribution and binding operation; it does not build an entry in its LSP cross-connect table. Therefore, label 80 is not processed by node I. Let's assume label 80 is associated with a certain class of service (say, delay) as well as with 192.168.3.0. Therefore, node H knows that any traffic that is destined for 192.168.3.0 can be sent out to node I on λ2 at interface a. Node J knows that a packet arriving on λ4 via interface b is intended for 192.168.3.0. Of course, node J must be O/E/O-capable, and convert the λ4 optical signal to an electrical signal so that it can examine and process the label. Likewise, node I is performing O/E/O operations as it converts λ2 to λ4.

- Note: Node I can certainly participate at the label level and be part of the LSP. This example keeps node I away from LSP management.

- Event 5: Thereafter, when node H receives a IP datagram destined for 192.168.3.0, it knows (due to say OSPF) that this address is reachable via node I. It also knows node I is reachable via interface a on λ2. Because of event 4, it appends label 80 to the IP traffic and sends the packet to node I.

- Event 6: Node I does not care about the MPLS label. Any traffic coming in from interface e or λ2, is switched to output interface f on λ4. Thus, this core router has performed only λ data plane operations, with O/E/O operations.

- Event 7: As the edge router to this domain, node J receives the packet via interface b on λ4. It converts the optical signal to an electrical signal and examines label 80, which reveals that node J is the end of the MPLS label switching path. Therefore, it removes (pops) label 80 and passes the IP datagram to the conventional layer 3 forwarding process for IP address look-up and final forwarding to 192.168.3.0.

Setting Up a Protection Path Between Nodes H, G, and J

In order to establish a protection (backup) path between the two edge routers, nodes H and J, similar events just described take place between H and J, and from a different core router, node G:

- Event 1: Node H has a full topology map of the other nodes and knows it can also reach node J (and 192.168.3.0) via node G.
- Event 2. Node G sets up its OSP cross-connect table to correlate (map) λ1 on interface g and λ1 on interface h to nodes H and J,

respectively. Thus, this LSP can use O/O/O lambda switching end-to-end.

- Event 3: Node G uses GMPLS, LMP or some other optical control plane protocol to configure λ1 between node H and node J. Therefore, node H knows it can reach node G on λ1 at interface c. Node H does not care (or know) about the OSP relationship of λ1 that node G has with node J.

- Event 4: Nodes H and J bind label 90 for all traffic with address 192.168.3.0 between them on their respective interfaces of c and d. Node G merely acts as a pass-through node for this label distribution and binding operation; it does not build an entry in its LSP cross-connect table. Let's assume label 90 is the exact same forwarding equivalence class as label 80. Therefore, node H knows that any traffic that is destined for 192.168.3.0 can also be sent out to node G on λ1 at interface c. However, this LSP is used as a protection path. The LSP represented by label 80 is the working (primary) path. As before, node J is configured to process labels, so it can terminate the LSP tunnel and pass the IP traffic to the user.

- Event 5: Thereafter, when node H receives an IP datagram destined for 192.168.3.0, it knows (due to, say, OSPF) that this address is reachable via node G, but node I is the primary node. It will not use the protection path unless the working path fails, or unless the network provider chooses to configure the system to use the backup path of load-leveling of traffic, or other network-specific functions.

In this example, node G has assumed the role of a pure O/O/O PXC, and no wavelength conversions are performed for this LSP.

Recovery and Use of Protection Path

For the next example, node I continues its role of a lambda cross-connect. The entry in its OSP cross-connect table correlates λ2 on interface e to λ4 on interface f. Again, node I (and G as well) is not concerned with MPLS label analysis, which would require label operations.

In the event that problems occur on the interfaces/links on the primary (working) path, the following events occur:

- Event 1: Node H discovers that the OSP between node H and node I is down by not receiving a control message (say, an LMP hello message, explained in Chapter 11) from node I within a set time. Alternately, node H could fail to receive a hello for the MPLS control plane via the Label Distribution Protocol (LMP), assuming Node I is running the MPLS control plane (which it is not in this example).

- Note: Of course, if an alternate wavelength or fiber in the link set between nodes H and I is available, then recovery can be made without resorting to protection switching to node G.
- Event 2: Node H consults its IP forwarding table (or better, its MPLS label forwarding table), and ascertains that 192.168.3.0 can be reached via a backup through node G. Due to previous label binding operations between nodes H and J, node H knows to append label 90 to the IP packet. Of course, node H also knows that $\lambda 1$ on interface c must be used for this backup LSP and OSP.
- Event 3: Node G receives the traffic. Just like node I for the primary path, node G does not care about the MPLS label. Any traffic coming in from interface g on $\lambda 1$ is switched to output interface h on $\lambda 1$. Unlike node I in the previous example, this core router has performed only O/O/O operations.
- Event 4: As the egress router to this domain, node J receives the packet via interface d on $\lambda 1$. It converts the optical signal to an electrical signal and examines label 90, which reveals that node J is the end of the MPLS label switching path. Therefore, it removes (pops) label 90, and passes the IP datagram to the conventional layer 3 forwarding process for IP address look-up and final forwarding to 192.168.3.0.

Expanding the Roles of Nodes G and I

This example kept nodes G and I isolated from the MPLS operations. As noted, the nodes do not need to be so constrained. They could participate in the label binding operations with nodes H and J. Like nodes H and J in the previous examples, Nodes G and I could use an optical control channel to detect problems, and resort to label and/or optical protection switching to recover.

However, if this expanded role is implemented, nodes G and I must be able to swap labels as part of the MPLS label switching operation. Thus, the role expansion places nodes G and I back into the job of being MPLS switches. Because of this restriction, my examples have confined the core routers' role to the optical data and control planes.

Also, by restricting core nodes to the optical plane, nodes G and I have less processing overhead than the nodes at the edge of the routing domain; that is, routers H and J.

NESTING THE LSPS AND OSPS

We have discussed the idea of confining the core nodes to the optical planes. Another example should help explain this concept. Figure 12–15 shows a network topology with an additional node in the backbone, router K. The figure also shows that two routing domains exist (they also existed in Figure 12–14, but are not as well-bounded as in Figure 12–15). Nodes H and J are edge routers, and nodes I, G, and K are core routers.

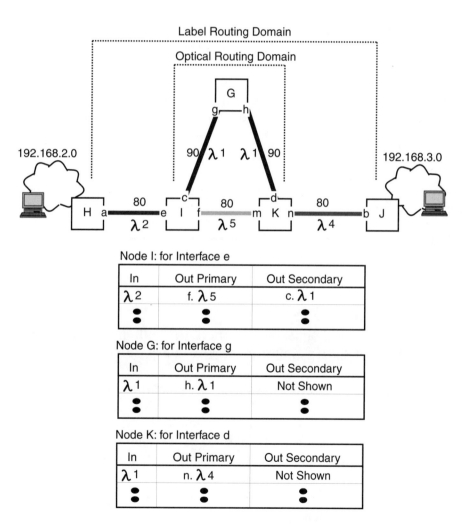

Node I: for Interface e

In	Out Primary	Out Secondary
$\lambda 2$	f. $\lambda 5$	c. $\lambda 1$
⋮	⋮	⋮

Node G: for Interface g

In	Out Primary	Out Secondary
$\lambda 1$	h. $\lambda 1$	Not Shown
⋮	⋮	⋮

Node K: for Interface d

In	Out Primary	Out Secondary
$\lambda 1$	n. $\lambda 4$	Not Shown
⋮	⋮	⋮

Figure 12–15   Nesting the routing domains.

The optical routing domain is nested within the label routing domain. The nesting approach means that nodes G, I, and K are not involved in label operations for ongoing payload, as suggested by the optical cross-connect tables shown at the bottom of Figure 12–15. It is the job of nodes H and J to correlate labels to the wavelengths associated with the optical routing domain. In this manner, the operations proceed as in previous examples, except that the error recovery is moved to the optical domain, and nodes H and J are no longer involved in error detection.

The relationships are as follows: (a) LSP 80 uses O/E/O for the OSPs at nodes I and K, and (b) LSP 90 uses O/O/O for the OSPs at node G.

There is one remaining problem with this scenario. The example in Figure 12–15 shows only one path to/from the optical backbone for nodes H and J. Consequently, if the links from these nodes to the network fail, the customers at nodes H and J are denied service. If up time and robustness are of paramount importance, then nodes H and J must be outfitted with alternate links to other core nodes, say, node G. This arrangement puts us back to the topology in Figure 12–14. The important point here is that the users sitting behind nodes H and J may not need 100% availability, and they may be willing to accept occasional downtime for a less-expensive configuration

To conclude the discussion of label and optical switching paths, let's assume the link between nodes I and K fails in Figure 12–15, and therefore, $\lambda 5$ is not available to convey the user payload between these two nodes. The following events take place to recover from this failure:

- Event 1: Node I does not receive acknowledgments to its LMP hello messages that it sent to node K on the optical control channel on interface f.

- Event 2: Node I times-out on the LMP hello procedure with node K, and consults its optical cross-connect table for a protection path.

- Event 3: Node I determines that the secondary (protection) path is $\lambda 1$ on interface c. It reconfigures the MEMS mirrors to (literally) reflect this observation. The traffic is diverted to node G. This operation also requires OEO $\lambda 2$ to $\lambda 1$ conversion.

- Event 3: Node G performs its ongoing optical cross-connect O/O/O operation.

- Event 4: So does node K with O/E/O operations, which also results in the traffic reaching node J, where the operations previously explained take place.

TOPOLOGY CHOICES FOR A NODE FAILURE

Thus far, the examples have focused on failures of optical links, with the optical nodes still up and running. In the event of failure of a node, the recovery scenario is more complex, and more expensive to implement. Nonetheless, it might be necessary, in the optical network core, to use BLSRs, BPSRs, or semi-meshed topologies discussed in Chapter 8. Whatever the topology may be, it is still desirable to keep the core nodes isolated from the upper layer MPLS label operations.

PLANE COUPLING AND DE-COUPLING

Notice that my explanations of the planes' interworkings show that the three data planes (IP, MPLS, and λ) are not coupled together. That is, a router can perform forwarding operations in a data plane without regard to the operations occurring in another data plane. But the control planes are coupled together.

As an example, an incoming IP datagram can be forwarded using the conventional IP routing table created by OSPF, IS-IS, or BGP. Alternatively, the datagram's destination address prefix can be mapped to an MPLS label by the IP and MPLS control planes' interactions. But thereafter, the labeled packet is processed only by the MPLS data plane. Likewise, the MPLS and λ control planes can interact to set up a relationship between labels and the OSP cross-connect table. Thereafter, wavelengths are processed only by the optical control plane, and the MPLS and IP headers are not examined.

Notice also that control plane interworking is needed to set up LSP and OSP protection paths. But once the protection paths are configured, protection switching can be performed at the optical level, without executing MPLS or IP operations.

Whether or not this approach will work is dependent upon how frequently control planes must be invoked. If LSPs and OSPs must be set up and torn down frequently, the resulting overhead will affect overall network performance. But this situation is a problem in any network that provides dynamic services and adaptive responses to customer requirements. Even with frequent control plane instantiations, keeping the core/backbone nodes focused on lambda switching and pushing IP/MPLS/λ control plane interactions to the edge routers should help considerably in ameliorating the overhead problem.

SOME END-TO-END WAVELENGTHS AND SOME NODE-TO-NODE WAVELENGTHS

A reasonable approach in implementing MPLS and optical planes is to try to set up end-to-end LSPs using the same wavelength. I am certain this possibility exists in large networks with large user populations; it is just like a leased line circuit, with the digital cross-connect fabric set up and remaining static. For those applications that do not fit a fixed, static profile, GMPLS can be used to try to allocate compatible wavelengths, and, if unsuccessful, to confine the core switches to a fast lambda conversion routine, but not label processing.

Some papers state that (eventually) wavelength conversion performed with tunable devices will perform at sufficient speeds to make the issue of wavelength conversion a moot point. Perhaps so, but in the meantime, a conservative and prudent apprach to MPLS label and lambda interworking is a cornerstone to an effective 3rd generation optical Internet.

GRANULARITY OF LABELS VS. WAVELENGTH SUPPORT

Regardless of the pros and cons of building systems that integrate the features of MPLS with the optical capabilities, the issue of label granularity must be carefully weighed against the number of wavelengths to support/transport each label.

To explain this important point, consider Figure 12–16. Node H is connected to node I with one fiber link set, and node I is connected to nodes G and K with one fiber link set to each node. Node H needs to send labeled packets to both nodes G and K. If node I is to perform photonic switching, node H cannot send MPLS packets destined for nodes G and H to node I on the same wavelength. If this situation does occur, node I must resort to O/E/O operations, convert the optical signal to an electrical signal, interpret the label value, make a switching decision, and convert the electrical signal back to an optical signal for transport to either node G or K.

Therefore, for an optical internet that operates with all three control planes (IP, MPLS, and λ) to be effective, the following situations should exist:

- There should be an ability to aggregate many IP address prefixes at the ingress node for O/O/O transport to the egress node. That is, the LSP and the associated wavelength should not change through the backbone network (and with some exceptions, the user-to-user LSP tunnel should extend through the network anyway).

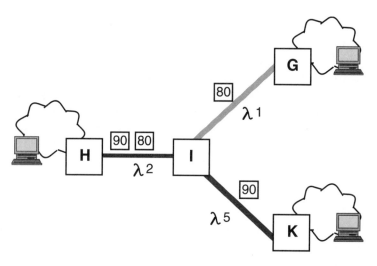

Figure 12–16   Label and wavelength granularity.

- Core nodes in the backbone can execute the O/E/O control planes to set up and correlate TE MPLS LSPs with the OSP cross-connect tables, and thereafter use the O/O/O data plane for ongoing traffic transfer.
- The interior nodes can use O/O/O-oriented λ protection switching, as described in this chapter, or, in the event of a problem, a node can resort to O/E/O control plane operations to reconstruct both the LSP and contributing OSPs.
- If the optical nodes and links are of high quality (and downtime is rare), the frequency of executions of the O/E/O-oriented control planes to allow core nodes to recover from occasional problems should not place an undue burden on the resources of the network.
- Notwithstanding these points, IP address aggregation is important to both the LSPs and the OSPs.

APPROACH TO THE PROBLEM OF LSP AND OSP INTERWORKING

In conclusion, at this early stage in the evolution of 3rd generation transport networks, one of the big challenges is to be able to keep the backbone confined to O/O/O operations most of the time, push the O/E/O operations of IP, MPLS, λ mapping to the ingress and egress nodes, and try to aggregate as many IP address prefixes into as few labels as possible.

Opponents of this approach will surely state that this gross aggregation approach will work against the important issue of supporting (and charging for) tailored QOS for each user (or a small subset of a community of users). After all, aggregating multiple users to one label with different QOS needs defeats one of the goals of a 3rd generation transport network: providing tailored QOS for individual users.

I do not hold this view. When the optical network has evolved to a multi-terabit transport system, the core network's performance will be such a high capacity that a node will not have the time to tailor its behavior to meet each user's performance requirements. Nor should it have to do so; the network will be operating at such a high bit rate and providing such low delay, that the issue of QOS support will be addressed only at the edge nodes of the network, those that provide ingress and egress for the customers' traffic.

Then why even bother with QOS provisioning and monitoring at the user-network interface (UNI) to and from the edge nodes? If the network is so all-powerful, why not just eliminate the time-consuming QOS and traffic policing functions?

The answer is two-fold. First, QOS and traffic policing remain essential in order for the network provider to charge for its services, and to regulate traffic at the (probable) bandwidth-constrained UNI. Second, the idea of a transport network that has all the capacity it needs is still just that: an idea.

From the standpoint of the optical fiber itself: Yes, it is known that enough cable can be laid to support any foreseeable demand. The ultimate challenge is to also design the optical nodes *and* the many servers and routers in the backbone to operate at a capacity in consonance with optical fiber. We return to this critical issue at the end of this book.

MEMS AND OPTICAL SWITCHING RE-EXAMINED

The optical switch technology is far from mature, and the interworking of IP, MPLS, and wavelengths is in its infancy. But, as noted in the preface to this book, we are looking forward to what might evolve in 3G transport networks and optical Internets. For all these wonderful IP, MPLS, and wavelength networks to come into being, MEMS and other optical switching technologies must be improved considerably, both in speed and reliability. But most people in the industry think the scenarios described in this chapter will be in existence in a few years. We must wait and see.

For a review of the state of optical switches and MEMS, I recommend [FULL01] as follow-up reading.

THERMO-OPTIC SWITCHES

There are other optical switches under development. The MEMS has gained favor and therefore has been highlighted in this chapter. However, as of this writing, it is not clear whether or not the optical switches are going to need switching matrices that support thousands of ports. It appears the MEMS technology is being pushed into the future, and very large photonic cross-connects have not reached a point of high demand.

Anyway, we shall wait to see what happens in the marketplace. For now, another optical switch that is being developed is the thermo-optical switch, also called a photonic waveguide. It is also built from silicon, and, like MEMS, it is very small. Its operation is shown in Figure 12–17. The light wave enters the switch at a splitter, which splits the beam and sends both copies down the waveguides. One of the pipes has its temperature changed by heating an electrical resistor. This heating changes the length of the waveguide, which results in the changing of the phase of the light passing through it. The two wavelengths reconverge at a coupler, which is capable of switching (or not switching) the waveguides onto an output port. In the example in Figure 12–17, wavelength 2 is switched onto output port 2, but wavelength 1 is not passed out of the switch.

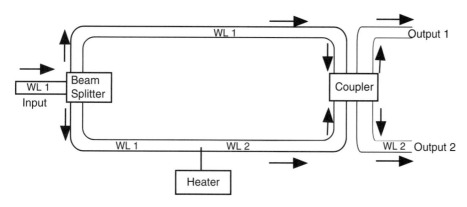

Figure 12–17   Thermo-optic switches.

Bubble Switches

Another optical switch fabric is the bubble switch, which is a very small bubble of fluid whose refraction index is the same as silica. This example also uses inkjet printer technology and is being developed by Agilent. The switching of the lightwave takes place if a bubble is in a fill hole. The fill hole can be filled with the refraction material dynamically, causing the light to bend and be transferred to another waveguide. If the fill hole is empty, the light continues through the original waveguide.

SUMMARY

The emerging third generation transport network will be capable of photonic switching, although O/O/O nodes are just now in the stages of development. The 3G transport systems will interwork the IP, MPLS, and λ control planes. The scenarios presented in this chapter represent one method of control plane interworking to support network switching requirements, and I expect the IETF working groups will soon publish their views on this important operation.

Whatever the specific method chosen, MPλS will require interactions between the MPLS and λ control planes. It is the data planes that should remain as loosely coupled as possible. I have presented such a scenario in this chapter.

13

ASON Operations at the User Network Interface (UNI) and the Network-to-Network Interface (NNI)

This chapter describes the emerging Internet specifications on the automatic switched optical network (ASON) operations at the UNI and NNI. These are important blueprints, for they establish rules for the interactions of user nodes, edge nodes, and interior nodes as they communicate with each other. The focus in this chapter is three-fold, and, of course, is related to information in other chapters: (a) managing bandwidth and providing bandwidth on demand, (b) rules for UNI interactions, and (c) rules for NNI interactions.

The material in this chapter is also related to some topics in Chapter 10 (see "Two General Models"). Also, be aware that NNI also means Network Node Interface.

OBJECTIVES OF THE ASON

The IETF has defined the following objectives for an ASON:

- Use of a standardized optical network control plane in order to achieve interoperability among the different vendor products.
- Ability to support rapid and automatic end-to-end provisioning of services within the network.

- On an individual service path basis, provide (if necessary) dynamic routing, restoration, usage-based accounting, policy-based quality of service features, and billing based on services rendered.
- Insofar as possible, keep one vendor's upgrade (vendor A) of the control plane transparent to another vendor (vendor B). This objective means that a control plane version upgrade should not have to be patched to all vendor systems in a multivendor network in order for vendor A's customers to obtain the benefit of the upgrade.
- Provide adequate security protection of the optical layer, particularly the control plane. Adequate security assumes that the service path can traverse multiple networks (e.g., different network administrations [domains]), and across NNIs, and receive proper and correct security services end to end. So, a domain assumes that its traffic is safe when the traffic traverses another domain.

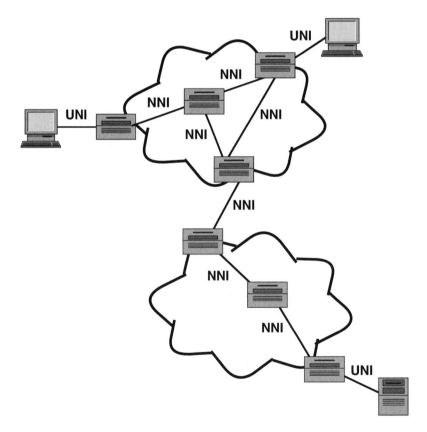

Figure 13–1   The UNI and the NNI.

- Allow the network service provider to control the usage of its network resources, giving the provider the ability to ensure mission-critical service paths (perhaps for high-paying customers) which are given priority over less important service paths.
- Emphasize the user of standards and open protocols.
- Ensure the scalability of the network.

THE UNI AND THE NNI

Logically enough, the UNI defines the operations between the user node and the ingress and egress network nodes, as seen in Figure 13–1. The NNI defines the operations between network nodes between networks, as well as within networks.

These two interfaces differ in some ways, and in others they are the same or identical. The services defined at the UNI are (a) neighbor discovery, (b) service discovery, and (c) signaling operations to create, manage, and modify an optical connection. The services defined for the NNI are (a) neighbor discovery, (b) topology and resource distribution (based on OSPF), (c) traffic engineering, and (d) signaling (based on CR-LDP or RSVP-TE).

MANAGING THE OPTICAL BANDWIDTH IN THE ASON

Bandwidth on demand has been provided by network operators for many years. Examples are the switched virtual circuits (SVCs) of X.25, Frame Relay, and ATM. The plain old dial-up services are another example (somewhat limited in its capabilities) of bandwidth on demand.

With the development of optical networks that provide tremendous bandwidth capacity, there is keen interest among customers, vendors, and network providers to deploy network offerings that provide optical bandwidth on demand. But the issue goes further than offering bandwidth on demand. The bandwidth capacity of optical networks is increasing each year by many orders of magnitude, and a pressing issue is to develop mechanisms to manage and control this vital network resource.

The present 1st and 2nd generation transport networks are preconfigured to provide bandwidth with proprietary element management systems (EMS), and they require crafting operations before the bandwidth is made available to the customer. Due to some manual operations involved in this crafting, and also because end-to-end provisioning often occurs through vendor-specific systems, it is not unusual that a long provisioning time is required before the service is made available to the customer. This situation occurs when the customer demands short provisioning times.

One idea of 3G transport systems is to migrate to a scheme in which the end user can dynamically request bandwidth from the network, and the network can dynamically find and reserve the required bandwidth for this user. Thereafter, the bandwidth is guaranteed, something like a leased, point-to-point circuit.

Inherent in optical bandwidth on demand is the ability of the user to (a) request a new connection to the network, (b) request a tear-down of an existing connection, (c) query the network about the characteristics of an ongoing connection, and (d) change parameters (and thus operating characteristics) of an ongoing connection.

Several efforts are underway to define standards for the management of bandwidth in optical networks. One effort is sponsored by the Open Domain Service Interconnect Coalition [ODSI01], and the other is sponsored by the Optical Interworking Forum [OIF01]. The IETF is taking the lead in the Internet standards area.[1] This next section provides a summary of the protocols and interfaces being defined by these two organizations and the IETF.

THE GENERAL APPROACH TO OPTICAL BANDWIDTH MANAGEMENT

Figure 13–2 shows an optical backbone in which three optical nodes (ON) are connected to the network users. The inside of the network has spare bandwidth available for its users. When a user needs some bandwidth, it sends a bandwidth request message to its local ON across a standardized UNI. The request message contains sufficient information for the network to know (a) the identification of the sending user, (b) the identification of the endpoint to which the sending user wants to send/receive traffic, and (c) the amount of bandwidth required for the connection.

---

[1]The best way to obtain up-to-date information on the working groups and their papers on optical networks is to go to www.ietf.org, click on working papers (or working groups), or key in a search for (a) optical and then (b) MPLS. These two subjects are closely associated with each other.

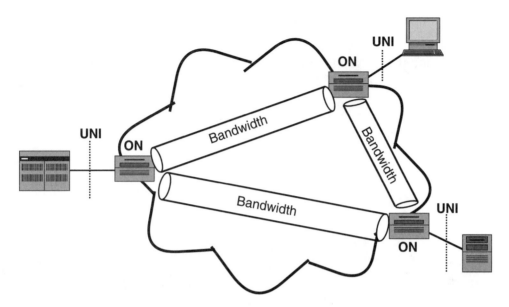

Figure 13–2   The optical bandwidth management arrangement.

Sound familiar? It should, because it is identical to the operations involved in an ATM, Frame Relay, or X.25 SVC connection on demand. A logical question to ask is why not create revisions to these currently-existing protocols since they are already available. The answer is that these emerging optical UNI specifications do not rely on conventional switched virtual circuit technologies. As we shall see, they use either the SONET overhead bytes (the DCC bytes in the section and line headers), or they use the resource reservation protocol (RSVP).

IETF OPTICAL CARRIER FRAMEWORK FOR THE UNI

The IETF is working on a model and framework for an optical carrier network [XUE01]. The general specification defines the carrier (network operator) service requirements for automatic switched optical networks (ASON). It guides the on-going efforts to develop a standard UNI and other interfaces to the optical layer (OL) control plane. It is a blueprint that describes the optical transport services for the UNI and is also based on the efforts of the OIF.

Focus on OC-48/STM-16 and Above

The primary focus is on the SONET/SDH tributaries of OC-48/STM-16 and above. While sub-rate extensions are discussed in a general way, it is important to emphasize that the philosophy, due to the nature of wavelength switching in an optical network, it is not practical to provision and switch user sub-rate signals (called user service paths) within an all-optical network. Therefore, it is necessary to include an optional low-granularity grooming optical networking function in the UNI architecture, called sub-rate UNI (UNI-SR). This interface extends to the user device and is defined as an extension to the UNI.

Table 13–1   Connection Granularity [XUE01]

SDH Name	SONET Name	Transported Signal
RS64	STS-192 Section	STM-64 (STS-192) signal without termination of any overhead (OH)
RS16	STS-192 Section	STM-16 (STS-48) signal without termination of any OH
MS16	STS-48 Line	STM-16 (STS-48); termination of RSOH possible
MS64	STS-192 Line	STM-64 (STS-192); termination of RSOH
VC-4-64c	STS-192c-SPE	VC-4-64c (STS-192c-SPE); termination of RSOH, MSOH and VC-4-64c TCM OH possible
VC-4-16c	STS48c-SPE	VC-4-16c (STS-192c-SPE); termination of RSOH, MSOH, and VC-4-16c TCM OH possible
VC-4-4c	STS-12c-SPE	VC-4-4c (STS-12c-SPE); termination of RSOH, MSOH, and VC-4-4c TCM OH possible
VC-4	STS-3c-SPE	VC-4 (STS-3c-SPE); termination of RSOH, MSOH, and VC-4 TCM OH possible.
VC-3	STS-1-SPE	VC-3 (STS-1-SPE); termination of RSOH, MSOH, and VC-3 TCM OH possible
VC-2	VC-2	VC-2 (VT6-SPE); termination of RSOH, MSOH, higher order VC-3/4 (STS-1-SPE) OH and VC-2 TCM OH possible
VC-12	VT2-SPE	VC-12 (VT-SPE); termination of RSOH, MSOH, higher order VC-3/4 (STS-1-SPE) OH and VC-12 TCM OH possible
VC-11	VT1.5-SPE	VC-11 (VT1.5-SPE); termination of RSOH, MSOH, higher order VC-3/4 (STS-1-SPE) OH and VC-11 TCM OH possible

UNI-SR (Subrates)

[XUE01] recommends the UNI-SR support the sub-rates listed in Table 13–1. Each subrate is referred to as an instance of connection granularity. If you are unfamiliar with the terms in Table 13–1, take a look at Chapters 5 and 6.

TYPES OF CONNECTIONS

As shown in Figure 13–3, three network connections are defined for the model: (a) optical channels, (b) optical paths, and (c) service paths. The optical channel defines an end-to-end physical connection between two termination points such as an ADM or an XC. Since it is defined as end-to-end through the network, it implies the concatenation of one or more optical fiber links or optical wavelength channels.

The optical path is the logical connection over the optical channel through the optical network. A good way to think of the optical path is that it is the optical frame (say SONET/SDH) running on the optical signal. The optical path does not extend past the edges of the network.

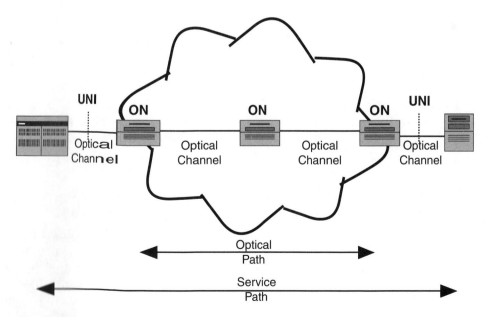

Figure 13–3   The network connections.

The service path is the logical end-to-end connection over an optical path. But "end-to-end" in this context means that the service path extends out to the user node (called the user edge device, or UED).

Connection Attributes

Some of the important aspects of optical bandwidth on demand, as defined in [XUE01], are the attributes associated with the connection. These attributes can be negotiated between the user and the network before the connection is established, or some of them can be modified during the connection. They are categorized as (a) identification attributes, (b) connection characteristic attributes, and (c) routing constraints attributes.

Identification Attributes

These attributes are used in the connection establishment operation and in the ongoing management of this connection. They include:

- Connection id: A globally unique identifier for the connection. This identifier is assigned by the network.
- Contract id: An identifier of who "owns" the connection. It is important for connection acceptance, billing, and appropriate suppo for SLAs, etc.
- User Group id: Identifier specifying groups of users that are ass ciated in a group.
- Connection Status: Describes the state of the connection.
- Connection Schedule: The date/time when the connection is d sired to be in service, and the earliest and latest date/time wh the connection will be disconnected.
- Destination Name: The name used to identify the node to which the connection is to be established.
- Destination Port Index: If individual ports are not given unique addresses, then a port index is required to identify them.
- Destination Channel (wavelength) id: When the network or end system allows multiplexing or switching at a finer granularity below the port level, the channel identifier is used to refer to specific channels below the port level. The destination channel identifier may be assigned by either the destination user or the network.
- Destination Sub-channel id: A further level of destination multiplexing.

- Source Name: The name used to identify the node from which the connection is to be established.
- Source Port Index: Similar to destination port index.
- Source Channel (wavelength) id: Similar to destination channel identifier.
- Source Sub-channel id: Similar to destination sub-channel ID.
- Third Party (Proxy) Attributes: Third party or proxy signaling identifies an entity other than the equipment directly connected to the interface.

Connection Characteristic Attributes

The next group of attributes relates to the physical and transmission characteristics of a connection. They are as follows:

- Framing: Designation of framing types such as: (a) SONET T1.105, (b) G.707, (c) Ethernet IEEE 802.3.x, (d) Digital wrapper G.709, (e) PDH, and (f) transparent (wavelength service).
- OH Termination Type: This field is framing-specific. For SONET and SDH framing, this field specifies to what degree the framing overhead bytes are terminated: (a) RS: signal without termination of any OH, (b) MS: signal with termination of RSOH (section OH) possible, and (c) VC: signal with termination of RSOH, MSOH, and TCM OH possible.
- Bandwidth: This attribute is also correlated to framing type. Its values will be consistent with the allowable values within the selected framing type. For SONET, this field will be used to indicate the bandwidth of the connection in terms of multiples of STS-1 (and VTx, if applicable), to allow for virtual concatenation. For SDH, this field will be used to indicate the bandwidth of the connection in terms of multiples of VC-4s/STM-1s (and VC-3, VC-12, and VC-11, if applicable), and should allow for virtual concatenation. For Ethernet, the values are in multiples of Mbit/s, so that Gigabit Ethernet is represented as 1000, and10GbE is represented as 10000.
- Directionality: This attribute will indicate whether the connection is uni-directional or bi-directional. SONET, SDH, and Ethernet are defined as bi-directional signals.
- Protection and restoration: Priority, protection, and restoration will be represented by two attributes:

- Service type: Specifies a class of service. A carrier may specify a range of different classes of service with predefined characteristics (e.g., restoration plans). The pre-defined service types correspond to different types of restoration (e.g., no restoration, 1+1 protection), connection set-up and hold priorities, reversion strategies for the connection after failures have been repaired, and retention strategies.
- Drop side protection: Refers to the protection between the user network elements and the optical network. Two different fields will be used to specify protection used at the two ends of the connection (i.e., different protection schemes can be used at both ends of the connection).

Routing Constraints Attributes

Various relationships may be defined between connections. For example, a user may request that multiple connections be diversely routed, that multiple connections be routed along the same shared physical route, that multiple connections be bundled together and treated as a single entity with a common set of attributes, or that a given connection be routed on the same path as an existing connection.

Two connections are diverse if they have no shared risk link groups (SRLG) in common. Diverse routing is frequently a requirement of sophisticated enterprise networks whose availability objectives may require that no single failure isolate a node or disconnect the network. The diversity requirement for such a network is best expressed by a matrix: If there are N connections involved between the same end points, then A[j,k] specifies whether connections j and k must be diverse.

Connections may initially be requested with the intention of adding a diversely routed connection at a future point in time. This allows requests to be individually handled while still providing diversity at a later date without service interruption.

As of this writing, the specifics of the routing attributes have not yet been defined.

THE NETWORK-TO-NETWORK INTERFACE (NNI)

The NNI is under development by the IETF Network Working Group [PAPA00]. The NNI model is shown in Figure 13–4. Several nodes and entities are shown in this figure that have not yet been explained. They are:

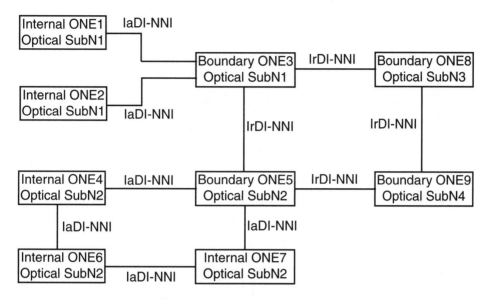

Figure 13–4   The NNI model [PAPA00].

- Optical network element (ONE): A network element belonging to the optical network. An optical network device could be an optical cross-connect (OXC), an optical ADM (OADM), etc.

- ONE controller: The owner of the UNI-N interface (since the UNI-N may not belong to the same device as the ONE) toward the UNI-C interface and/or the owner of the NNI interface.

- Boundary ONE: An optical network element belonging to the optical network whose controller includes an IrDI-NNI interface and an IaDI-NNI interface and/or a UNI-N interface.

- Internal ONE: An optical network element internal to the optical network (also referred as a termination incapable device) whose controller has only an IaDI-NNI interface.

- Client network element (CNE): A network element belonging to the client network. A client (C, that is, the customer) network element could be a SONET/SDH ADM, a SONET/SDH cross-connect, an ATM switch, an Ethernet switch, an IP router, etc.

- CNE controller: The owner of the UNI-C interface (since the UNI-C may not belong to the same device as the boundary CNE).

- Optical network controller (ONC): Logical entity within an optical sub-network terminating the NNI signaling.

- Intra-domain (IaDI)-NNI interface: The interface between internal ONE controllers belonging to the same optical sub-network or between internal ONE controllers belonging to distinct optical sub-networks.
- Inter-domain (IrDI)-NNI interface: The interface between boundary ONE controllers belonging to distinct optical networks.
- Generalized label switched path (GLSP): Point-to-point connection with specified attributes established between two termination points in the optical network. GLSPs are considered as bi-directional (and in a first phase as symmetric). A GLSP could be a fiber switched path, a lambda switched path or a TDM switched path (circuit).

In Figure 13–4, there are four optical subnetworks, four boundary ONEs, and five internal ONEs with the following relationships:

- Optical sub-network1 includes 2 internal ONEs and 1 boundary ONE
- Optical sub-network2 includes 3 internal ONEs and 1 boundary ONE
- Optical sub-network3 includes 1 boundary ONE
- Optical sub-network4 includes 1 boundary ONE

NNI Signaling Requirements

The following signaling transport mechanisms are defined for the NNI:

- In-band: Signaling messages are carried over a control-channel embedded in the logical link between the NNI interfaces of the peering ONE controllers. The control-channel is implemented through the use of optical channel layer (OCh) overhead bytes [G.70901] over which the NNI signaling channel is realized. For the SONST/SDH particular case, the control-channel could be implemented through line DCC bytes or other SONET/ SDH unused overhead bytes.
- Out-of-band: Signaling messages are carried over a control-channel embedded in the physical link between the NNI interfaces of the peering ONE controllers. The control-channel is implemented through the use of a dedicated wavelength included on a

(D)WDM fiber link over which the NNI signaling channel is realized. This channel is referenced as the optical supervisory channel (OSC). For the SONET/SDH particular case, a TDM sub-channel can be allocated for realizing the NNI signaling channel.

- Out-of-network: Signaling messages are carried over a dedicated and separated network between NNI agent interfaces of the peering ONC controllers or over a dedicated control-link between NNI interfaces of the peering ONE controllers. The dedicated physical-link is implemented through the use of one (or multiple) dedicated interface(s) over which the NNI signaling channel is realized.

Neighbor Discovery

The key objective of the neighbor discovery protocol (NDP) at the NNI is to provide the information needed to determine the neighbor identity (IPv4 address associated to the corresponding NNI) and neighbor connectivity over each link connecting internal ONEs or an internal ONE to a boundary ONE. The physical port and identity discovery provide the following information to the ONE:

- The ONE discovers the identity of the neighboring ONE by automatically discovering the IPv4 address assigned to the NNI interface.
- The ONE discovers the identity of the physical ports of each port connected to the neighboring ONE.

NNI Topology and Resource Distribution Protocol

The Topology and Resource Distribution Protocol (TRDP) is the mechanism provided to initially exchange and distribute the discovered logical-port-related information of the ONE included in an optical sub-network. This protocol runs across intra-domain NNI interfaces.

The TRDP protocol is an IGP protocol and is based on the following concepts:

- Maintaining the neighbor relationship with peering ONEs
- Flooding of the ONEs' logical link adjacencies
- Flooding of the ONEs' logical link state
- Flooding of the ONEs' logical link related information

NNI Protocol Mechanisms

We must move on in this chapter to study the ASON UNI and NNI signaling services. But before we do, note that this discussion on the NNI has been a highlight of the specification as defined in [PAPA00]. If you need the details for which to make detailed planning and general design decisions, you should consult this reference.

UNI AND NNI SIGNALING SERVICES

The UNI and NNI define five and four signaling services, respectively. The services are invoked by a UNI or NNI node sending a request message to another node or nodes, as shown in Figure 13–5. In turn, the receiving node must respond with a response message. Below is a summary of the functions of these services, and Table 13–2 will be helpful as you read about the services.

- Creation: This procedure is used to create a lightpath (end-to-end) from the source UNI, through one or more NNIs, to the destination UNI. The principal services achieved are a route calculation and determination, assignment of identifiers, and the allocation of resources. Table 13–2 lists and explains the parameters that are

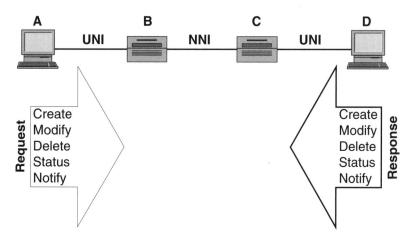

Figure 13–5   The UNI and NNI signaling services and messages.

Table 13–2   UNI and NNI Message Parameters

Parameter Name(s)	Parameter Function
Bandwidth-framing	Values will be consistent with the allowable values within the selected framing type, such as Ethernet, SONET, SDH, ATM, IP, etc.
Carrier ID	ID of carrier that created connection request
Contract ID	Owner of the connection
Directionality	Indication if connection is uni-directional or bi-directional
Diversity	Possible needs for lightpaths to traverse different conduits, etc.
Explicit route	Information on the constrained route through the optical network(s)
Max signaling delay	Maximum delay in executing signaling procedures to establish a connection
Network protection	Degree and type of NNI protection switching (1:1, etc.)
Priority-preemption	Under study, but will allow the preemption of certain GLSP processes
Record route	Information on the route taken by the GLSP
Result code	Diagnostic information
SDH/SONET options	Specific to SDH/SONET OAM procedures
Side protection	Refers to the protection between the user network elements and the optical network (1:1, 1+1, etc.)
Termination ID	ID of an optical channel that defines an end-to-end physical connection between two termination points in the network by concatenating one or more optical links or optical wavelength channels
User group ID	Identifier specifying groups of users that are associated in a group. This identifier is particularly important for virtual private optical networks (VPONs).
Priority	protection and restoration: priority, protection and represented by two attributes: service type and side protection
Service type	A class of service dealing with protection plan options; pertains to priority of connection robustness

associated with the create request and response messages. Some of these parameters are also coded in the modify, delete, status, and notification messages.

- Modification: This procedure is used to modify an existing light-path. There are restrictions on what can be modified, and include only GLSP-related parameters: (a) priority value, user-group ID, and maximum signaling delay.

- Deletion: This procedure reverses the creation procedure and tears down the lightpath. It is destructive, and the create procedure must be executed if a ligthpath is needed once again. It needs only the following parameters in its messages: (a) source and destination points, (b) GLSP ID, and (c) result code.
- Status: This procedure is used to provide status information between UNI and NNI nodes about the results of the other procedures. It reports on the success or failure of ongoing operations, such as a creation request.
- Notification: This service is available only at the UNI, and is used by the UNI-C to notify the NNI node about the status of a G.LSP at the UNI.

SUMMARY

The success of the ODSI and OIF work, and the associated IETF activities in relation to the UNI and NNI specifications, remain to be seen. Several vendor interoperability tests by the ODSI and OIF have been successfully completed, and by-and-large they have met with favorable reactions in the industry. I refer you to [ODSI01] and [OIF01] for more information of UNI and NNI operations.

14

ATM vs. IP in Optical Internets

This chapter discusses the issues surrounding the use of IP in optical networks. Since many existing 2G transport backbone networks run IP over ATM, the chapter examines the pros and cons of IP over optical vs. ATM over optical. (The chapter assumes you are familiar with ATM.)

Framing and encapsulation are important operations in an internet as well as in an optical network, and we analyze the pros and cons of several encapsulation and framing standards published by the ITU-T and the IETF.

IP OVER ATM OVER SONET

The prevalent approach today for moving IP traffic over a wide area network (WAN) is to use the services of ATM and SONET, as shown in Figure 14–1. This practice is called IP over ATM over SONET since IP is a layer 3 protocol, operating over ATM and SONET.

For these services to operate correctly, and for different vendors to be able to interwork their products together, many rules are needed. Here are some examples:

- Mapping of IP addresses into ATM virtual circuits
- Mapping of ATM cells into SONET payloads

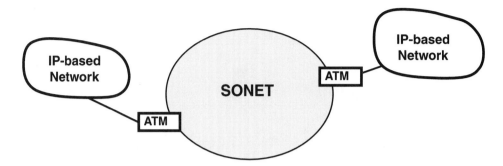

Figure 14–1   Running IP over ATM over SONET.

- Boundary alignments (octet alignments) of IP and ATM octets in the SONET payload envelope
- Correlation (if necessary) of ATM alarms to SONET OAM messages (of which there are many)
- Agreement on specifications for the IP to ATM encapsulation headers

THE OSI AND INTERNET LAYERED MODELS

For the analysis of several subjects in this chapter, it will prove helpful to use the OSI and Internet layered reference models as a reference. Figure 14–2 shows the models.

The layers of the OSI reference model, the Internet model, and the layers of vendor's models, such as IBM's Systems Network Architecture (SNA), contain the communications functions at the lower three layers. From the OSI perspective, it is intended that the upper four layers reside in the host computers.

This does not mean that the lower three layers reside only in the network. In order to affect complete communications, the services in the lower three layers also exist at the host machine. End-to-end communications, however, occur between the hosts by invoking the upper four layers, and between the hosts and the network by invoking the lower three layers. This concept is shown in Figure 14–2(a) with the arrows drawn between the layers in the hosts and the network.

The "network" in the figure means the placement of the layers in perhaps hundreds of components (such as ATM switches and IP-based routers), although only one is shown.

Also, although the upper layers are not shown residing in the network nodes (such as routers), they do indeed exist in these components. But they are usually not invoked for the ongoing transport of user payload. They are executed to support operations within the network, such as setting up sessions between routers. In some situations, the upper

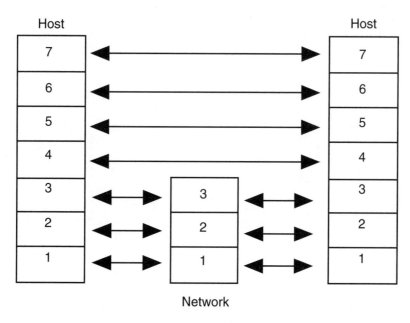

(a) The OSI Model

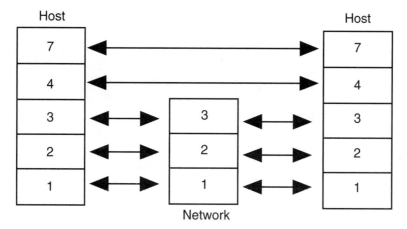

(b) The Internet Model

Figure 14–2   The OSI and Internet layered models.

layers are invoked between the network node and the host; one example is the establishment of TCP sockets between a host and a router in a mobile network for the support of traffic integrity operations, such as flow control, sequencing, and acknowledgments of traffic.

Figure 14–2(b) shows the Internet model. It does not include layer 5, the session layer. With rare exceptions, it does not include layer 6, the presentation layer, although the Simple Network Management Protocol (SNMP) uses a subset of layer 6. Therefore, layers 5 and 6 are not shown in Figure 14–2(b).

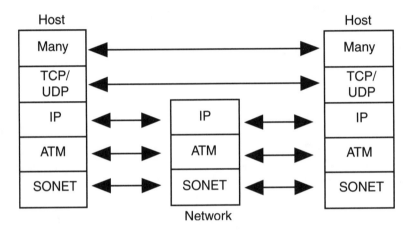

(a) The Internet Core Protocols (and SONET)

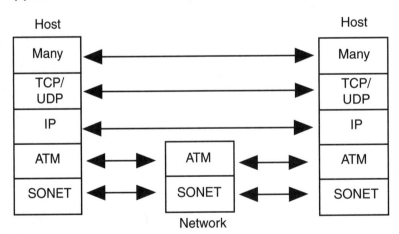

(b)With ATM as a Bearer Service

Figure 14–3   Typical protocol placements.

Placement of Core Protocols

Figure 14–3(a) shows the placements of the Internet core protocols in the Internet model. The two lower layers are operating with ATM and SONET. IP is operating at layer 3, with TCP/UDP at layer 4. At layer 7, a wide variety of protocols exists to support applications such as email, file transfer, network management, route discovery, Web browsing, etc.

Figure 14–3(b) shows a typical protocol stack in which IP is not used for IP address-based forwarding. In IP's place is ATM. This approach is considerably more efficient than the network protocol stack in Figure 14–3(a) because ATM replaces IP as the forwarding protocol. Virtual circuit switching using ATM is preferable to IP address forwarding because it is much faster.

PPP and L2TP

The point-to-point protocol (PPP), shown in Figure 14–4(a), is widely used in the Internet and intranets. PPP is used to encapsulate network layer packets over a serial communications link. The protocol allows two machines on a point-to-point communications channel to negotiate the particular types of network layer protocols (such as IP) that are to be used during a session. It also allows the two machines to negotiate other types of operations, such as the use of compression and authentication procedures. After this negotiation occurs, PPP is used to carry the network layer protocol data units (PDUs) in the I field of an HDLC-type frame.

The layer 2 tunneling protocol (L2TP), shown in Figure 14–4(b), was introduced to allow the use of the PPP procedures between different networks and multiple communications links. With L2TP, PPP is extended as an encapsulation and negotiation protocol to allow the transport of PPP and user traffic between different networks and nodes.

One principal reason for the advent of L2TP is the need to dial in to a network access server (NAS) that may reside at a remote location. While this NAS may be accessed through the dial-up link, it may be that the NAS is located in another network. L2TP allows all the PPP operations to be used between machines in different networks. With the implementation of L2TP, an end user establishes a layer 2 connection to an access concentrator such as a modem bank, an ADSL bank, etc. Thereafter, the concentrator is responsible for creating a L2TP tunnel and sending the specific PPP packets to a network access server (NAS).

Figure 14–4(c) is similar to a previous layered stack and shows a typical protocol stack in the network if IP is not used for IP address-based forwarding. In IP's place is ATM. L2TP is used in this stack.

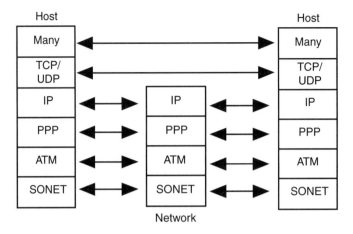

(a) Using PPP

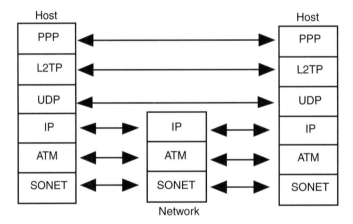

(b) Using PPP and L2TP

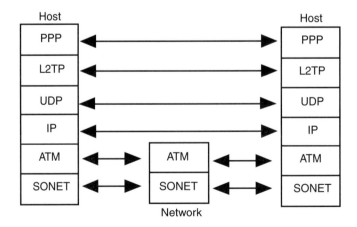

(c) With ATM as the Forwarding Protocol

Figure 14–4   Using PPP and L2TP.

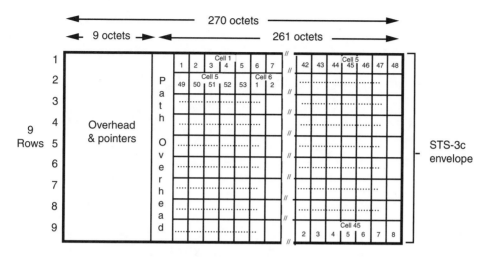

Note: Example shows the first cell aligned exactly in the beginning of the payload area. It may be positioned anywhere in the payload.

Figure 14–5   ATM over SONET or SDH.

ATM IN THE SONET/SDH PAYLOAD ENVELOPE

Figure 14–5 shows how ATM cells are mapped into a SONET or SDH payload envelope. The payload pointers can be used to locate the beginning of the first cell. Additionally, cell delineation is achieved by the receivers locking onto the 5 bytes that satisfy the HEC operations. In this manner, the receiver knows where a cell is positioned in the envelope. The receiver also is able to detect an empty cell.

It is unlikely that cells would be positioned at the first byte of the payload. If they are, an STS-3c system can carry 44 cells, and bytes 1–8 of the 45th cell. The remainder of the 45th cell is placed in the next SONET frame. So, a cell can cross the tributary/container frame boundary.

PPP IN THE SONET PAYLOAD ENVELOPE

Request for comments (RFC) 1619 defines the rules for running the point-to-point protocol (PPP) over SONET. See Figure 14–6. Since SONET is a physical point-to-point circuit, PPP over SONET should be a straightforward operation. This section paraphrases RFC 1619 (which is quite terse).

There are ambiguities in this RFC, and some implementers have complained to me about some difficulty in using it as an authoritative guide. One complaint deals with the rules on octet alignment of the PPP payload in the SONET SPE. Anyway, listed below are the major rules as outlined in RFC 1619:

- PPP treats the SONET network as octet-oriented synchronous links.
- The PPP octet stream is mapped into the SONET synchronous payload envelope (SPE), with the PPP octet boundaries aligned with the SPE octet boundaries.
- Scrambling is not used.
- The path signal label (C2) is intended to indicate the contents of the SPE. The experimental value of 207 (cf hex) is used to indicate PPP.
- The multiframe indicator (H4) is currently unused and must be zero.
- The basic rate for PPP over SONET is that of STS-3c at 155.520 Mbit/s.
- The available information bandwidth is 149.760 Mbit/s, which is the STS-3c SPE with section, line, and path overhead removed. This operation is the same mapping used for ATM and FDDI.

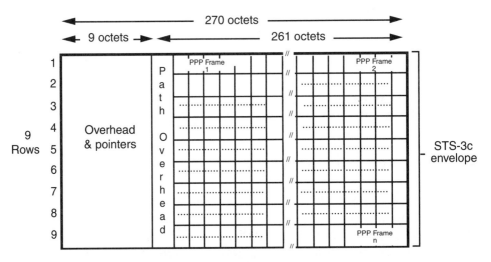

Figure 14–6   PPP over SONET.

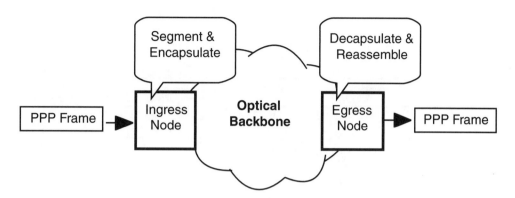

Figure 14–7   Operations at the Ingress and Egress nodes.

PREVALENT APPROACH IN TODAY'S INTERNETS

Before IP and PPP are encapsulated into SONET, they (typically) are first encapsulated into an ATM cell. Figure 14–7 shows that the IP/PPP traffic (the PPP frame) is accepted at the ATM switch, which is acting as the ingress node to the optical network. At this node, the PPP frame is segmented into ATM cells. The ATM switch also adds an encapsulation header; it is used to identify the type of traffic being carried in the cell, such as PPP, AppleTalk, SNA, etc. The ATM cell is then encapsulated into the optical payload, such as a SONET payload envelope.

At the egress node, the process is reversed. The SONET header, as well as the ATM header, is stripped away, leaving only the original PPP frame. The 48-byte segments are reassembled into the PPP frame. This frame is the same image as the frame presented to the ingress switch.

ENCAPSULATION/FRAMING RULES

As noted, before IP and PPP are encapsulated into SONET, they are first encapsulated into an ATM cell. Figure 14–8 shows the relationship of running IP over ATM, with emphasis on the CP-AAL5 and the ATM layers. ATM adaptation layer, type 5 (AAL5) performs its conventional segmentation and reassembly functions by delineating the traffic into 48-byte data units with the addition of an 8-byte trailer as part of the last data unit.

The error detection operation is provided by the AAL5 CRC-32 calculation over the PDU, and the padding field (PAD) is used to fill in the CPCS SDU to an even increment of 48 bytes.

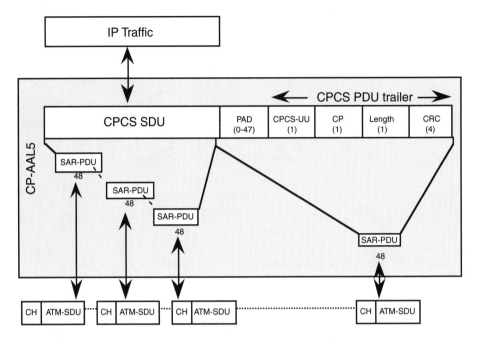

Figure 14–8   Classical IP over ATM.

ATM and Frame Relay Framing Formats

While the emphasis thus far at layer 2 has been on ATM, Frame Relay should not be excluded, because it has a big presence in the industry. The emphasis will remain on ATM, but we will include some discussions on Frame Relay as well.

Figure 14–9 shows the formatting and identification conventions for Frame Relay frames and AAL5 common part convergence sublayer (CPCS) PDUs with IP traffic. The Frame Relay frame and the AAL5 CPCS PDU use several industry standards for these operations. They are:

- *Control:* The control field, as established in HDLC standards. It is 1 byte in length.
- *NLPID:* The network level protocol ID, as established in the ISO/IEC TR 9577 standard. It is 1 byte in length.
- *OUI:* The organizationally unique ID, as established in RFCs 826, 1042, and cited in many other RFCs. It is 3 bytes in length.
- *PID:* The protocol ID, published as an Internet standard. It is also called Ethertype. It is 2 bytes in length.

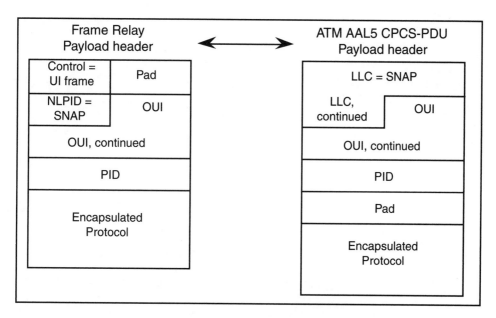

Figure 14–9   Formatting and identification conventions.

- *LLC:* The logical link protocol, as established in the IEEE 802.x standards. It is 3 bytes in length and includes three 1-byte fields: (a) source service access point (SAP), (b) destination SAP, and (c) the HDLC control field. The SAPs are usually set to 0xAA, and are not used (they defer to the subnetwork access protocol (SNAP)).
- *SNAP:* A header that includes OUI and PID.

The convention for the figures that follow is: one line entry in the figure represents two bytes. The exception is the last entry, which is payload and is variable in length.

If it appears to you that some of these fields perform redundant operations, your perception is correct. Due to the fragmented evolution of encapsulation headers, different groups have developed their own standards. In some situations, the result is that one encapsulation header identifies another encapsulation header. For example, in some systems the ISO NCPID identifies a SNAP header. Then the SNAP header identifies the OUI and PID fields. To be charitable, it is messy.

Encapsulation Field Values

As depicted in Figure 14–10, for the encapsulation of IP datagrams, the NLPID in the Frame Relay payload header of 0xCC (the reserved

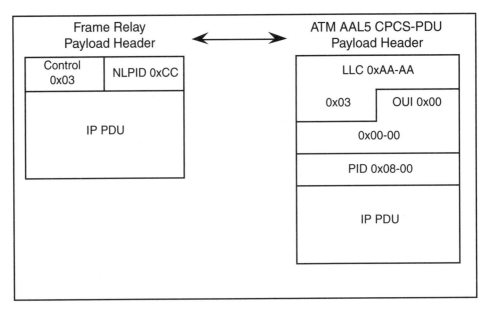

Figure 14–10   Frame relay/ATM payload header for IP PDUs.

NLPID value for IP) performs the same functions as the PID value of 0x08–00 (the reserved PID value for IP). In the AAL5 CPCS-PDU payload header, the OUI is set to 0x00–00–00.

Encapsulation Options with SNAP

The encapsulation methods are an important part of the debate regarding ATM vs. IP over SONET. Therefore, it is a good idea to look at several encapsulation alternatives.

Since many systems run IP over PPP, a logical approach is to use the ATM SNAP header (the PID field) to identify that PPP follows IP. This ID is a registered Internet number of 0x88–0B, reserved for PPP. This value is also the registered Ethertype value for PPP. This idea is shown in Figure 14–11. (Note that one header identifies another header, and so on. Again, a bit messy.)

An important aspect of this scenario is the fact that PPP headers and trailers must be taken into account as part of the overall overhead. It can be confusing, for the following scenarios (among others) can exist:

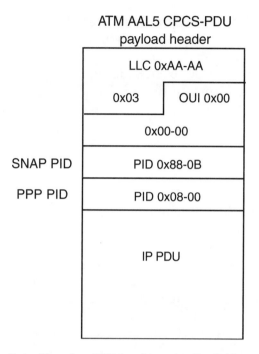

ATM AAL5 CPCS-PDU payload header

Note: The other PPP header and trailer fields are not shown here. They reside in the area titled "PPP PID."

Figure 14–11   Using SNAP to identify PPP PID.

- IP over PPP over ATM over SONET
- IP over ATM over SONET
- IP over (just) PPP's PID over ATM over SONET

The third item can be a point of confusion. Let's clarify this entry. Some of the PPP overhead fields may not be used:

- *Beginning and Ending Flags:* Usage depends on implementations.
- *Address:* Not used, set to all 1s (but may be examined in some systems).
- *Control:* Not used, set to HDLC's unnumbered information (UI) (but may be examined in some systems).
- *FCS:* Usage depends on implementation.

You could state, "Why does it matter? If PPP is in both the IP and IP/ATM stacks, then it's a wash." Not quite; in the ATM stack, the specific implementation of PPP may push the payload into another ATM cell. If only a small part of this cell's 48-byte payload is needed, the remainder is filled with the padding bytes. This situation leads to a lot of overhead. On the other hand, if there is little or no padding needed, the situation is not a serious problem. We return to these issues later in the chapter.

THE PPP PACKET

Let's take a look at the PPP packet. The PPP packet uses the HDLC frame as stipulated in ISO 3309–1979 (and amended by ISO 3309–1984/ PDAD1). Figure 14–12 shows this format. The flag sequence is the standard HDLC flag of 01111110 (0x7E); the address field is set to all 1s (Hex FF) which signifies an all stations address. PPP does not use individual station addresses because it is a point-to-point protocol. The control field is set to identify a HDLC unnumbered information (UI) command. Its value is 00000011 (0x03). The I (information) field carries the fields of the upper layer protocols, typically IP, UDP TCP, and a layer 7 protocol.

The protocol field is used to identify the traffic that is encapsulated into the I field of the frame, such as IP, OSPF, etc. The field values are assigned by the Internet, and the values beginning with a 0 identify the network protocol that resides in the I field. Values beginning with 8 identify a control protocol that is used to negotiate the protocols that will

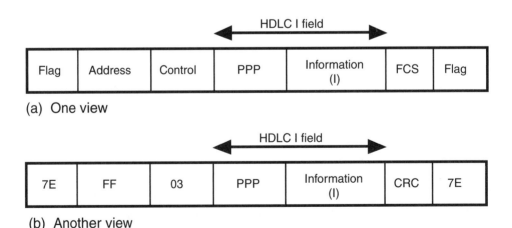

(a) One view

(b) Another view

Figure 14–12   The PPP format.

actually be used. For example, IP is identified with the value of 0021, and the protocol used to negotiate IP operations during a PPP setup is 8021 (the IP control protocol).

THE ATM VS. IP DEBATE

Table 14–1 provides a comparison of IP and ATM. The Attributes column defines the capability of the attribute, and the next two columns explain how the two protocols support or do not support the attribute.

Table 14–1   Comparisons of IP and ATM

Attribute	IP	Cell Relay (ATM)
QOS support?	Very little (Note 1)	Extensive
Application support?	Asynchronous data (not designed for voice)	Asynchronous, synchronous voice, video, data
Connection mode?	Connectionless	Connection-oriented
Congestion management?	None (Note 2)	Extensive
Identifying traffic? (Note 3)	IP address	Virtual circuit ID: The VPI/VCI and an OSI address
Congestion notification?	None	The CN bits in the PTI field
Traffic tagging?	None (Note 4)	The cell loss priority (CLP) bit
PDU size?	Variable (a datagram)	Fixed at 48 bytes (a cell)
Sequence numbers	None	Cell header, no; for payload, depends on payload type
ACKs/NAKs/ Resends?	None	Only for signaling traffic (SVCs)
Protection switching	Not defined	Yes
Location?	In user machine (PC, etc.) and in routers and switches	Rarely in user machine, usually in routers and switches
Marketplace?	Quite prevalent	Prevalent

Note 1: The addition of MPLS and DiffServ/RSVP changes "Very little" to "Extensive."
Note 2: The addition of DiffServ and RSVP-TE changes "None" to "Extensive."
Note 3: For ATM, addresses are used initially for the virtual circuit provisioning. Thereafter, virtual circuit IDs are used. For IP, the DiffServ codepoint and/or the MPLS label can be used in place of the cumbersome IP address.
Note 4: The addition of DiffServ changes "none" to "extreme."

This table is important in regard to the IP vs. ATM debate. It shows that many capabilities that ATM provides are not available with IP. The conclusion drawn is that IP cannot be a direct replacement for ATM. It follows that removing ATM from the SONET stack translates into substantially reduced features and services to the user.

ATM opponents consider ATM too expensive. ATM is indeed "pricey." Yet the issue is not as simple as it may seem. ATM provides a very wide array of services, well beyond what IP provides (which is very little). If IP is going to provide ATM-like features (and most people agree that they are needed), several supporting protocols must be added to IP, such as MPLS and DiffServ.

If dynamic call processing is to be provided for telephone and video users, services like ATM's switched virtual call (SVC) must be added to the IP arsenal. This means protocols such as Megaco, MGCP, and SIP must become part of the IP network.

ATM is going to be a prevalent technology for quite some time. But it should also be emphasized that the combinations of IP/MPLS/DiffServ/ RSVP-TE and several other supporting technologies can replace ATM completely, and provide all the functionality that ATM now provides.

OVERHEAD OF IP AND ATM

As noted, one of the big issues today is the overhead of running IP over ATM versus the overhead of IP over an alternative, say, directly over SONET. Figure 14–13 provides some general information on the differences in the number of bytes needed for these two approaches.

The payload is assumed to be 40 bytes, to keep the comparisons consistent. Both protocol stacks have the same overhead at the upper layers since they are both supporting the same upper layer protocols, TCP, and IP.

The difference lies at the layers below IP. ATM uses the 3-byte LLC and the 5-byte SNAP (containing the 3-byte OUI and the 2-byte PID). The IP-only stack does not use these headers.

Please note the "note" in Figure 14–13. The ATM stack may not have to carry the full PPP headers and trailers across the network. It can extract the PPP PID field and map it into the SNAP PID field, then reconstruct the PPP headers and trailers at the egress to the network, if needed. This may be feasible since the flags, address fields, and control fields are present, but never change. Whether this is possible depends on the vendor's design of the ATM node.

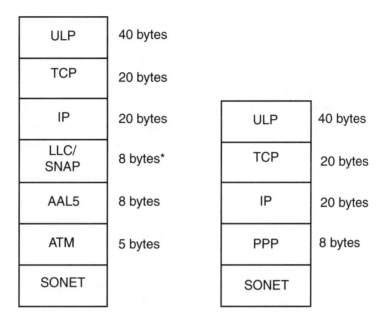

* Note: If PPP is under IP, the SNAP PID can so indicate.

Figure 14–13   Comparisons of overhead.

Also, note that the total number of bytes passed to ATM is more than a 48-byte payload. Consequently, the traffic must be placed in more than one ATM cell; the details on this operation are shown next.

Is the ATM Overhead Tolerable?

The answer to the question "Is the ATM overhead tolerable?" will depend upon who supplies the answer. If the question is answered by a network manager on a private campus, the answer is likely to be yes. This manager is probably not paying hard dollars for bandwidth from a public WAN backbone operator. The attractive features of ATM may make the overhead less of an issue.[1]

---

[1]The same answer (yes) might come from a user of ATM who does not know ATM is being used. An example: some of the DSL modems being installed today run ATM between the user's site and the service provider's site. A more likely answer from this person would be, "I have no idea." I am one of those DSL users, and I do not like the fact that my DSL local loop is running ATM, because I know of the overhead it consumes. I also want to know what my service provider is doing with ATM in my DSL node.

The major problem occurs when a backbone customer is paying for bandwidth and is running the ATM stack. For example, ISPs pay for this overhead when they use a carrier's links. Their incentive is to eliminate ATM and run IP directly over SONET.

Another factor is the overhead of processing AAL, even though AAL5 should not be processed in the backbone network. Interfaces with OC-12 (STS-12c) now have ATM SAR chips. Interfaces are now available for OC-48 (STS-48c) for support of direct PPP/HDLC mappings.

THREE ENCAPSULATION METHODS

In this part of our analysis, we examine three methods of encapsulation:

1. Running IP and a full PPP frame over ATM
2. Running IP and only the PID field of PPP over ATM
3. Running IP and a full PPP frame directly over the physical layer

Method 1: Conventional Approach

For method 1, three ATM cells are needed to transport a 40-byte payload. Figure 14–14 shows why. First, 96 bytes are presented to AAL5. Previous discussions explains how these bytes are used (40 for ULP, 20 for TCP, 20 for IP, 8 for PPP, and 8 for LLC and SNAP (the OUI and PID)).

This unit has the AAL5 trailer appended to it and is divided into 48-byte segments. The padding field is used to round out the traffic to an even increment of 48 bytes. With the 96 bytes and the 8 bytes contributed by AAL5, the unit is 104 bytes. Thus the padding field is 40 bytes (104 + 40 = 144 bytes / 48 bytes per cell = 3 ATM service data units (SDUs). The third SAR-PDU contains only the 8-byte AAL5 trailer and 40 bytes of padding. Next, the three 5-byte cell headers are appended to the service data units to yield a total of 144 + 15 = 159 bytes.

Recall that the original payload was 40 bytes of ULP, plus the 20 bytes each of the TCP and IP headers, the 8 bytes for PPP and the 8 bytes for the LLC and SNAP fields. Thus, the ratio of payload to overhead is 96:159.

Well, maybe; it depends on how one defines overhead. The LLC and SNAP (OUI and PID) should be considered overhead when counting

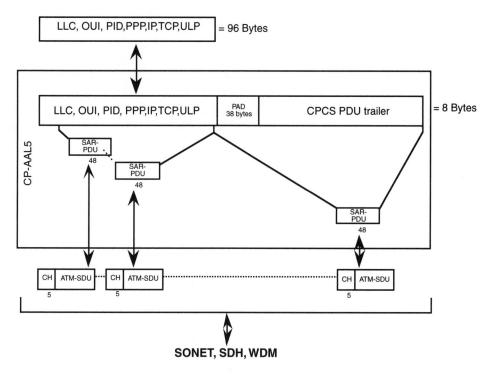

Figure 14–14   Operations to support Method 1.

bytes, since the ATM bearer service requires their use. If ATM is not used, LLC and SNAP are not needed. One could argue that the ratio of payload to overhead is 88:174 (minus the 8 bytes of LLC and SNAP). I think it fairer to use this latter ratio, especially when comparing ATM to IP. Consequently, in this example the use of ATM carries nearly an 80% overhead penalty.

Method 2: Lightweight PPP

For method 2, the PPP flags, address field, control field, and CRC field are stripped away before the payload is presented to CP-AAL5. Thus, 6 bytes are removed. The value used to identify PPP is carried in the ATM PID field (0x88–0B). Recall that this method requires the egress node to reconstruct these fields for presentation to the receiving application (if it needs them). These fields do not change, and the

ATM/SONET payload alignment can be performed with the SONET pointers or the ATM HEC field.

Let's see what it gives us; see Figure 14–15. The submitted unit to CP-AAL5 is now 90 bytes (because the two 1-byte flags, the 1-byte address field, the 1-byte control field, and the 2-byte CRC field are not present). The 8-byte AAL5 trailer is added to yield a unit of 98 bytes.

Three ATM cells are still needed: 98 / 48 = 2, with a remainder of 2 bytes. Therefore, the third cell contains 2 bytes of data, 38 bytes of padding, and the 8-byte AAL5 trailer.

So, deleting the PPP protocol control information did not reduce the number of ATM cells needed to support this IP packet.

However, if the system uses any one or a combination of three standardized options, the payload can be decreased substantially before it is presented to CP-AAL5, leading to the use of fewer than three ATM cells.

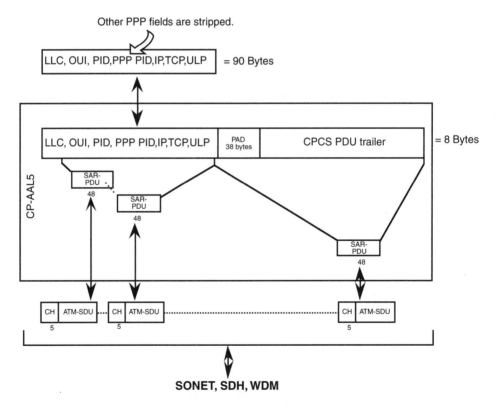

Figure 14–15   Operations to support Method 2.

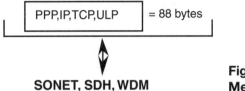

SONET, SDH, WDM

Figure 14–16   Operations to support Method 3.

These options are: (a) PPP PID field compression, (b) IP header compression, (c) TCP header compression.

Indeed, all methods are improved by the use of these techniques, not just method 2. Check your RFCs for information on these important compression operations.

Method 3: Eliminating ATM

For method 3, as illustrated in Figure 14–16, ATM is not used. Instead, PPP, IP, and the upper layer protocols are run directly over the physical layer. Obviously, this approach changes the payload-to-overhead ratio significantly. The overhead-associated LLC, SNAP, AAL5, and ATM are not needed.

For our analysis of these three methods, it might be concluded that there is no choice but to eliminate ATM. If the reduction of overhead is the only consideration, that is a valid conclusion. However, it was noted that ATM has many features, such as QOS traffic policing operations, and extensive diagnostic capabilities. If ATM is removed, so are its many features.

SUMMARY

The debate regarding IP vs. ATM has been going on for several years. In its simplest from, it revolves around the overhead of ATM and its fixed-length size. Whether or not these attributes of ATM are a handicap to its use is dependent on those that use ATM.

It is a good idea to check network provider tariffs and determine if any possible (and probable) ATM overhead is being charged back to you. I expect this discovery will affect your opinions about the ATM vs. IP debate.

But, regardless of this debate, IP is here to stay. ATM is here to stay as well, at least for a long time. Eventually, I think ATM will be replaced by MPLS and supporting protocols, such as DiffServ, CR-LDP, and RSVP-TE.

15

Optical Internets: Evolving to a 3G Architecture

The subject of IP/MPLS/optical interworking resurfaces in this chapter in relation to the migration of the Internet to a 3G transport network. A 3G transport Internet? This idea means the Internet takes on the characteristics of traditional transport networks such as those that are supported by the traditional carriers, such as AT&T, MCI Worldcom, BT, Mercury, France Telecom, etc.

At this point in the evolution to 3G, the Internet is not taking on the complete role of these transport networks. But it is likely to take on many of the characteristics of legacy transport networks, and it will surely evolve to interwork with the vital SS7 and AIN/IN resources that are owned and operated by the traditional carriers.

The first part of the chapter picks up on the IP/MPLS/optical interworking subject and provides some more examples of how this powerful protocol assembly will evolve. The next part deals with the issues of Internet and legacy transport network interworkings, and brings the IP-based call processing architectures into the discussion.

MIGRATION TO IP OPTICAL NETWORKING

Today's backbone networks are made up of SONET/SDH technology, with the access networks operating at OC-3 and OC-12, and the long-haul systems operating at OC-48 and OC-192. It is anticipated that

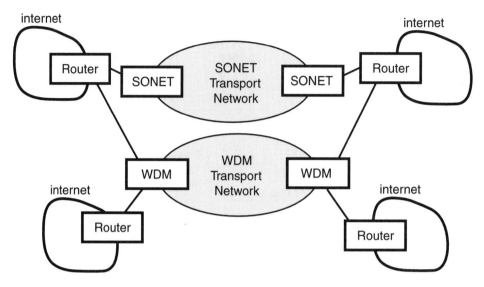

Figure 15–1   Migration to IP optical networking.

WDM will be deployed with IP operating directly over it in the near future. Figure 15–1 shows a probable migration scenario. An edge router rests between the internets and the optical networks. Based on the destination of the traffic and available technology, the traffic is either sent through the SONET TDM transport network or the WDM transport network. This approach is attractive because a migration can take place without disruption to the existing transport network.

IP AND THE OPTICAL BACKBONE

Figure 15–2 shows an example of an optical backbone network that supports IP. This technology is new and has not yet seen extensive deployment. Nonetheless, a number of companies are developing optical routers, and the U.S. Department of Defense Advanced Research Projects Agency (DARPA) is funding an effort among several companies and universities. It is called all-optical label swapping (AOLS).

The routers attached to the optical backbone routers are connected through copper or fiber. For this example, let's assume the router has its interface to the network edge node configured with WDM. The optical router is tasked with managing each WDM channel in relation to the

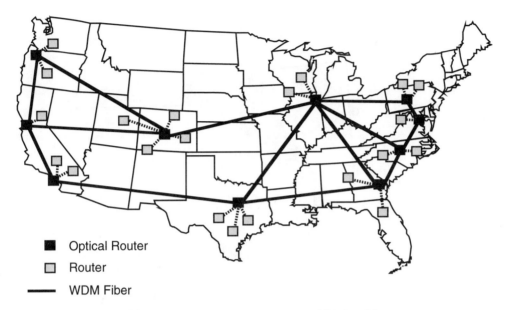

Optical Router

Router

—— **WDM Fiber**

Figure 15–2   Example of an optical/IP backbone.

router interfaces as well as the WDM interfaces associated with the backbone links.

Channels must be added, dropped, bridged, and passed through, perhaps on all the interfaces. In addition, these operations should reflect the state of the network traffic.

Example of IP and λ Forwarding

Figure 15–3 shows a scheme for supporting IP traffic through the optical network. Be aware that all possible add, drops, inserts, and pass-throughs are not shown, nor are the channels coming from the Chicago node. Notwithstanding this general view, the depiction accurately reflects a IP router-to-λ configuration. These routers are configured to support WDM.

The following channel relationships exist:

- *Node A:* This router adds a WDM channel to the WADM interface to Chicago. The channel is also dropped at node B.
- *Node B:* This router adds a WDM channel to the WADM interface to Chicago. In turn, this channel is dropped at node A. Since the channels from nodes A and B are made available to these two

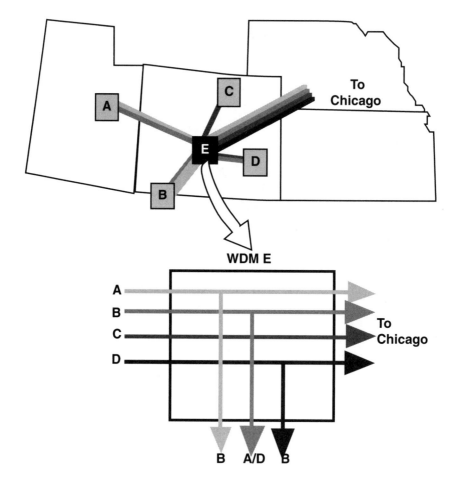

Figure 15–3   Adding, dropping, and cross-connecting IP traffic between routers.

nodes, we can assume they have a lot of traffic to exchange with each other. Node B also has a drop relationship with Node D.

- *Node C:* Node C has no WDM channel relationships with the other router nodes, only to Chicago. Perhaps this router connects to sites that process classified information and is not made available to the other routers.

- *Node D:* Node D has a WDM channel dropped to node B, as well to the interface to Chicago.

Therefore, the following WDM channel relationships exist between these four IP/λ nodes:

- A $\Rightarrow$ B
- B $\Rightarrow$ A
- B $\Rightarrow$ D
- D $\Rightarrow$ B

IP Subnets

IP and associated protocols, such as OSPF, TCP, etc., use IP addresses, and forwarding and route discovery operations are based on using these addresses. An IP optical network must be able to correlate destination addresses in the IP packet to a route in the optical network.

One possibility of how this service might be realized is offered in Figure 15–4, which shows that traffic has been forwarded from the optical router in Denver to the Chicago node. This node is tasked with forwarding the IP traffic to nodes G, H, I, and J. At these nodes are IP-based internets, identified with the IP address prefixes shown in the figure (some IP addresses are reserved and/or set aside for special use; this simple example assumes all these addresses are available).

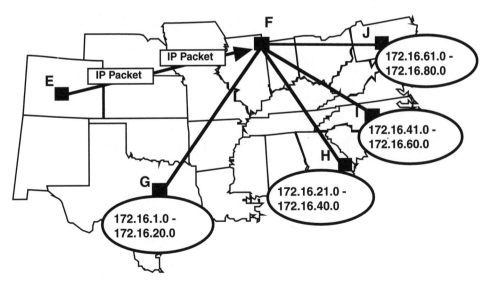

Note: For simplicity, some reserved addresses are used in this example.

Figure 15–4   IP subnets.

This address configuration presents some attractive implementation opportunities. Since the address prefixes are contiguous, it is possible to correlate a wavelength with a group of address prefixes.

However, this view is not one shared by AOLS, and I do not think mapping prefixes to a wavelength is the best long-range solution. A better approach is to use labels and map the labels to a wavelength (as defined in Chapter 12). We will examine this operation shortly.

Support of Non-optical Nodes

The previous example is altered slightly. Figure 15–5 shows that the optical node E in Colorado also supports native-mode IP on, say, DS3, or OC-3 interfaces. In order to route the IP traffic to the correct destination, node E is configured with a mapping table. This table associates IP address prefixes with a wavelength.

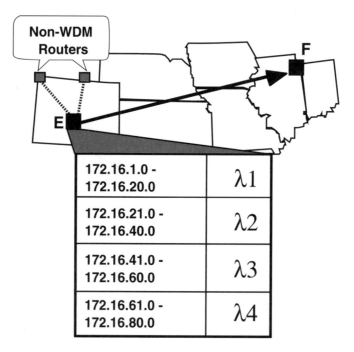

172.16.1.0 - 172.16.20.0	$\lambda 1$
172.16.21.0 - 172.16.40.0	$\lambda 2$
172.16.41.0 - 172.16.60.0	$\lambda 3$
172.16.61.0 - 172.16.80.0	$\lambda 4$

Figure 15–5   Node E accepts native IP packets and maps to WDM channels.

When an IP packet is received at node E, it examines the IP address in the packet header and maps the IP packet onto the associated WDM channel.

This process is performed at an edge device, that is, a node that sits at the boundary of the WDM network. In some of our previous examples, node E also acts as a node in the backbone WDM network.

The decision to use a node for both an edge and a backbone node should be weighed carefully. The IP address analysis and the associated IP-to-WDM channel mapping may consume more overhead than an optical backbone node can afford. In that case, the task of IP-WDM mapping can be pushed out to another router, assuming that the router is so designed. This scenario was shown earlier.

Some of the WDM channels on the fiber between nodes E and F are shown in Figure 15–6; they represent an expanded view of previous illustrations. We are using four wavelengths for the purpose of explaining IP-WDM concepts. The actual number of wavelengths, of course, is implementation-specific.

As shown in Figure 15–7, the incoming IP packets arrive at the link interfaces at node E. Through the use of its IP/λ mapping table, the node places the packets onto an outgoing queue that is associated with a wavelength on a specific outgoing interface. The next task is to transmit these packets out of the optical interface. This task entails an electro-optical conversion process wherein the electrical bits in the buffer are translated to the associated optical bits for transmission onto the fiber.

Figure 15–6   Some of the WDM channels.

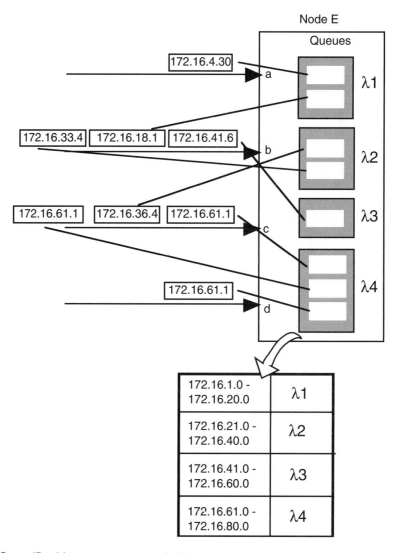

Note: Some IP addresses are reserved; this example assumes that all addresses shown are available for use.

Figure 15–7   Mapping the IP addresses to the WDM channels.

PLACING MPLS INTO THE PICTURE

Thus far, the examples show the mapping of IP prefix addresses onto wavelengths. This operation is certainly feasible, and some networks that do not need the features of MPLS can opt for this implementation. For other networks, another approach is to: (a) first map IP addresses to MPLS labels, and (b) then map the labels to wavelengths. The reason for bringing MPLS into the picture is to exploit the traffic engineering and scaling capabilities of MPLS, as well as other attributes explained in Chapter 9.

As shown in Figure 15–8, a set of IP addresses (or address prefixes) can be aggregated into a single MPLS label. The MPLS specification provides a number of rules on aggregation and on how the labels are set up between label switching routers (LSRs). For this discussion, perhaps you can see the opportunity to use WDM channels to support label switching. We will examine this idea next.

If label switching networks continue to grow (and they surely will), there will be opportunities to interwork and combine label switching routers (LSRs) with optical routers. As Figure 15–9 shows, native-mode IP networks will continue to exist for many years; in fact, there is little incentive to push label or WDM technology into local area networks or conventional point-to-point local loops. To do so would entail changing

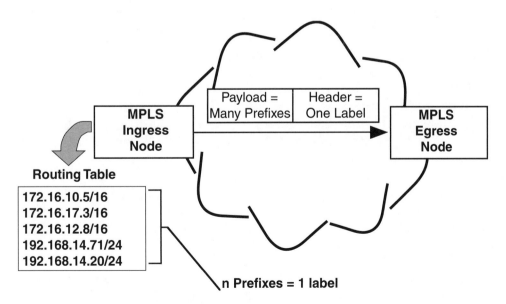

Figure 15–8   Aggregating addresses into a label.

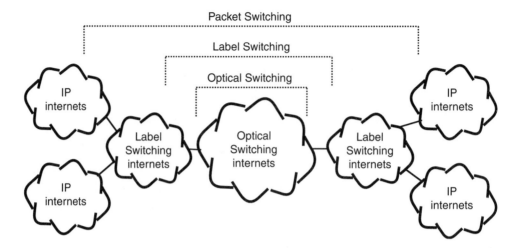

Figure 15–9   Interworking WDM and label switching internets.

the software and hardware architecture of user machines, such as PCs, palm units, etc.

So, this part of an internet stays the same, and the interfaces from a router back to the user computers are conventional Ethernet, PPP, DSL, V.90, cable modem, and so on. The router's interfaces out to the network will be MPLS, WDM, and probably a melding of the two.

This nested approach allows the network administrator to set up different switching domains in an organized fashion. In Figure 15–9, the packet switching domain uses IP in the data plane and OSPF, IS-IS, and BGP in the control plane. The label switching domain uses MPLS forwarding in the data plane and CR-LDP, OSPF (extensions), and RSVP-TE in the control plane. The optical switching domain uses lambda OSP switching in the data plane and GMPLS, LMP, and perhaps others (as they emerge) in the control plane.

Figure 15–10 shows how the different internet nodes interwork with each other. At node E in Denver, native IP packets are received from attached routers (not shown in this figure). The following events take place to relay the traffic to node F in Chicago for distribution to nodes G, H, I, and J.

- *Event 1:* Previously, OSPF, IS-IS, or BGP has discovered the addresses associated with hosts attached to nodes G, H, I and J. This information is stored in a routing table at node E.

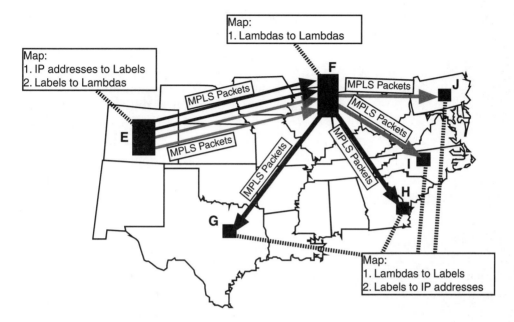

Figure 15–10   End-to-end operations.

- *Event 2:* Upon node E receiving an IP packet, it accesses the routing table to determine the next node that is to receive this packet. This next node is node F.
- *Event 3:* By previous configurations (using a label binding protocol, such as LDP or RSVP-TE), node E knows (a) the outgoing interface for this packet, and (b) the associated label. Therefore, node E appends the MPLS label header to the IP packet.
- *Event 4:* Furthermore, by previous configurations (using an λ "binding" protocol, such as GMPLS or LMP), node E also knows the specific wavelength that is to be used for this packet.
- *Event 5:* Node E maps the label to the appropriate wavelength on the appropriate interface, then sends the packet (to node F).
- *Event 6:* For this example, Node F is operating as a O/O/O PXC for data plane operations. Due to the prior execution of the optical control plane, node F knows that the wavelength associated with a specific fiber interface is to be optically cross-connected to one of its downstream neighbor nodes (that is, nodes G, H, I, or J).
- *Event 7:* Using the configured MEMS fabric (configured as a result of GMPLS or LMP), node F relays the packet to the appropriate

output interface to, say, node G. The λ used is the same on each OSP (say, $\lambda 1$).

- *Event 8:* Node G in Dallas is a egress node to both the MPLS and optical routing domain. It receives the packet on a specific wavelength on its input interface with node F. Its optical and MPLS cross-connect tables (again, pre-configured earlier with the IP, MPLS, and optical control planes) reveal that the packet has reached the end of the label switching path, as well as the optical switching path.

- *Event 9:* Therefore, node G resorts to O/E/O operations, terminating the LSP and OSP, and passes the native-IP packet to the relevant subnet.

Figure 15–11 shows the operations for mapping the MPLS labels in the packet header to a WDM channel. Obviously, these concepts are similar to the IP address prefix mappings discussed earlier.

Which leads to the questions, "Why bother with the labels? Why not just map the IP addresses directly into the WDM channels?" The answer is that under some situations, it might be sufficient for the edge router to map an IP address prefix directly into the WDM channel. However, this situation may not be the same for all networks. For example, it is highly unlikely that WADM nodes will be prevalent in local and campus networks, at least not to any great extent (for a number of years). The same holds true in wide area backbones, but to a lesser degree.

The point is that label switching networks are prevalent and growing. When WDM nodes begin to be integrated into IP-based networks, we will then see a convergence of label switching and WDM.

Therefore, IP to wavelength mapping may have a niche in the industry. The prevalent view, however, is that the IP to label and then to wavelength mapping will emerge as the dominant technology.

Some additional thoughts about Figure 15–11 might prove helpful. The four wavelengths now have labels associated with them. If the optical network has the capability to negotiate end-to-end wavelength reservations, then the core optical nodes (node F in this example) do not have to process the MPLS label during data transfer. For example, $\lambda 1$ is mapped from node E, through F, to G. Consequently, wavelength conversion is not required at node F.

The table at the bottom of Figure 15–11 shows that each wavelength is associated with one of the end nodes of an LSP, nodes G, H, I, or J. This information can be used by node E when it receives a GMPLS request from node F for wavelength allocations pertaining to certain sites. It can determine if the required wavelength is available for use.

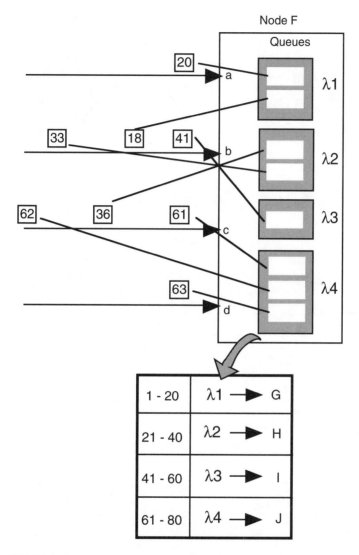

Note: Some MPLS labels are reserved; this example assumes that all labels are available for use.

Figure 15–11   Mapping MPLS labels to WDM channels.

PUTTING IT TOGETHER

To conclude the examples of optical internet operations, Figure 15–12 shows that the switching table entries provide sufficient information to move an IP datagram from node E to the next node in the path, which is node F.

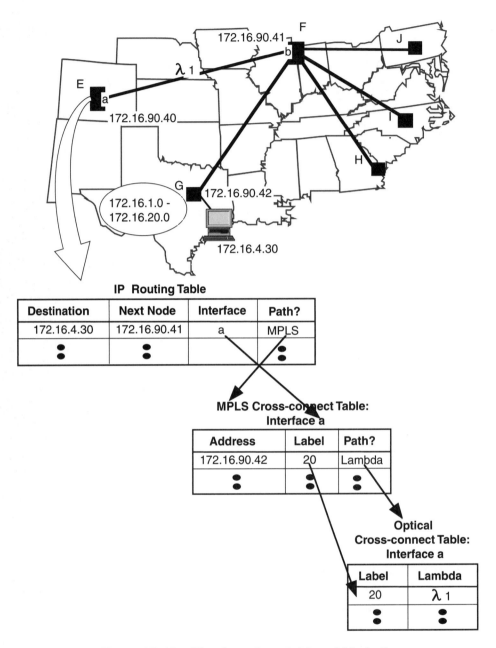

IP Routing Table

Destination	Next Node	Interface	Path?
172.16.4.30	172.16.90.41	a	MPLS
⋮	⋮		⋮

MPLS Cross-connect Table:
Interface a

Address	Label	Path?
172.16.90.42	20	Lambda
⋮	⋮	⋮

Optical
Cross-connect Table:
Interface a

Label	Lambda
20	λ 1
⋮	⋮

Figure 15–12   The data plane tables at Node E.

The three tables are parts of the IP, MPLS, and λ data planes. Recall that these tables are created by the IP, MPLS, and λ control planes. In an operational system, the tables would contain more entries, but those shown are sufficient for our examination. The tables can be implemented in any fashion the node designer wants; for efficiency, they should be in the form of ASICs, or especially designed chip sets. Also, nodes E, F, and G have been assigned IP addresses to aid in explaining the operations in these examples.

The three tables (more formally known as forwarding information bases) perform the following services.

IP Routing Table

- *Destination:* Through OSPF, IS-IS, or BGP, node E knows about address 172.16.4.30.
- *Next Node:* Also courtesy of the IP routing protocols, node E knows that the next node to receive this IP datagram is node F, assigned address 172.16.90.41.
- *Interface:* Node E knows the output link (interface) to node F is a.
- *Path?:* The entry of "MPLS" alerts node E that the interface is configured for MPLS operations. Had it been coded as, say, "IP," then node E would have resorted to conventional IP forwarding. However, for this operation, an MPLS LSP is used. So, the Path? value states the path to node F is an MPLS path, and it acts as an index into the MPLS table for interface a. Also note that had the Path? value been coded as "Lambda," it would have alerted node E to resort to IP to λ mapping, which is not shown in this example. In any of these cases, the decisions are made by the network administrator.[1]

MPLS Cross-connect Table: Interface a

- *Address:* The address of 172.16.90.42 is the address for node G. This is the address for the next logical, adjacent MPLS node. As explained in earlier chapters, MPLS does not require an LSP to be

---

[1]Today's routers are not yet set up to allow these types of configuration commands to be entered into the router's operating system. Before long, routers will have these capabilities.

set up at each node in the path. If you have forgotten about this aspect of MPLS, review the material in Chapters 9, 10, and 12, for it is an important component in supporting the interworking of label and lambda switching.

- *Label:* Label 20 is associated with the LSP between nodes E and G. You may be wondering how this table identifies the LSP, since it contains only the end of the LSP tunnel's address (172.16.90.42). This table is created and stored by and at node E, so it surely knows its own address (172.16.90.40).
- *Path?:* This entry of "Lambda" alerts node E that the interface is configured for wavelength operations. Thus, this entry acts as an index into the optical cross-connect table for interface a.

Optical Cross-connect Table: Interface a

- *Label:* The label value of 20 is another index that points to the wavelength that is assigned to MPLS packets with labels of 20 in their headers.
- *Lambda:* The traffic can now be sent to node F on λ 1 from interface a.

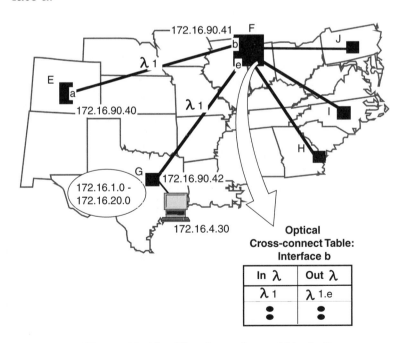

Figure 15–13   The data plane at Node F.

Figure 15–13 shows the optical cross connect table at node F for its interface b. The other tables are not needed for this operation, since prior control plane procedures mapped λ1 from node E's a interface to λ1 on node F's e interface. In this specific example, node F does not participate in the LSP between nodes E and G

The optical cross-connect table at node F, shown in Figure 15–13, is not necessarily a table. It could be the state of the MEMS mirrors in the switching fabric. To show this idea, the example is re-rendered in Figure 15–14.

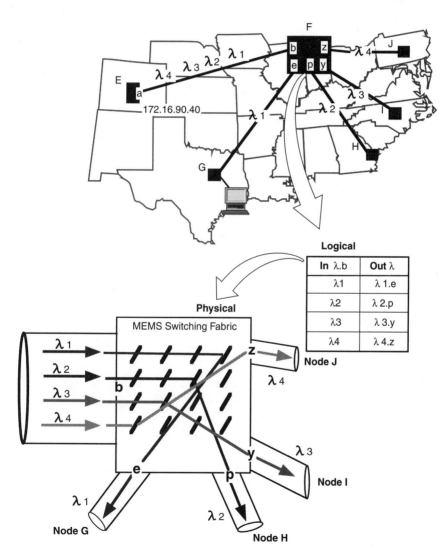

In λ.b	Out λ
λ1	λ 1.e
λ2	λ 2.p
λ3	λ 3.y
λ4	λ 4.z

Figure 15–14   The logical view and a MEMS physical
implementation.

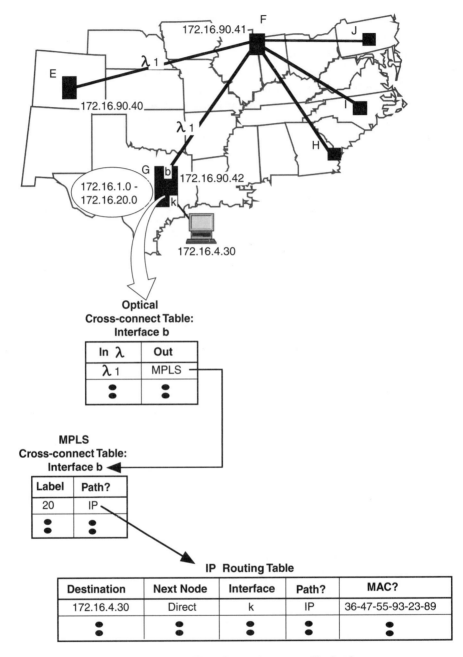

172.16.90.41

E
172.16.90.40

λ1

λ1

G
**172.16.1.0 -
172.16.20.0**
b
172.16.90.42
k

172.16.4.30

**Optical
Cross-connect Table:
Interface b**

In λ	Out
λ1	MPLS
• •	• •

**MPLS
Cross-connect Table:
Interface b**

Label	Path?
20	IP
• •	• •

IP Routing Table

Destination	Next Node	Interface	Path?	MAC?
172.16.4.30	Direct	k	IP	36-47-55-93-23-89
• •	• •	• •	• •	• •

Figure 15–15   The data planes at Node G.

Here, the optical cross-connect table shows the relationships of the incoming ports and wavelengths to the outgoing ports and wavelengths. In addition, the MEMS mirrors show how they reflect the switched OSPs from the input port b to four output ports: e, p, y, and z.

Figure 15–15 shows the data planes at node G. As we look at each entry, we see that the operations at node G are almost the reverse of those at node E. And this make good sense, since node E is the source of the MPLS LSP and node G is the end of the LSP. Also, it is possible that the tables at all nodes are similar in their structure. I have shown those entries that are relevant to this example.

Optical Cross-connect Table: Interface b

- *In λ:* Wavelength 1's OUT entry identifies the end of the lightpath.
- *Out:* The "MPLS" entry points to the MPLS table for interface b.

MPLS Cross-connect Table: Interface b

- *Label:* Label 20 coming into interface b identifies the next label to be used on the next LSP segment, or, in this example, IP procedures.
- *Path?:* The value of "IP" identifies the end of the MPLS LSP. Therefore, the node "pops" label 20 off the packet to reveal the IP header. The IP routing table is consulted.

IP Routing Table

- *Destination:* Destination address 172.16.4.30 is examined.
- *Next Node:* The next node entry reveals that there is no next node. This address is attached to a subnet on node G.
- *Interface:* The interface to which node 172.16.4.30 is connected is found on node G's interface k.
- *Path?:* Interface k is a native IP address, so it is not necessary to build an LSP to node 172.16.4.30. (If this entry were coded "MPLS," node G would create a new MPLS tunnel and index into

the MPLS tunnel for its appropriate outgoing interface, but this is not needed here.)

- *MAC?:* A LAN MAC address of 36-47-55-93-23-89 is associated with IP address 172.16.4.30. This entry means that the link on interface k is an Ethernet link. Therefore, node G can encapsulate the IP datagram into the Ethernet frame and deliver the traffic to node 172.16.4.30.

Issues in MPLS/Optical Plane Interworking

Some of the issues of interworking MPLS and the optical plane are discussed in Chapters 10 and 12. For this discussion, it is important to pick up on some of these thoughts in these chapters, and express some problems with label networks, specifically, MPLS interworking with PXCs [AWDU01] and [RAJA02].

There are no analogs of label merging in the optical domain. This implies that a PXC cannot merge several wavelengths into one wavelength. I do not view this situation as an insurmountable problem, but it will require label merging to be performed at the edge LSR. Then the label (or labels) can be mapped to a wavelength.

Most designers do not favor converting the wavelength back to electrical signals within the network, so the network operator must have a complete knowledge of the QOS requirements and (of course) the destination of the user traffic. Thus, constrained routing should be employed to set up the LSP and associated optical trails.

Another distinction is that a PXC cannot perform the equivalent of label push-and-pop operations in the optical domain. One again, this operation must be performed at an edge device and must be kept transparent to the PXC nodes within the network, as shown in these examples in relation to node F.

My final statement on this important issue is that it seems quite reasonable to expect that the core optical network will not process IP datagrams in its data plane, but it is equally reasonable to expect the core network to be able to support the interworkings of the IP, MPLS, and λ control planes. In this manner, the network is designed to give the best performance for payload processing and to have the capabilities to configure, maintain, protect, restore, and tear down the optical facilities, as they support IP and MPLS.

PROTOCOL STACK ALTERNATIVES

Figure 15–16 shows several protocol stacks that either exist now or will be deployed in the near future. My view is that all these implementations have a place in a communications network and it is a matter of deciding which protocol stack is appropriate for the specific network requirement.

There has been an increased awareness of the benefits of the SONET technology over the past few years. At the same time, it also recognized that the cost and overhead of SONET may not be warranted in some situations.

One situation that comes to mind is a simple point-to-point link between two buildings on a campus. The rich functionality and expense of SONET may be overkill for this situation. The network manager may not need all the diagnostics and alarms that go hand-in-hand with SONET.

But the issue goes further than the use or non-use of SONET for certain topologies. As we have examined in this book, the issue also involves the use or non-use of ATM. As noted earlier, some critics of ATM state that ATM has too much overhead and is too expensive for certain applications and topologies.

It is obvious that the deployment of SONET and ATM is not appropriate in many cases. But it should also be understood that an

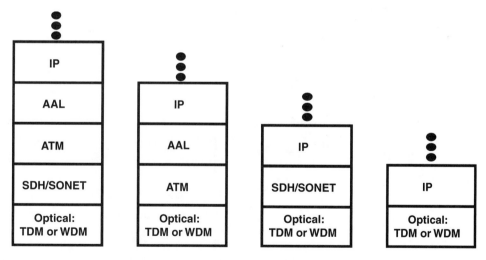

Notes: (1) IP may be running on top of PPP, not shown here.
         (2) For PONs and metropolitan networks, Ethernet is replacing ATM.

Figure 15–16   Protocol stack alternatives.

implementation without SONET will not have the superior provisioning, backup, and OAM capabilities that are built into SONET. Likewise, an ATM-less implementation will not have ATM's traffic management capabilities. If they are not needed, then don't use them, but recognize the implications of such a scaled-down system and what it means to the network administrator and the customers who use the system.

Revisiting the Digital Wrapper

The protocol stack arrangements shown in Figure 15–16 are accurate depictions of the alternatives. However, as shown in Figure 15–17, there should be another layer in these protocols stacks for the following situations: (a) The SONET layer is removed, and (b) WDM is employed. If SONET is not used, there is no method to organize the traffic on the

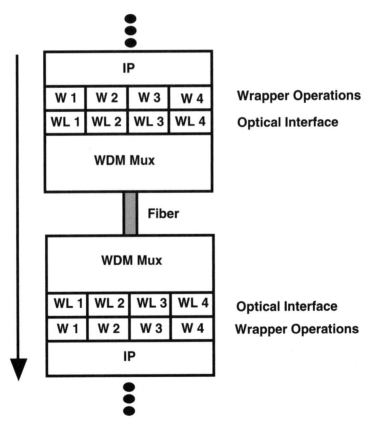

Figure 15–17   The shim or digital wrapper header.

fiber. Remember that SONET has headers and slotting arrangements that identify the virtual tributaries (VTs). If WDM is employed, it makes sense to add a header to the traffic as it enters the optical transmission system in order to carry information about the type of traffic and where the traffic is going.

Figure 15–17 shows these ideas. The header is called a shim header, or a digital wrapper. I am using the "lean stack" in this example: IP traffic runs directly over WDM. IP traffic has a shim header or digital wrapper placed around it at each input wavelength transmitter. In addition to containing information about the traffic, the information may also be used to switch the optical signals from one fiber to another in an optical switch.

INTERNETWORKING SS7 AND LEGACY TRANSPORT NETWORKS AND THE INTERNET

One of the common criticisms of the Internet that is voiced by some people is the absence of the many features that are common to telephony systems, such as high-quality voice calls, call forwarding, call screening, caller ID, and so forth. These features are quite important to many telephone users and are a vital part of the services that produce revenue for telephony service providers.

The initial Internet telephony products are called voice over IP (VoIP), and they are not intended to be a complete "telephone network." To be able to provide full-feature telephony services, a "transport Internet" must be able to avail itself to the SS7 technology, the lynchpin for telephony service features, and the foundation for the advanced intelligent network (AIN) services.

Reinvention or Use of the Telco Platform

If the telco platform is not used, the services that are part of SS7 must be "reinvented" by the Internet tasks forces—considered by many in the telephony industry to be a ridiculous alternative. Maybe so, maybe not: Several of the IP call processing protocols (such as SIP and Megaco) have begun to define service features, such as call waiting.

At any rate, the large SS7 vendors, such as Lucent, Nortel Networks, etc., are developing IP/SS7 gateways, and many products will be available in 2002.

The Integration of the Telephone and Internet Service Providers

In the United States, where deregulation legislation is taking effect, there is a lot of activity in the service providers' acquisitions and mergers. In addition, as voice-over data becomes more pervasive, the traditional data-only ISPs are increasing their interfaces into the traditional telephony architecture, such as the LEC equipment and SS7. Figure 15–18 shows the emerging architecture.

The customer still uses an LEC to connect to the ISP. The data traffic is exchanged through the ISP, the ISP's Internet and to the other user

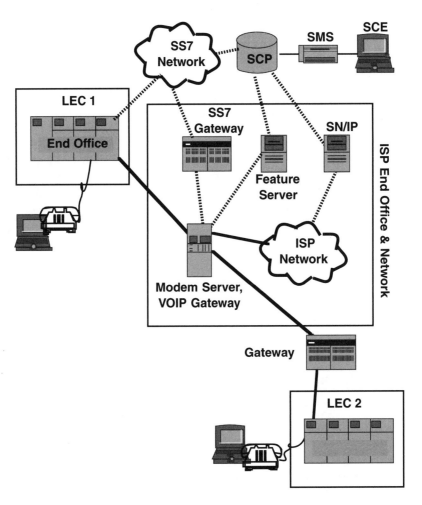

Figure 15–18   Integration of the telephone and ISPs.

(the "called" party). The ISP's network access server supports a modem pool and acts as a VoIP gateway.

In this example, the ISP is acting as an IXC by transporting the IP traffic over the ISP's network. The "ISP Network" in this figure also denotes the ISP's connection with the Internet.

Figure 15–18 also shows the interworking of the ISP with SS7 and the intelligent network (IN) components (shown at the top of the figure). The modem server connects to the IN components through an SS7 network or through a feature server, which, in turn, connects to the service control point (SCP). The SCP to feature server connection is authenticated with RADIUS. The job of the SCP is to allow the ISP to exploit the IN capabilities (billing, call screening, etc.), plus IP-specific features such as routing and billing by volume.

The IN service node and intelligent peripheral are also shown in this figure as part of the ISP architecture. This specific configuration will eventually be commonplace, but it is unusual at this stage of the evolution toward integrating voice and data networks. Moreover, the SN/IP operations may be part of the feature server node. The end offices are using the traditional circuit switches. Eventually, they will be replaced with packet switches.

THE INTERNET TRANSPORT NETWORK PROTOCOL STACK

Figure 15–19 shows a possible protocol stack for a transport network that is IP-based. By IP-based, I mean that the network uses IP and its companion protocols. Here is a brief description of the entites in this protocol stack:

- *Optical Layer:* This layer has been the focus of this book. With the use of 3G technologies, such as OTN architecture, ASON for dynamic services, etc. Obviously, this layer assumes a huge role in the 3G optical Internet.
- *Digital Wrapper:* The digital wrapper may be merged with the MPLS label.
- *MPLS:* This label switching technology will be used to implement constrained routes and other traffic engineering operations. For the foreseeable future, ATM and Frame Relay will provide services similar to the label switching services of MPLS. In addition, Diff-

The Web: HTTP, URLs, XML, DNS							
Voice	Video	Data	Control (OSPF, IS-IS, BGP)	Control (RSVP-TE, OSPF-TE, LDP)	Control (SIP, Megaco, H.323)	Control Wireless	Control (Legacy Telco)
RTP	RTP						
UDP, SCTP	UDP, SCTP	TCP	TCP/ UDP, or no L_4	TCP/ UDP, or no L_4	TCP/ UDP	TCP/ UDP	
IP							
PPP							
MPLS (and or Ethernet/ATM/Frame Relay), with 802.x or DiffServ Support							
Digital Wrapper (perhaps merged with MPLS)							
Optical Layer (TDM, WDM, OTN, ASON, UNI, NNI)							

Medium

Figure 15–19   The Internet transport protocol stack.

Serv will eventually take over the traffic monitoring and policing functions of ATM and Frame Relay.

- *Note:* The role of Ethernet in PONs and metropolitan optical networks will be significant. Its presence in a wide area backbone transport is not a major issue at this time.
- *PPP:* This protocol with its many extensions (such as L2TP) will continue to play a key role in dial-up protocols, including interworking with some of the security aspects of the control planes.

- *IP:* This protocol forms the basis for addressing and packet forwarding. As Figure 15–19 suggests, all upper layer protocols (with the exception of the current legacy telco control plane) run on top of IP.

- *UDP / TCP / SCTP or No L_4:* Depending on the specific needs of an upper layer protocol, UDP, SCTP, or TCP may or may not be invoked. Figure 17–18 shows the most likely scenarios. (Note: OSPF does not operate with a L_4 protocol, but directly on top of IP.

- *Voice:* Packetized voice will operate over the Real Time Protocol (RTP).

- *Video:* Packetized video will operate over the RTP.

- *Data:* Most data applications will continue to use TCP.

- *Control (OSPF, IS-IS, BGP):* Conventional route advertising and route discovery will continue to use the IP-based routing protocols.

- *Control (RSVP-TE, OSPF-TE, LDP):* MPLS will use this control plane to advertise labels and addresses and to create bindings for an LSP, and a constrained route LSP.

- *Control (SIP, Megaco, H.323):* This emerging control plane will support VoIP and many service features associated with the telephone network.

- *Control (Wireless):* The network side of mobile, wireless networks will migrate to the use of the layer stack shown in Figure 15–19. But this migration will take quite some time. In the meantime, many of the control plane procedures will continue to be based on the legacy teleco control plane and of course the mobile-specific protocols, such as roaming, and registration.

- *Control (Legacy Telco):* This control plane will continue to dominate transport networks at the upper layers, pehaps indefinitely. There are those in the industry who would like to see the IP telephony control plane (SIP, Megaco, H.232, etc.) replace SS7 protocols such as ISUP. But don't hold your breath for this to occur any time soon.

- *The Web:* No, don't hold your breath, but all the IP-based upper layer protocols in Figure 15–19 are designed to interwork gracefully with the Web architecture, including the domain name system (DNS). This gives the IP-based protocols a decided advantage over the legacy telco technologies, which are not designed for Web interactions.

CONCLUSIONS

Well, that's it. Originally, my conclusions for this chapter and book were placed here, but one of my reviewers suggested that they be placed in the preface to this book. That's where they are, if you want to read them again.

I hope you have enjoyed reading this book and that you find it a useful addition to your library. I enjoyed writing it and I thank you for reading it.

Appendix A
The T1 Family

T1 LINE CONFIGURATIONS

Today, the majority of T1 offerings digitize the voice signal through a variety of analog-to-digital techniques. Whatever the encoding technique, once the analog images are translated to digital bit streams, the T1 system is able to time division multiplex (TDM) voice and data together in 24 user slots within each T1 frame.

Figure A–1 shows a T1 configuration. There is no typical configuration for these systems. They can range from a simple point-to-point topology shown here, wherein two T1 multiplexers operate on one link, or they can employ with digital cross-connect systems (DCS) that add, drop, and/or switch payload as necessary across multiple links.

Voice, data, and video images can use one digital "pipe." Data transmissions are terminated through a statistical time division multiplexer (STDM), which then uses the TDM to groom the traffic across the transmission line through a T1 channel service unit (CSU) or other equipment, such as a data service unit (DSU) or a combined DSU and CSU. The purpose of the CSU is to convert signals at the user device to signals acceptable to the digital line (and vice versa at the receiver). The CSU performs clocking and signal regeneration on the channels. It also performs functions such as line conditioning (equalization), which keeps the signal's performance consistent across the channel bandwidth, signal reshaping, which reconstitutes the binary pulse stream, and loop-back

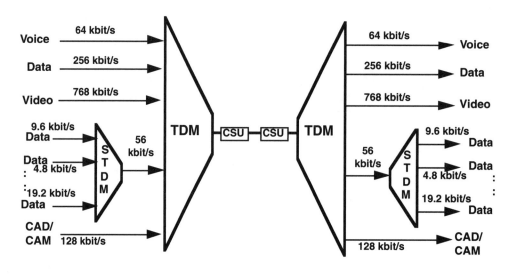

Where:
    CAD/CAM   Computer assisted design/computer assisted manufacturing
    CSU   Channel service unit
    STDM   Statistical time division multiplexer
    TDM   Time division multiplexer

Figure A–1   Possible topology for a digital carrier system.

testing, which entails the transmission of test signals between the DSU and the network carrier's equipment.

The bandwidth of a line can be divided into various T1 subrates. For example, a video system could utilize a 768 kbit/s band, the STDM, in turn, could multiplex various data rates up to a 56 kbit/s rate and perhaps a CAD/CAM operation could utilize 128 kbit/s of the bandwidth.

THE DIGITAL NETWORK

The U. S. T1-based digital network has been under development for over thirty years. During this time, a hierarchy of transmission levels (low speeds to high speeds) has been implemented through time division multiplexers, channel banks and digital cross-connects. These levels are designated by digital signal (DS) numbers ranging from DS0 to DS4.

DS1 Frame Format

Each basic channel operates at 64 kbit/s signal. This signal is called a digital signal level 0, or DS0. The 0 means that the signal is not multiplexed (digital signal, 0 level of multiplexing). The multiplexed 24 DS0 signals are collectively called DS1 (digital signal, first level of multiplexing). Let us see how DS1 is formed.

A few simple calculations are needed at this point in the discussion in order to understand the DS1 signal. After each of the 24 channels in a channel bank (terminal) has been sampled, quantized, and encoded, the resultant pulse train (bit stream) is called a *frame*. A frame has a time duration of 125 microseconds (μsec) (1 second/8000 samples = .000125). The bit duration is 648 nanoseconds (nsec): 125 μs/193 = 648 nsec. Further, each PAM sample is encoded into an eight-bit 5.184 nsec word: 648 nsec × 8 = 5.148 μsec.

The frame contains 24 eight-bit binary words, as depicted in Figure A–2. At the end of channel 24, an additional bit (the F bit) is appended to the frame. This bit becomes the 193rd bit of a frame and is used for framing (synchronization) and a variety of operations and maintenance services.

These calculations provide an insight into the DS1 bit rate. We just learned that the pulse code modulation (PCM) terminal produces 24 8-bit words, plus the F bit. The sampling rate of each channel in the system is 8000 times per second. Thus, 8000 x 193 bits per frame = 1,544,000 bits per second, or 1.544 Mbit/s, which is the DS1 line bit rate (see Table A–1). This DS1 signal is transmitted onto the T1 TDM cable facilities.

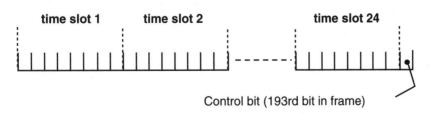

(a) 1.544 Mbit/s frame.

Figure A–2   The T1 frame and coding scheme.

Library Resource Center
Renton Technical College
3000 N.E. 4th St.
Renton, WA 98056

Table A–1   Digital Signal at the First Level (DS1)

24	Channels or words
× 8	Bits per word
192	*Word bits* / frame
+ 1	*F* bit
193	Bits per complete frame
× 8000	Sampling rate/second
1,544,000	bit/s or 1.544 Mbit/s

NORTH AMERICAN ASYNCHRONOUS DIGITAL HIERARCHY

When the digital network was in its early stages of development, common clocks (such as a primary reference source) were not available. In order to synchronize the switches, terminals, and multiplexers to a common rate, bit stuffing was used to bring lower-rate signals into a common higher rate.

Five levels of multiplexing exist within the North American asynchronous digital hierarchy (see Figure A–3). Starting with the 1.544 Mbit/s DS1, each level of the hierarchy increases a facility's channel capacity. The current systems are capable of handling over 24,000 channels. There are several types of asynchronous digital multiplexers/demultiplexers that support this hierarchy, and they are described in this section.

A DS1 signal may be combined with another DS1 signal to produce a 3.152 Mbit/s signal containing 48 voice frequency (VF) channels. The multiplexer used for this operation is called an M1C mux, which means first level in, combined level out. This level is called a digital signal at the first level combined, or DS1C.

The combination of four DS1s to produce a 6.312 Mbit/s bit stream is called a digital signal at the second level, or DS2. It supports 96 voice channels. The multiplexers used for this operation are called M12, which means first level signals in, second level out.

Figure A–3 also shows the relationship of the digital signal cross-connect (DSX, also called a digital cross-connect) to the hierarchy. These components are equipment frames containing jack panels that serve as channel bank and multiplexer cross-connect interfaces in the telco office. The frames are named DSX-0, DSX-1, DSX-1C, DSX-3, and DSX-4 for each of the six DS rates (DSX-0 and DSX-4 are not shown in Figure A–3). Each frame connects equipment that operates at the respective DSn rate.

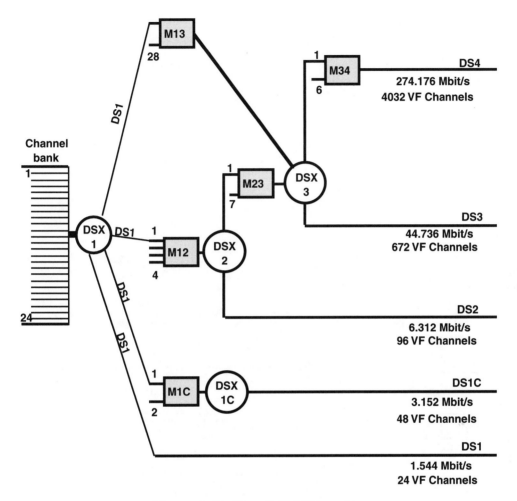

Figure A–3   The digital hierarchy.

The DSX-0 is employed for connecting and terminating digital data system (DDS) equipment.

The DSX-1, DSX-1C, and DSX-2 have several common features, such as monitoring and patching jacks, accommodations for conventional telephone plugs, order-wire terminations, and tracer lamps (to identify the two ends of a cross-connection). As shown in Figure A–3, the DSX-1 connects to a channel bank (and other equipment, explained later). The DSXs are 110-ohm balanced points. The DSX-3 and DSX-4 are similar to the DSX-1, DSX-1C, and DSX-2 except they are 75-ohm coaxial interfaces.

It is important to distinguish between a DSX and a DCS, which is also called a digital cross-connect. The DSC is considerably more intelligent. It is software controlled and uses time-slot interchange (TSI) to transfer slots between input and output lines. DCSs eliminate channel banks at interfaces where channels are transferred between carrier

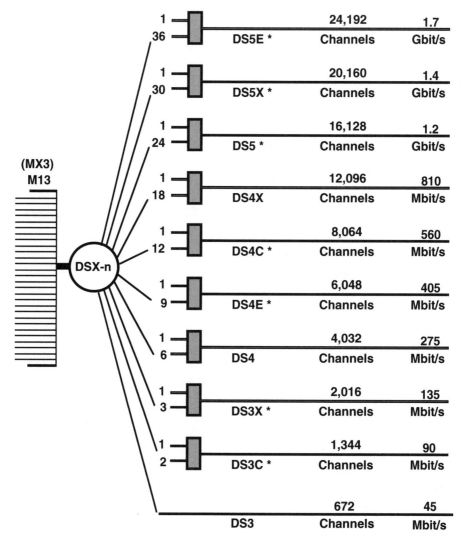

Note: * = not standardized

Figure A–4   North American Asynchronous Digital Hierarchy.

systems. DCS operations are explained in more detail later in this chapter and in Chapter 5.

One of the most common types of multiplexers is the MX3. It accepts up to 28 DS1 signals, 14 DS1C signals, or 7 DS2 signals as inputs, and creates a DS3 signal as its output. These multiplexers are called MX3 (with X designating the level in), meaning M13 for first level in and third level out, or M23 for second level in and third level out.

The final (formally defined) level within the North American asynchronous digital network is the DS4, which produces a 274.176 Mbit/s signal with 4,032 voice channels. An M34 mux is used for producing this digital level.

There are also several other common (but not standard) levels (shown in Figure A–4). These are: (a) the 90 Mbit/s DS3C, (b) the 135 Mbit/s DS3X, (c) the 405 Mbit/s DS4E, (d) the 560 Mbit/s DS4C, and (e) the 1.2, 1.4, and 1.7 Gbit/s systems. These systems accept DS3 as their inputs. The DS3C system accepts two DS3 inputs, the DS3X system accepts three DS3 inputs, and the DS4E system accepts nine DS3 inputs. The "E" indicates "extended." The signal is not high enough to be called a DS4C, which is a 560 Mbit/s system transmits 12 DS3 signals. The reader should check the vendors' offerings for equipment operating above DS4, due to the lack of standards at these levels.

SUBSCRIBER-TYPE SYSTEMS

Subscriber-type PCM systems are available that use the same quantizing and encoding processes as the D2, D3, and D4 systems explained previously (see Figure A–5). These systems are also software programmable for voice and data circuits just as the D4 and D5 channel banks are. They are capable of SF/ESF, AMI/B8ZS, and ADPCM (LBRV) operations. The main difference is that one terminal is located in the central office while the other is in the field near or on the customer's location. They may be referred also to as a *pair gain system*, a *digital loop carrier,* or a *subscriber loop carrier*. Some of them can also extend a leased DS1 and/or DS3 to the customer's premise for his own use.

Subscriber-type systems support a wide variety of applications by various operating companies. One of the more popular uses is providing service to developing areas for new subdivisions where an existing cable plant is insufficient. A system can provide the service immediately and permanently, or it can be moved to another location (if growth in the area eventually justifies a central office). Regardless of whether the service is

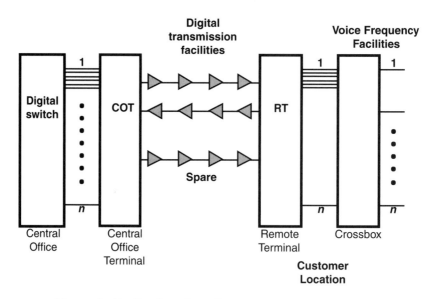

Figure A–5   Basic subscriber system arrangement.

permanent or temporary, a subscriber system is easy to engineer and install on short notice. An example is a new industrial park experiencing
sudden and unexpected growth, resulting in demands for service exceeding the available loop plant. The system can be installed and operating
within a few weeks. Also, many companies use these systems to provide
for temporary service to large functions such as business conventions or
sporting events.

There are other reasons to justify the placement of a subscriber loop
carrier in the loop plant. First, the copper pairs serving the subscribers
will be much shorter, thus overcoming distance limitations in providing
the newer services. Second, shortening the customer loop decreases the
exposure to power-line interference with its resultant degradation and
noise impact on these circuits. Flexibility is further enhanced by the
1200-ohm loop capability of the remote terminal. Third, electronics allow
the future ability to provide new services quickly. The distance from the
central office to the remote terminal is limited only by the copper DS1
span line performance. Today, most of these systems employ fiber optics,
so there is very little distance limitation. Subscriber loop carriers provide
applications for videoconferencing and local area networks (LANs) links.

Subscriber carrier systems provide several functions which channel
banks do not because they are in the local loop. These are as follows:
ringing, coin collection, party lines, remote terminals, and subscriber line
testing as well as batteries for backup power and fan units when not installed in a controlled environment.

References

[AGRA92] Agrawal, G. P., *Fiber-Optic Communication Systems*, John Wiley, New York, 1992.

[ASHW01] Ashwood-Smith, Peter, et al., "Generalized MPLS: Signaling Functional Description," draft-ietf-mpls-generalized-signaling-05.txt, July, 2001.

[AWDU99] Awduche, W., et al., "Requirements for Traffic Engineering Over MPLS," RFC 2702, September, 1999.

[AWDU01] Awduche, Daniel O., et al., "Multiprotocol Lambda Switching: Combining MPLS Traffic Engineering Control with Optical Cross-connects," draft-awduche-mpls-te-optical-03.txt, April, 2001.

[BELL99] Bell Labs, "Bell Labs Trends and Developments," Volume 3, Number 1, Spring, 1999.

[BELL01] Bellato, Alberto, et al., "Optical Transport Networks GMPLS Control Framework," draft-bellato-ccamp-g709-framework-00.txt, June, 2001.

[BERN01] Bernstein, L. et al, Optical InterDomain Routing Considerations, draft-bernstein-optical-bgp-01.txt, July, 2001.

[BISH01] Bishop, D. J., Giles, C. R., Das, S., "The Rise of Optical Switching," *Scientific American,* January, 2001.

[BLAC91] Black, Uyless, *OSI: A Model for Computer Communications Standards,* Prentice Hall, 1991.

[BLAC01] Black, Uyless, and Waters, Sharleen, *SONET and T1: Architectures for Digital Transport Networks,* Second Edition, Prentice Hall, 2001.

[BLAC02] Black, Uyless, *MPLS and Label Switching Networks,* Second Edition, Prentice Hall, 2002.

[BLUM01] Blumenthal, Daniel J., "Routing Packets with Light," *Scientific American,* January, 2001.

[BROR01] Brorson, S., et al., "Link Management Protocol (LMP) for DWDM Optical Line Systems," IETF draft-fredette-lmp-wdm-02.txt, July, 2001.

317

[CHIU01] Chiu, Angela, et al., "Impairments and Other Constraints on Optical Layer Routing," draft-ietf-ipo-impairments-00.txt, May, 2001.

[CHRA99] Chraplyvy, Andrew R., "High Capacity Lightwave Transmission Experiments," *Bell Labs Technical Journal,* January-March, 1999.

[DUTT98] Dutton, Harry, Jr., *Understanding Optical Communications,* Prentice Hall, 1998.

[FERN00] Fernandez, M., and Kruglic, E., "MEMS Technology Users in a New Age in Optical Switching," *Lightwave,* August, 2000.

[FREE00] Freeland, Daren, et al., "Considerations on the Development of an Optical Control Plane," draft-freeland-octrl-cons-01.txt, November, 2000.

[FULL01] Fuller, Meghan, "Startup's Switchless Switch Targets Network Edge," *Lightwave,* October, 2001.

[G.70901] "Interface for the Optical Transport Network," ITU-T Recommendation G.709, February, 2001.

[G.87200] "Architecture of Optical Transport Networks," ITU-T Recommendation G.872, 2000.

[GILE99] Giles, C. R., and Spector, Magaly, "The Wavelength Add/Drop Multiplexor for Lightwave Communication Networks," *Bell Labs Technical Journal,* January-March, 1999.

[JACK99] Jackman, Neil A., et al., "Optical Cross-connects for Optical Networking," *Bell Labs Technical Journal* , January-March, 1999.

[JOHN99] Johnson, Steven R., and Nichols, Virginia L., "Advanced Optical Networking— Lucent's MONET Network Elements," *Bell Labs Technical Journal,* January-March, 1999.

[KAMI97] Kaminow, I. P., and Koch, T. L. (Eds.), *Optical Fiber Telecommunications IIIA,* Academic Press, 1997.

[KOLE00] Kolesar, Paul, and Buck, Preston, "The 62.5 vs. 50 Micron Debate," *Lightwave,* April, 2000.

[LANG01] Lang, Jonathan, P., et al., "Link Management Protocol (LMP)," IETF draft-lang-mpls-lmp-02.text, September, 2001.

[LEE01] Lee, Young, et al., Protection Scheme for Optical Channel Concatention, draft-ylee-protection-occ-00.txt, June 2001.

[LIGH01a] "Optical Units Reference," Available from: www.lightreading.com.

[MANN01] Mannie, Eric, "GMPLS Extensions for SONET and SDH Control," draft-ietf-ccamp-gmple-sdh-os.txt, June, 2001.

[NORT98] Nortel Networks, "S/SMDS TransportNode: Best-in-Class Portfolio of High-Capacity Solutions," Document No. 56088.16/11-98, Issue 2, November 10, 1998.

[NORT99a] Nortel Networks, "Positioning OC-12 TBM Networks for the 21st Century," Document No. 56107.16/02-99, Issue 1, February 25, 1999.

[NORT99b] Nortel Networks, "Highways of Light," *Nortel Networks Telesis,* Volume 101, 1999.

[ODSI01] www.odsi-coalition.com provides the specifications and source code for ODSI's work on optical bandwidth on demand.

[OIF01] www.oiforum.com provides information on the OIF's work on an optical network user-network interface (UNI).

[PAPA00] Papadimitriou, D., et al., "Optical Network-to-Network Interface Framework and Requirements," draft-papadimitriou-onni-frame-01.txt, November, 2000.

[PODZ00] Podzimek, Cheri, and Harmon, Dan, "Expanding the Network Diameter," *Lightwave,* May, 2000.

[RAJA02] Rajagopalan, Bala, et al., "IP over Optical Internets: A Framework," draft-ietf-ipo-framework-00.txt, no create date provided, expiration date is 13/2002.

[RAMA98] Ramaswami, Rajiv, and Sivarajan, Kumar N., *Optical Networks: A Practical Perspective*, Morgan Kaufman Publishers, San Francisco, 1998.

[REFI99] Refi, James J., "Optical Fibers for Optical Networking," *Bell Labs Technical Journal,* January-March, 1999.

[RYAN01] Ryan, Jim, "ITU G.655 Adopts Higher Dispersion for DWDM," *Lightwave,* September, 2001.

[STRI01] Strix, Gary, "The Triumph of the Light," *Scientific American,* January, 2001.

[T1X1.501] ANSI T1X1.05, "Need for Concatenating Optical Channels to Create Transparent High Bandwidth Channels," 2001.

[XUE01] Xue, Yong, "Carrier Optical Services Framework and Associated UNI Requirements," draft-many-carrier-framework-uni-00.txt, May, 2001.

[XU01] Xu, Yangguang, et al., "Intra-Domain GMPLS Control Plane Architecture for Automatically Switched Transport Network," draft-xu-ccamp-gmpls-arch-intra-domain-00.txt, September, 2001.

Acronyms

A/D
A-NZDF
AAL: ATM adaptation layer
AAL5: ATM adaptation layer type 5
ADM: add-drop multiplexer
AIN: advanced intelligent network
AIS: alarm indication signal
ANSI: American National Standards Institute
AOLS: all-optical label swapping
APS: automatic protection switching
ASE: amplifier spontaneous emission
ASIC: application-specific integrated circuit
ASON: automatic switched optical network
ATM: asynchronous transfer mode

AU: administrative unit
AUG: administrative unit group
BER: bit error rate
BGP: border gateway protocol
BIP: bit interleaved parity
BITS: building integrated timing supply
BLSR: bi-directional line-switched ring
BOD: bandwidth of demand
BPSR: bi-directional path switched ring
BPV: bipolar violation
BSNT: bit stream without octet timing
BSOT: bit stream with octet timing
C: container
CAD/CAM: computer assisted design/computer assisted manufacturing
CATV: cable TV
CBR: constant bit rate

CCid: control channel id
CH: cell header
CMIP: common management information protocol
CNE: client network element
CNLS: connectionless network
CO: central office (also: connection-oriented)
CP: common part
CPCS: common part convergence sublayer
CPE: customer premises equipment
CPI: common part indication
CPU: central processing unit
CR-LDP: constraint-based LDP
CRC: cyclic redundancy check
CS: cross-connect
CSU: channel service unit

DARPA: Defense Advanced Research Projects Agency
DCC: data communications channel
DCS: digital cross-connect system (also: digital cross-connect)
DDS: digital data system
DLC: digital loop carrier
DNS: domain name system
DQDB: dual queue dual bus
DRAM: dynamic random-access memory
DS: digital signal
DS0: digital signal level 0
DSF: dispersion-shifted fiber
DSU: data service unit
DSX: digital signal cross-connect
DWDM: dense wave division multiplexing
DWHdr: digital wrapper and header
E/O: electrical-to-optical converter
EDF: erbium-doped fiber
EDFA: erbium-doped fiber amplifier
EMS: element management system
ESI: external synchronization interface
ETSI: European Telecommunications Standard Institute
FCS: frame check sequence
FDDI: fiber distributed data interface
FDM: frequency division multiplexing
FEC: forward error correction (also: forwarding equivalence class)

FERF: far end receive failure
FF: fractional frequency
FS: feature server
FSC: fiber-switch capable
FTTC: fiber to the curb
FTTH: fiber to the home
G-PID: generalized PID
GCC: general communication channel
GFP: generic framing procedure
GLR: generalized label request
GLSP: generalized label switched path
GMPLS: generalized MPLS
HDLC: high-level data link control
HEC: header error control
HO-POH: higher order path overhead
I: information
IaDi: intra-domain
ID: identifier
IEC: International Electrotechnical Commission
IETF: Internet Engineering Task Force
IGP: Internal gateway protocol
IN: intelligent network
IP: Internet protocol
IPX: Internet Protocol X (vender-specific IP)
IS-IS: Intermediate system-to-intermediate system
ISDN: Integrated services digital network
ISO: International Standards Organization
ISP: Internet service provider
ISUP: ISDN user part

ITU: International Telecommunication Union
ITU-T: International Telecommunication Union—Telecommunication Standardization Sector
L2TP: layer 2 tunneling protocol
LAN: local area network
LASER: light amplification by stimulated emission of radiation
LDP: label distribution protocol
LEC: local exchange carrier
LI: length indicator
LLC: logical link control
LMP: link management protocol
LO-POH: lower order path overhead
LOF: loss of frame
LOH: line overhead
LOL: loss of light
LOP: loss of pointer
LOS: loss of signal
LSC: lambda-switch capable
LSP: label switched path (also: label switching path)
LSR: label switching router
LTE: line terminating equipment
MEMS: microelectromechanical systems
MONET: multi-wavelength optical networking consortium
MOR: multi-wavelength optical repeater

MPλS: multiprotocol lambda switching

MPLS: multiprotocol label switching

MPLS TE: MPLS traffic engineering

MSOH: multiplex section overhead

MTU: maximum transmission unit size

MUX: multiplexer

NAS: network access server

NCC: number of contiguous components

NDP: neighbor discovery protocol

NHLFE: next hop label forwarding entry

NLPID: network level protocol id

NM: nanometers

NNI: network node interface (also: network-to-network interface)

non-BOD: non-bandwidth of demand

NVC: number of virtual components

NZDF: non-zero dispersion fiber

OADM: optical ADM

OAM: operations, administration, and maintenance

OC: optical carrier (also: optical channel)

OCC: optical channel carrier

OCG: optical carrier group

Och: optical channel

ODSI: open domain service interconnect coalition

ODSI: optical domain service interconnect

ODU: optical channel data unit

ODUk: optical channel data unit

OFA: optical fiber amplifier

OH: overhead

OIF: optical interworking forum

OIF IrDi: inter-domain

OL: optical layer

OLN: optical line terminal

OLS: optical link system (also: optical line system)

OMS: optical multiplex section

OMU: optical mux unit

ON: optical node

ONC: optical network controller

ONE: optical network element

ONU: optical network unit

OOS: overhead signal

OPS: optical physical section

OPUk: optical channel payload unit

OSC: optical supervisory channel

OSI: open systems interconnection

OSNR: optical signal-to-noise ratio

OSP: optical switching path (also: optical switched path)

OSPF: open shortest path first

OTM: optical transport module

OTN: optical transport network

OTS: optical transmission section

OTU: optical transport unit

OTUk: optical channel transport unit

OUI: organizationally unique id

OXC: optical cross-connect (also: optical/electrical cross-connect)

PAD: padding (also: padding field)

PBX: private branch exchange

PCM: pulse code modulation

PDH: pleischronous digital hierarchy

PDU: protocol data unit

PID: protocol id

PLI: PDU length indicator

PMD: polarization-mode dispersion

PNNI: private network-to-network interface

POH: path overhead bit

PON: passive optical network

POP: point of presence

PPP: point-to-point protocol

PRS: primary reference source

PT: payload type

PTE: path terminating equipment

PTT: Postal, Telephone, and Telegraph Ministries

PXC: photonic cross-connect (also: optical/optical cross-connect)

QOS: quality of service

RAI: remote alarm indication

RCC: requested contiguous concatenation

RDT: remote digital terminal

RESV: reservation

RFC: request for comments

RS: regenerator section

RSOH: regenerator section overhead

RSVP: resource reservation protocol

RSVP-TE: RSVP traffic engineering

RTP: real time protocol

SA: service adapter

SAR: segmentation and reassembly sublayer

SCE: service creation environment

SCP: service control point

SCTP: stream control transmission protocol

SD: signal degrade

SDH: synchronous digital hierarchy

SDU: service data unit

SIP: session initiation protocol

SLA: service level agreement

SMDS: switched multimegabit data service

SMS: serviced management system

SN: service node

SNA: systems network architecture

SNAP: subnetwork access protocol

SNMP: simple network management protocol

SOH: section overhead

SONET/SDH: synchronous optical network/synchronous digital hierarchy

SOP: state of polarization

SPE: synchronous payload envelope

SRLG: shared risk link group identifier

SS: signaling system

SS7: signaling system number 7

SSM: synchronization status message

ST: signal type

STDM: statistical time division multiplexer

STE: section terminating equipment

STM: synchronous transport module

STP: signaling transfer point

STS: synchronous transport signal

SVC: switched virtual circuit or call

T: transparency

TDM: time division multiplexing (also: timedivision multiplexer; time-division multiplex capable)

TE: traffic engineer

TIA: Telecommunications Industry Association

TL: transaction language

TLV: type-length-value

TRDP: topology and resource distribution protocol

TSI: time-slot interchange

TU: tributary unit

TUG: TU group

UED: user edge device

UI: unit interval (also: unnumbered information)

UNI: user-network interface

UNI-SR: UNI sub-rate

USF: unshifted fiber (also: dispersion-unshifted fiber)

UU: user-to-user information

VC: virtual controller (also: virtual container)

VF: voice frequency

VoIP: voice over IP

VPN: virtual private network

VT: virtual tributary

VTG: virtual tributary group

WADM: wavelength ADM

WAN: wide area network

WDM: wave division multiplexing (also: wavelength division multiplexing)

WECO: Western Electric Co.

WFIB: wavelength forwarding information base

Index

Page numbers ending in "f" refer to figures. Page numbers ending in "t" refer to tables.

Prentice Hall: Professional Technical Reference

Back Forward Reload Home Search Guide Images Print Security Stop

PH
PTR

http://www.phptr.com/

www.phptr.com

PRENTICE HALL

Professional Technical Reference
Tomorrow's Solutions for Today's Professionals.

Keep Up-to-Date with
PH PTR Online!

We strive to stay on the cutting edge of what's happening in professional computer science and engineering. Here's a bit of what you'll find when you stop by **www.phptr.com**:

Special interest areas offering our latest books, book series, software, features of the month, related links and other useful information to help you get the job done.

Deals, deals, deals! Come to our promotions section for the latest bargains offered to you exclusively from our retailers.

Need to find a bookstore? Chances are, there's a bookseller near you that carries a broad selection of PTR titles. Locate a Magnet bookstore near you at www.phptr.com.

What's new at PH PTR? We don't just publish books for the professional community, we're a part of it. Check out our convention schedule, join an author chat, get the latest reviews and press releases on topics of interest to you.

Subscribe today! Join PH PTR's monthly email newsletter!

Want to be kept up-to-date on your area of interest? Choose a targeted category on our website, and we'll keep you informed of the latest PH PTR products, author events, reviews and conferences in your interest area.

Visit our mailroom to subscribe today! **http://www.phptr.com/mail_lists**